PHILOSOPHY AND TRUTH
Selections from Nietzsche's Notebooks of the early 1870's

Friedrich Nietzsche

Edited and Translated
with an Introduction and Notes

by

DANIEL BREAZEA

HUMANITIES PRESS INTERNATIONAL, INC.
New Jersey ◇ London

First published 1979

This paperback edition first published 1990 by
Humanities Press International, Inc., Atlantic Highlands, N.J.,
and 3 Henrietta Street, London WC2E 8LU.

© Daniel Breazeale, 1979

Reprinted 1991, 1992

Library of Congress Cataloging in Publication Data
Nietzsche, Friedrich Wilhelm, 1844–1900.
    Philosophy and truth: selections from
Nietzsche's notebooks of the early 1870's
    Includes bibliographical references.
    I. Philosophy—Collected works.   I. Breazeale,
Daniel.   II. Title.
B3312.E5B73   193   76–53746
ISBN 0–391–03671–8 (Pbk.)

British Library Cataloging in Publication Data
Nietzsche, Friedrich 1844–1900
    Philosophy and truth : selections from Nietzsche's
    notebooks of the early 1870's.
    1. German philosophy
    I. Title   II. Breazeale, Daniel
    193
ISBN 0–391–03671–8

Printed in the United States of America

PHILOSOPHY AND TRUTH
Selections from Nietzsche's Notebooks of the early 1870's

To Nicole Danielle

Contents

Acknowledgments

On behalf of the readers of this volume, I would like to thank the following four persons who contributed so much toward keeping it free of errors: Anesti and Barbara Andrea, who patiently compared my translation to the German original and made countless suggestions which have been incorporated in the final version; Viviane Breazeale, who carefully read and corrected successive versions of the manuscript; and Pat Harris, who cheerfully prepared the final typescript. Without the cooperation and assistance of these four persons this book would not have been possible.

Preface

Going through a philosopher's unpublished notebooks seems to have even less justification than reading his mail. His letters were at least intended to be read by someone else. But by what right do we read, translate, and publish his notebooks—those private workshops of the mind in which he tries out ideas he may later reject, practices for public performances, and ingenuously records his worst and most trivial as well as his better and more considered thoughts? The indiscretion appears compounded in the case of a thinker like Nietzsche who, for twenty years, published almost one book per year and whose creative life ended abruptly, leaving him no time to arrange or edit his private papers in any way. Of course, this is the age of scholarly specialists who claim for themselves the indefeasible right to know absolutely everything about the victim of their research. But surely these can be left to pursue their obsession in the half-light of archives and to study their subject in his original language.

Here is a volume consisting largely of English translations of selections from Nietzsche's unpublished papers and notebooks from the years 1872-1876. Though it will be of considerable interest to "Nietzsche specialists," it is not intended primarily for them. The objections to a publication of this sort can be set aside only if the material in question is of truly exceptional interest and importance, either because it provides essential information about the intellectual development of a thinker or because of the intrinsic significance of its content, and if there exists a sufficiently large number of serious readers, sufficiently interested in and informed concerning the figure in question to be able to profit from the publication of such writings.

In the case of Nietzsche, the second condition is certainly satisfied today. After nearly a century, Nietzsche has begun to receive the same serious consideration as a philosopher in English speaking countries which has been common for fifty years in German and French speaking lands. His writings are no longer in the sole possession of enthusiasts and polemicists. Thanks in no small part to the recent number of excellent English translations of his writings and serious studies of his philosophy, the realization is growing that this rather unlikely and odd thinker occupies a central position in the history of thought and culture. There exists today a large number of English readers anxious to learn more about and from Nietzsche.

For such readers the "texts" translated in this volume will be an exciting discovery. For some, the major value of these selections will be the substantial contribution they can make to our understanding of Nietzsche's intellectual development during what was perhaps the most crucial and poorly understood period of his life. For others, including myself, these writings will be even more highly prized for the contribution which they can make to a further and deeper understanding of Nietzsche's views on a number of topics of special interest to contemporary philosophers, especially epistemological topics. Readers interested in Nietzsche's theory of knowledge and truth are often frustrated by his none too frequent published remarks on these topics, and by the absence of sustained, discursive exposition from such passages. However, as the material translated in this volume shows, Nietzsche was capable of elaborating his epistemological views at much greater length and with much more emphasis upon arguments and evidence than one is accustomed to find in his published remarks on the subject. No one interested in Nietzsche's theory of knowledge can afford to neglect the notebooks of the early 1870's. There are, of course, valuable discussions of many other topics in these notebooks: the contemporary meaning of ancient culture, for example, or the nature of philosophy and its relation to art, science, and general culture. Thus these writings can be *helpful* for clarifying and supplementing Nietzsche's published remarks on a number of subjects, and for understanding his thoughts on certain subjects (e.g. epistemology) they are *essential*.

There is an additional consideration which I have had in view in publishing these texts. They do make an important contribution both to our understanding of Nietzsche's intellectual development and to our clearer understanding of Nietzsche's views on several very important subjects. In the end, however, why does one read Nietzsche, or any philosopher? I would like to believe that one becomes involved in the serious study of a particular thinker—Locke, for example, or Plato—because one has found that one is able to *learn* much more from this author than from most others. The final reason why I have taken the trouble to edit and translate these writings is because I think that in them Nietzsche says some things which are worthy of the serious attention of intelligent people.

Finally, I am not unaware of a certain irony in presenting these unpublished writings of Nietzsche's accompanied by so much obvious scholarly baggage: elaborate notes and critical apparatus. It is what Nietzsche would have called a thoroughly "Alexandrian" production, and if ever there was a critic, in practice as well as in theory, of "Alexandrianism" it was Nietzsche. My sole reason for burdening Nietzsche's texts in this way is my desire to make these writings accessible to as wide a circle of readers as possible. Due to the special and fragmentary character of these writings, it would appear to me to be irresponsible not to provide my readers with a minimal amount of editorial and critical guidance. Irony is not always to be avoided—especially when it is unavoidable.

Note to the Paperback Edition

I am gratified that these translations from Nietzsche's *Nachlass* should have attracted sufficient interest among English readers to merit a paperback edition. This paperback edition differs from the first only in a few minor respects. A number of typographical and other errors in the first edition have been corrected, and the late Walter Kaufmann's Forword has been omitted.

Since the publication of the original edition, all of the texts in this volume have appeared in the new critical edition of Nietzsche's *Werke* edited by Giorgio Colli and Mazzino Montinari and published by Walter de Gruyter [= *WKG*]. Where appropriate, references to volume and page numbers of this new edition of the German text have been inserted within square brackets. Also, references to the manuscript sources and dates of Nietzsche's notes have been revised in the light of the philological information contained in *WKG*. Though the new critical edition of Nietzsche's notebooks includes many passages not published in any of the earlier editions of Nietzsche's *Nachlass*, and though some of the passages that were published in earlier editions of the same are slightly altered in the new German edition, such additions and changes are not reflected in the present volume, which thus remains a collection of *selections* from Nietzsche's early notebooks.

Finally, I should like to thank Robert Rabel and Yolanda Estes for their valuable assistance with the many corrections to the text of this paperback edition.

Introduction

Nietzsche's productive intellectual life came to an end early in January 1889, just as the life of his writings, his life's work, was beginning. The first university lectures on his philosophy had already been held, and an acute observer might have detected on the horizon the first glimmer of that widespread attention which he had labored so long and, as he thought, fruitlessly to obtain for his ideas.

At the time of his collapse, Nietzsche had already prepared for the printer several books which had not yet appeared. Yet these made up only the smallest part of an immense literary estate of unpublished writings, consisting of relatively polished manuscripts, rough drafts of published books, lecture notes, musical compositions, letters, dozens of notebooks, and hundreds of loose pages of notes and plans. Included in this material were writings from every period of Nietzsche's life and on the widest variety of subjects, all in the most chaotic disarray.

The publication of the literary remains (*Nachlass*), under the personal supervision of Nietzsche's rather unscrupulous sister, began almost immediately after his collapse and continued as his fame grew. At first, the greatest attention was understandably focused on the unpublished writings of the late 1880's. During his last productive years Nietzsche had often referred to a projected *magnum opus*, work upon which was constantly being interrupted by other literary projects. Nevertheless, he did amass a large body of manuscript material, consisting mostly of plans and very rough notes, for this project. An editorial selection and arrangement of some of this material was eventually published under the title *The Will to Power*, but unfortunately, neither Nietzsche's editors nor readers were always careful in the use they made of this fascinating text. It was frequently represented and read as if it were a book written by Nietzsche himself, indeed, as his crowning achievement. But by no means all of the *Nachlass* of the 1800's was included in *WM*,[1] nor was any of the unpublished material from earlier decades. Much, but by no

---

[1] *WM* = *Will to Power*. References to Nietzsche's writings are normally made by abbreviation of the *German* title, followed by *section* number. A list of Nietzsche's writings and a key to the abbreviations used in this volume may be found at the end of the introductory material.

means all, of the remaining unpublished writings were gradually published, sometimes in severely edited form, in the various editions of Nietzsche's "Complete Works" which were published over the years.

Owing in part to the unfortunate misrepresentation of *The Will to Power* as a book written by Nietzsche, as well as to the suspect editorial policies of the "Nietzsche Archives" and to the sophisticated use which certain Nazi interpreters of Nietzsche made of his unpublished writings, there is wide-spread confusion concerning the legitimate role of the *Nachlass* in our understanding and interpretation of Nietzsche's thought. Since all of the selections translated in this volume are from the *Nachlass*, the issue of its significance cannot be avoided.

I believe that, when properly employed, Nietzsche's unpublished notes and manuscripts can make an important, and in some cases essential, contribution to our understanding of his philosophy and its development. I further believe that the *Nachlass* is "properly employed" when the following three rules are adhered to—rules which, had they been observed in the past, would have prevented many misunderstandings. (1) Quotations from and references to Nietzsche's unpublished writings should always be identified as such. For no matter how much significance one assigns to any particular passage in the *Nachlass*, the unalterable fact remains that none of this material was published by Nietzsche himself or even intended by him for publication in the form in which we find it. This fact is particularly significant in regard to the early *Nachlass*, which Nietzsche could have revised for publication but often did not, perhaps for very good reasons. Any responsible use of the *Nachlass* must not conceal this information. (2) When views expressed in the *Nachlass* seem to conflict with views encountered in Nietzsche's published writings, mention must be made of this conflict. Indeed, even where there is no such direct conflict, it is a good general procedure to supplement any reference to *Nachlass* material with some reference to Nietzsche's published thoughts on the same subject. (3) Priority should always be given to published over unpublished remarks on the same topic; nothing in the *Nachlass* should be taken to supersede Nietzsche's published views of the same period, and under no circumstances should the *Nachlass* be thought to contain Nietzsche's "real" philosophy or opinions, in contrast with his published, "exoteric" writings.

If the above rules are adhered to then most of the qualms concerning the use of Nietzsche's *Nachlass* can be set aside, in which case there remains no good reason why one should not avail oneself of the pleasure and opportunity of studying Nietzsche's unpublished as well as published writings.[2] But this conclusion is much too negative, for the

----

[2]This conclusion ignores the additional problem of the integrity of the avail-

Nachlass contains many notes which are not merely harmless, but which make a valuable and very positive contribution to our understanding of Nietzsche. This general claim is especially true of Nietzsche's unpublished writings from the early 1870's (from which all of the selections in this volume are drawn). But before trying to assess the value and importance of these writings it might be useful to survey, first, Nietzsche's own varied activities during the years in question and the place of these writings therein and, secondly, the character of these manuscripts and notebooks themselves.

The Decisive Decade

The publication in 1878 of *Human, All-too-Human (MAMa)* seems to mark an obvious turning point in Nietzsche's personal life and intellectual career. The contrast between this book, as radical in form as in content, and his previously published writings is very striking. Little could have prepared readers of *The Birth of Tragedy* or the four *Untimely Meditations* for this explosive new book. As Nietzsche himself later remarked more than once, it was with *MAMa* that he first found the genuine path toward becoming himself.[3] Thus it is widely accepted that there was a crucial "break" in Nietzsche's career sometime just before the publication of *MAMa*. The main evidence for this view is the difference in manner and matter between the writings which precede and those which follow this juncture.

But though Nietzsche himself called explicit attention to the innovative character and special significance of *MAMa,* he denied any corresponding radical break in his own intellectual development. As he said (apparently with some surprise) many years later in a letter to Georg

---

able printed texts of Nietzsche's *Nachlass*. (See "Note on the Texts," below.) It would, of course, be best to have the *Nachlass* in the form in which it was left by Nietzsche rather than in the editorial arrangement of *GOA*, which has been the textual basis for almost all later editions of Nietzsche's *Works*. It will be years before the new edition (*WKG*) is complete, but enough of the *Nachlass* has already been printed in *WKG* to warrant some conclusions about the editorial policies of the earlier editors. In general, a comparison of the original texts with the "edited" versions corroborates a point made some years ago by Walter Kaufmann, namely, that the earlier editors had no desire to distort or falsify Nietzsche's philosophical views. Thus for the purpose of understanding Nietzsche's thought (as opposed to his life) there is considerably less danger in relying upon the early editions of the *Nachlass* than is sometimes feared. See Kaufmann's "Appendix" to his *Nietzsche: Philosopher, Psychologist, Antichrist,* 4th ed. (Princeton: Princeton University Press, 1974).

[3]See *EH*, III, "MAMa" as well as the 1886 preface to *MAMb&c*.

Brandes on May 4, 1888: "it all hangs together; it was on the right road for years." Indeed, for him *MAMa* was primarily significant as the first of his writings in which he found the courage to express publicly and unambiguously certain ideas which he had long since arrived at but had lacked the confidence to publish. In other words, what was revolutionary for Nietzsche in *MAMa* was that it was in this book that he first found a public voice which was genuinely his own. Thus he explained the apparent "break" between the four *Untimely Meditations* and *Human, All-too-Human*: the earlier writings have to be *antedated*, most of them give voice to ideas developed even before *The Birth of Tragedy*–ideas which in many cases he had already privately come to doubt. "For my own self," he explained, "I was already in the midst of moral skepticism and dissolution, *that is to say,* just as much involved *in the critique as in the deepening of all previous pessimism.* And already I believed (as the people say) 'in nothing at all any more'—including Schopenhauer. Just at this time I produced a work which has been kept secret: *On Truth and Lies in a Nonmoral Sense.*"[4] This passage is quite important, for in it Nietzsche not only affirms the continuity of his own intellectual development during the period in question (the early 1870's), but claims that the evidence for this affirmation is to be found in certain unpublished writings of the period.

Authors are notoriously unreliable guides to their own intellectual development and many readers might be inclined to dismiss Nietzsche's own remarks on this subject as transparent attempts to reconstruct his own past in a form more pleasing to himself. However, we need not rely upon his testimony in this matter; a substantial portion of the *Nachlass* in question is readily available. Thus, the unpublished writings of this period are key documents for any interpretation of Nietzsche's intellectual development—whether they provide evidence for the continuity of his thinking or show instead the sudden emergence of new perspectives and concerns. That Nietzsche himself attached special importance to the unpublished writings of this period may be inferred from the extraordinary references in his published writings and correspondence to these same unpublished writings. But before turning to an examination of the *Nachlass* of the early 1870's, a brief survey of the "public" side of Nietzsche's career during this period is in order.

In the spring of 1869, at the age of twenty-four, Nietzsche arrived at Basel, where he remained as a professor of Classical Philology for the next ten years. His teaching duties included, not just lectures and seminars at the university, but also instruction in the lower division *Pädagogium* attached to the university. The specialized topics upon which he lectured included: Greek and Latin poetry, Greek and Latin rhetoric, elements of philology, Latin grammar, Greek drama and religion, the

---

[4]1886 Preface to *MAMb* and *MAMc*.

Pre-Platonic philosophers, and the Platonic dialogues. In addition, during the early years of his professorship, he gave several well-attended public lectures, including an inaugural lecture on Homer (May 1869), two lectures on ancient tragedy and Socrates (spring 1870), and a series of five lectures on education (*ZB*, January-March 1872). Academic routine was interrupted for the first time in the summer of 1870, when Nietzsche volunteered to serve as a medical orderly during the Franco-Prussian war. After a brief period of service, ended by a general collapse of his health, he returned to Basel, but he never regained his full good health and was forced on that account to take convalescent leaves from his academic duties, first in the winter of 1875-6 and then again in the winter and spring of 1876-7.

It was of course also during the early Basel years that Nietzsche was personally and intellectually closest to Wagner. Immediately after moving to Basel he established a warm personal contact with the Wagner household at nearby Tribschen, which he maintained until the Wagners' departure for Bayreuth in the spring of 1872. Quite a bit of effort was devoted by the young professor to a variety of literary and non-literary schemes for furthering the Wagnerian cause during the period between 1869 and 1876.

During this same period Nietzsche wrote and published five books: *The Birth of Tragedy* (written 1870-1, first edition 1872, second edition 1874) and the four *Untimely Meditations*: on Strauss (*UBa*, written spring 1873, published 1873), on history (*UBb*, written fall 1873, published 1874), on Schopenhauer (*UBc*, written spring-summer 1874, published 1874), and on Wagner (*UBd*, written spring 1875, published 1876). *Human, All-too-Human* was written in 1876 and 1877 and published in 1878.

Yet this by no means tells the entire story, for in addition to his academic duties and the work involved in writing the books listed above, Nietzsche was involved in a number of other literary and philosophical projects. His correspondence during these years is filled with references to literary efforts and intellectual projects which were never published. Included among these are: a public manifesto and appeal on behalf of the Bayreuth project ("*Bayreuther Horizontbetrachtung*," January 1873) and a number of notes and drafts for additional "Untimely Meditations," most notably the large amount of manuscript material assembled for one on philology (*WP*, 1874-5). But overshadowing these projects are the many plans and notes which Nietzsche amassed for a major book which was to be concerned with a number of closely interconnected themes—the nature of philosophy, the philosopher's relation to culture, the analysis of truth and knowledge, the meaning and value of the demand for absolute truth: all of which were to be treated within the framework of an historical exposition of the ancient Greek philosophers. In his correspondence of the period Nietzsche referred to this general project under a variety of different names, but the plans and notes which he made for it (and which have since been published in the various editions of his *Nachlass*) have come to be known under the collective title of Nietzsche's "Philosophers' Book" (*Philosophenbuch*).[5]

The History of Nietzsche's "Philosophers' Book"

In the spring of 1872, Nietzsche delivered his series of public lectures "On the Future of our Educational Institutions." He seemed generally pleased with these lectures and expressed his intention to revise and expand them for publication. By the end of August the same year, however, he was writing to his friend Erwin Rohde that he had decided to set aside the revision of the lectures on education and to redirect his energies. The nature of his new undertaking is not specified, beyond the cryptic words: "My projects are now somewhat confused. And yet I feel myself to be always upon a *single* track—there is no confusion, and if time only permits, I will expose them to the light of day. My summer's occupation with the Pre-Platonic philosophers has been especially fruitful."[6] What Nietzsche refers to here is the course on the Pre-Platonic philosophers which he gave during the summer semester of 1872. This course of lectures, which he offered on four different occasions, was clearly his personal favorite and was the one upon which he worked the hardest, especially during the summer semester of 1872.[7]

Judging from the letters of this period, the new project quickly came to absorb the center of Nietzsche's attention. On November 21, 1872 he wrote to Rohde: "I am considering arranging my next book[8] as a

---

[5]To be precise, what is usually designated as Nietzsche's "*Philosophenbuch*" consists of two parts: an "historical" half consisting of *Pt/G,* plus various notes for its continuation, and a "theoretical" half, consisting of *P, PAK, WL.* and *WWK.* Thus what is translated in this volume is the entire "theoretical" part of the "*Philosophenbuch,*" plus three other selections from the same period which seem to me to belong to the same general circle of problems and concerns. For further details concerning the individual selections, see the "Note on the Texts" below.

[6]Letter to Rohde, August 26, 1872. In the notes before 1875 Nietzsche almost invariably speaks of the "Pre-Platonic" rather than Pre-Socratic philosophers. This is significant because it indicates that he considered Socrates to be not simply the radical new spokesman for "theoretical optimism" which he is 'depicted as being in *GT,* but to be part of a single line of *development,* leading back to Thales. So understood, Socrates is himself at least as much of an end as a beginning.

[7]See letter to Rohde, June 11, 1872. Regarding the various versions of the lectures on Pre-Platonic philosophy, cf. below "Note on Texts, Translation, and Annotation," n. 4.

[8]*Schrift,* literally "writing." This is Nietzsche's favorite word for his own literary productions.

Festschrift for the year 1874 and Bayreuth; perhaps it will bear the title *The Last Philosopher.*" Then again, on December 7 he wrote to Rohde: "*The Philosopher*, my unhatched intellectual egg, still exists only in my mind—as colorful and as worth hunting for as a beautiful Easter egg is for good children."

The weeks immediately following Christmas of 1872 were devoted to propagandizing for Wagner, but by January 31, 1873 Nietzsche was again writing to Rohde: "By the way, I am once again writing on the old Greek philosophers, and one day or another a manuscript will arrive for you, as a sample." This promise was repeated in another letter of February 21. What is apparently the same project was mentioned again in a letter of February 8, 1873 to his mother and sister, though this time under a different title: "Besides I have been busy, and if health and the Easter vacation permit, then I will be finished with a new book before the beginning of the summer. The title will probably be *Philosophy in the Tragic Age of the Greeks.*" Yet another title appears in a letter of February 24 to Carl von Gersdorf, in which Nietzsche wrote: "My book grows and forms itself into a companion piece to the *Birth* [*of Tragedy*]. Perhaps the title will be *The Philosopher as Cultural Physician*," adding that he hopes to surprise Wagner with it on his birthday (May 22). The character of the book in question is described in more detail in a letter to Malwida von Meysenbug written at the end of the same month:

> I now long for sunshine and some cheerfulness, especially in order to be able to finish a manuscript dealing with philosophical matters and upon which I have worked with genuine love. In this manuscript all the great philosophers who lived during the tragic age of the Greeks, that is to say, during the sixth and fifth centuries, appear. It is most remarkable that the Greeks philosophized at all during this period—even more, how they philosophized!
>
> Wish something cheerful and cheering for me, so that I may find the desire and courage for this labor and for its completion, especially during the Easter vacation, when I have a few free days. With this book I return to a supremely practical problem of culture. I am occasionally worried and afraid.

For the next month Nietzsche continued his intermittent work on this project, writing to Rohde on March 22: "I hope to be far enough along to send you a large section of my very slowly gestating book on Greek philosophy for provisional examination. Nothing is set concerning the title, but if it were to be called *The Philosopher as Cultural Physician*, you would see thereby that I am concerned with a fine general problem and not merely with an historical one." But what is perhaps the most informative reference to this project in any of his letters is found in one written to von Gersdorff in April 5, 1873:

> I will be bringing to Bayreuth a manuscript, *Philosophy in the Tragic Age of the Greeks*, to present there. The whole thing is still very far from being in

publishable form. I am becoming more and more strict with myself and must still wait some time before attempting yet another version (the *fourth* presentation of the same theme). It was also necessary for me to pursue the most peculiar studies for this end—I even touched fearlessly upon mathematics, then mechanics, chemical atomic theory, etc. I have again convinced myself in the most magnificent manner of what the Greeks were and are. The distance from Thales to Socrates is simply enormous.

After returning from Easter at Bayreuth Nietzsche wrote the book on Strauss and hit upon the idea of a series of "Untimely Meditations." Over the next years he devoted more and more of his time and energy to this new project—though the new project was of a type which allowed him to incorporate almost anything into its format.[9] The projected book on philosophy and the Greeks was not, however, completely abandoned. Indeed, most of the summer of 1873 was devoted to a new presentation of the epistemological theme first broached in the previously mentioned writings on philosophy and the Greeks. And in the fall of 1873 many of his previously developed thoughts on the nature of philosophy were incorporated into the notes for what was apparently to be an "Untimely Meditation" on the subject of philosophy (*Die Philosophie im Bedrängniss*). This project did not advance very far, though some of the notes assembled for it were later employed in the book on Schopenhauer (*UBc*). Finally, near the end of 1875 Nietzsche once again returned to the theme of Pre-Platonic philosophy, this time with special reference to the contrast between "science" and "wisdom." This was, however, to be his last attempt at that project which had featured so prominently in his plans since the summer of 1872.[10]

---

[9]Nietzsche's basic intention in projecting the series of "Untimely Meditations" was to lay down an advance barrage against as many aspects of contemporary life as possible. But from the beginning he saw this as a project to be *followed* by the presentation of his own more constructive thoughts. Thus in separate letters to Rohde (March 19, 1874) and von Meysebug (October 25, 1874) he describes the projected series of "Untimely Meditations" as a five year project for purging himself of all of his hostile and negative thoughts and feelings. He never lost sight of the *responsibilities* he had thereby assumed, or the relation between his destructive and constructive work. In this regard, cf. the following autobiographical fragment from 1885-7 (*GOA*, XIV, p. 381 = *MA*, XIV, p. 339): "For me, my 'Untimely Ones' signify *promises*. What they are for others, I do not know. Believe me, I would have ceased living a long time ago if I had turned aside even a single step from these promises! Perhaps there will yet come a person who will discover that from *Human, All-too-Human* on, I have done nothing but fulfill my own promises."

[10]Actually, though there is no indication that Nietzsche began serious work on the projected book on philosophy and the Greeks before 1872, there is some evidence that he had at least hit upon the idea of such a book several years

Without abandoning our relatively external point of view, we are able to reach the following conclusions about the *Nachlass* of the early 1870's: Between the summer of 1872 and the end of 1875, but particularly in the year between the fall of 1872 and the fall of 1873, Nietzsche was compiling notes for a major book which was, in some sense, to be a "companion piece" to *The Birth of Tragedy*, a book which was to include a presentation of the history of Pre-Platonic philosophy but which was not envisioned to be a merely historical study. On the contrary, the book was supposed to be concerned with a "fine general problem," with a "supremely practical problem of culture." Finally, in order to pursue this project Nietzsche had had to involve himself in an intense study of science and the theory of knowledge.

One point, however, is quite clear: Nietzsche never arrived at any single, clear, and definite plan for the projected book; instead, he drafted dozens of different outlines, compiled hundreds of pages of notes, and experimented with a variety of ways of organizing and presenting his accumulated thoughts on the subject. The indeterminate character as well as the several sides of the projected book are reflected in the various tentative titles which Nietzsche assigned to it over the years: "The Last Philosopher," "The Philosopher," "Philosophy in the Tragic Age of the Greeks," "The Philosopher as Cultural Physician," "The Justification of Philosophy by the Greeks," "Plato and his Predecessors,"[11] "On Truth and Lies in a Nonmoral Sense," "Philosophy in Hard Times," and "The Struggle between Science and Wisdom."

Something else which is clearly evident is that the projected work involved the thorough integration of "theoretical," "historical," and

---

earlier, in 1870. The evidence in question is a page in notebook P I 15 on which the following three titles appear, one after the other:

"The Birth of Tragedy
The Philosophers of the Tragic Age
On the Future of our Educational Institutions"

Since the lectures on education were not given until the spring of 1872 and the work on the book on Greek philosophers did not begin until the late summer or fall of that year, this is a remarkable note. It is printed on p. 78 of Karl Schlechta and Anni Anders', *Friedrich Nietzsche. Von den verborgenen Anfangen seines Philosophierens* (Stuttgart-Bad Cannstadt: Frommann, 1962). [see *WKG*, III, 3, p. 66].

[11]According to the first *Nachbericht* to *GOA*, X, p. 501, the title "Plato and his Predecessors" dates from the summer of 1876 when Nietzsche considered—and quickly abandoned—a plan to expand his project to include Plato. The other title, "The Justification of Philosophy by the Greeks," occurs as an isolated entry in notebook P I 20b (Summer 1872 to the beginning of 1873) and is printed in *GOA*, X, p. 502 [= *WKG*. III, 4, p. 104].

"practical" problems. What Nietzsche had in mind was not a work of three chapters: an "historical" presentation of the development of Pre-Platonic philosophy, a "theoretical" analysis of problems of knowledge and truth, and a "practical" consideration of the value of the knowledge drive and the relation between philosophy and culture. All three of these themes were clearly meant to figure prominently in the projected book, but by no means was any one of them to be treated independently of the other two. On the contrary, the evidence is that Nietzsche wished to use his analyses of knowledge and culture to illuminate the history of Greek philosophy at the same time that he used that history to illustrate and explain his conclusions regarding knowledge and culture. It is true that certain of the manuscripts which Nietzsche worked on in connection with the projected book were of a relatively purely "historical" or "theoretical" character. The well-known *Philosophy in the Tragic Age of the Greeks* is an instance of the first type. But as Nietzsche explained in his letter of April 5, 1873 to von Gersdorff, he did not consider *PtZG* to be a separately publishable work, and the reason for this judgment was not any lack of completeness in its historical exposition, but rather its *merely* historical character. It seems quite clear that, in 1873 anyway,[12] Nietzsche considered the manuscript of *PtZG* to be little more than a bare skeleton waiting to be fleshed out, an historical armature for the support of arguments and conclusions concerning the general problems of philosophy, culture, and knowledge. Similarly, the relatively "theoretical" manuscripts, such as "On Truth and Lies in a Nonmoral Sense", were not intended for separate publication, but were meant to be integrated with a narrative history of Pre-Platonic philosophy.

Unfortunately, the projected book which would successfully weave together all of these threads was never written. Perhaps it was never written precisely because Nietzsche was not able to integrate the various themes to his own satisfaction. All that we have are the diverse notes, plans, and drafts which Nietzsche compiled during the time he was working on this project. *Philosophy in the Tragic Age of the Greeks,* which is a relatively finished historical survey of the development of ancient philosophy, is the best known selection from this material, but it is only a small part of the book which Nietzsche planned to write. There are, in addition, a number of other "texts" (most of them editorial compilations

---

[12]Of course it is possible that Nietzsche might, at some later date, have considered publishing *PtZG* separately. Indeed, this seems to have been the case. In the spring of 1874 he had a fair copy of the manuscript made, in which he made a few corrections in his own hand at some later time. Finally, in 1879 when he thought he was dying and tried to make arrangements for the disposition of his papers, he dictated the second short preface to *PtZG*. It is nevertheless certain that *PtZG* was not originally intended to be published as an independent work.

from the notebooks of the same period) which deal much more explicitly with the "theoretical" questions which were to be treated in the unwritten book on philosophy and the Greeks. Most of these additional notes are translated in the present volume. Some preliminary idea of the importance and interest of these unpublished writings may be gained from a more detailed consideration of the major themes and questions with which they are concerned.

Culture

If there is any theme unquestionably audible in everything that Nietzsche wrote it is the theme of culture, the problem of civilization: what is it? how has it been achieved? how can it be preserved? These questions are investigated again and again in the unpublished, as in the published writings of the early 1870's. Though there is nothing in the notebooks on this topic which will surprise anyone well acquainted with Nietzsche's published writings, a reader unfamiliar with Nietzsche's basic theory of culture may benefit from a few words on the subject.

Nietzsche's fundamental idea of culture is the Goethean one of harmonious manifoldness or unity in diversity. Culture is not an artificial homogeneity imposed by external restraints or ascetic self-denial, but an organic unity *cultivated* on the very soil of discord and difference: "the concept of culture as a new and improved *physis*, with no inner and outer, no dissemblance and convention, the concept of culture as unanimity of living, thinking, seeming, and willing."[13] One of Nietzsche's most important discoveries was the unifying function of values and goals and his interpretation of them as essential instruments for the creation and preservation of culture.

What gives Nietzsche's remarks on this subject their special urgency, however, is his conviction—which increased with the years—that modern "culture" lacks genuine unity and is thus no true culture at all. To use one of his favorite words, modern culture is a "motley" culture, one which displays its weakness by its tolerance and eclecticism, as well as in its all-pervasive dichotomy between inner and outer, private and public life.[14] Thus modern culture is a false or counterfeit culture. From this observation it is a short step to forecasting the imminent collapse of Western civilization. Consequently, Nietzsche's meditations upon culture usually occur within the context of an analysis of the disintegration of modern culture. But from the beginning, Nietzsche's purpose in con-

---

[13]*UBb*, 10. Regarding the meaning of *"physis"* in this definition, see below, *PB*, n. 68. Also, compare this definition of culture with the definition in *PB*, 48 of culture as "a single temperament and key composed of many originally hostile forces, which now enable a melody to be played."

ducting such investigations was not to draw from them the cold comfort of the Schopenhauerian pessimist who privately rejoices to see his theory confirmed in practice; instead, his task was "to comprehend *the internal coherence and necessity of every true culture*" (*P*, 33) in order to be able to minister to the diseased culture of the present. The reason for Nietzsche's interest in the general question of culture is made explicit in section 25 of *MAMa*: "If mankind is not to destroy itself . . . there must be discovered, as a scientific criterion for ecumenical goals, a *knowledge of the conditions of culture* which surpasses all previous levels of such knowledge. Herein lies the immense task for the great minds of the next century." The search for "ecumenical goals," i.e. goals which could subordinate and unify all lesser goals and could thus serve what Zarathustra called "the meaning of the earth," occupied the center of Nietzsche's attentions in his later books. But in the earlier published and unpublished writings his main concern was with the *prior* task of determining the general nature and preconditions of culture as such and its relation to other forces.

Cultural unity is impossible apart from some form of *mastery*: this is Nietzsche's first conclusion concerning culture. In order for culture to be possible at all there must be hierarchy, obedience, subordination, and subjugation. What Nietzsche later called "the pathos of distance" is a prerequisite for any culture whatsoever, for only out of such a pathos can a person or class gain the feeling of justified self-confidence required by the creators of cultural unity, the confidence to legislate "greatness." Culture demands such creator/commanders, precisely because "the *culture* of a people is manifest in the unifying mastery of their drives" (*P*, 46), and because such "unifying mastery" is achieved only by subordinating what is "small" to what is "great." Where this distinction is not admitted, there no culture can spring up or survive; and where a culture does exist its character is determined by the character of this distinction, for "culture depends upon the way in which one defines what is 'great.' "[15]

_____

[14]See *UBb*, 4 and *UBd*, 5 for early versions of this indictment of modernity, which was sharpened and intensified in Nietzsche's later works.

[15]See VII, B, 7 (below). This theory of culture might appear to have definite social and political implications. Nietzsche himself certainly thought so and did not hesitate to draw them, hesitantly in his published writings of the early 1870's and forthrightly in certain unpublished writings of the same period (most notably, the important essay on the Greek state, *GS*, and the first and third of the lectures on education, *LB*): Social hierarchy is the precondition for culture, which can only be built upon a broad base of human toil; the achievements of "the genius" of culture presuppose the labors of "the slaves." Thus, on the one hand, culture is always the possession of a socially privileged elite; but on the other, the function of this elite is to impose a saving unity upon (and thus, in Nietzsche's words, to "justify") the society as a whole.

Another important feature of Nietzsche's account of culture is the striking similarity he found between cultural unity and *artistic* unity. Through unity of style a work of art displays just that "harmonious manifoldness" which is the sign of culture. Furthermore the unity of the work of art is like the unity of a culture in that it is no mere external or formal unity. Style is as integral to culture as it is to art, both of which are destroyed by the insistence upon separating form and content. Hence Nietzsche often used aesthetic terminology to describe culture as "above all, the unity of artistic style in all the expressions of a people's life" (*UBa*, 1). This affinity between cultural and artistic unity was no doubt instrumental in directing him toward *art* in his search for forces capable of cultural regeneration.

But though the artist might seem a prime candidate for the role of cultural founder, there are two other obvious candidates: the religious teacher ("saint"), and the philosopher.[16] Each of these figures seems sufficiently infected with "the pathos of distance" to be able to define what is great for a people, and history offers at least as many examples of cultures which seem to have their roots in religion and philosophy as it does of those based upon art. Thus one of the issues which Nietzsche explored, particularly in his notebooks of the early 1870's, is the relative ability of the artist, the saint, and the philosopher to impose cultural unity upon a people and an age. A distinguishing feature of this exploration is Nietzsche's attempt to recognize and to understand historical differences between types of cultures. Specifically, he distinguished between: the mythical cultures which preceded classical antiquity, the "tragic culture" of Greece in the sixth and fifth centuries B.C.; the "Alexandrian culture" of late antiquity, decadent modern culture, and the kind of genuine new culture which might be created under present conditions.[17]

It is important to keep these historical distinctions in mind when interpreting Nietzsche's conflicting remarks on culture (e.g. some of the notes translated in this volume appear to support the view that philosophy can serve as a foundation for culture, whereas others seem to deny it.) The appearance of contradiction is easily removed by introducing the above historical distinctions; for what might indeed have served as a viable foundation for culture at one time (e.g. religion in the age before

---

[16]This trinity of genius—saint, philosopher, and artist—is thoroughly Schopenhauerian, though Nietzsche's conclusions regarding the cultural significance of the three is profoundly un-Schopenhauerian. One explanation of this difference is Schopenhauer's complete lack of any historical sense.

[17]Implicit in *GT*, these historical distinctions between types of cultures are most fully developed in the notes assembled for the unwritten "Meditation" on philology. These notes, *WP*, are especially concerned with the necessary hostility between antique and modern culture. See especially *WP*, 20, 30 and 40.

antiquity) may be utterly incapable of playing the same role at a later date and under different circumstances. Thus from the fact that philosophy was *once* able to shape and determine a culture it does not follow that it is *now* able to do so.

What Nietzsche wished to learn from his general and historical study of culture were the conditions for cultural renewal in the modern world. But to answer this question he had to face squarely two closely related and distinctive characteristics of modern times, both of which would seem to work against the very possibility of establishing (or re-establishing) the kind of cultural unity analyzed by Nietzsche. The first of these two defining characteristics of modernity is its principled opposition to every form of mastery or subjugation, especially its opposition to any form of spiritual tyranny. To the extent, therefore, that culture requires mastery and mastery presupposes hierarchy, modern proponents of culture must set themselves squarely against one of the strongest currents of their age, for "we desire to regain mastery over that which has been totally released."[18]

Secondly, the modern world is above all the world of "science"—in the broad sense of disciplined, theoretically grounded inquiry into the true nature of things.[19] However far short he may actually fall of his goal, the modern, "enlightened" man is determined to banish every vestige of illusion from himself and his world, to direct the merciless light of rational inquiry into even the darkest and most hallowed recesses of the spirit. Such a man is absolutely unwilling to settle for anything less than what he consideres "true"—and what he considers true is only what he can measure and weigh. Everything must be brought before the bar of conscious reflection and there tried. But every past culture seemed to Nietzsche to have drawn its driving energy from an unconscious and unexamined center of vitality and to have propagated itself largely by means of illusions. Consequently, the problem of modern culture cannot be separated from the problem of modern science.

The first question is: can any genuine culture satisfy the stringent requirements of modern scientific consciousness? Can we add a fourth figure to our list of cultural founders: the man of science who establishes a "scientific culture"? Will such a culture thrive without any illusions? Or is this expectation only the biggest illusion of all? But an even more fundamental question has to do with the *legitimacy* of modern scientific consciousness itself. What does it demand when it demands "knowledge"

---

[18]*P*, 36. For a description of the modern age and its opposition to spiritual tyranny, see *MAMa*, 261.

[19]The ordinary German word for science (*Wissenschaft*, which is sometimes translated as "scholarship") has this broad connotation. See below, *P*, n. 14. In what follows I shall be using "science" in this broader sense, which is by no means synonymous with "*natural* science."

and "truth"? Can such demands be satisfied, even in principle? If not, what is the *meaning* and *value* of the demand for truth—both originally and now? In other words, during the early 1870's Nietzsche's general interest in culture led him to an investigation of the problem of a culture "based upon knowledge," and in order to investigate this possibility he was forced to delve rather deeply into narrower questions concerning the nature, origin, and value of knowing. The notebooks of this period contain the closest thing Nietzsche ever wrote to a coherent and sustained exposition of his "theory of knowledge."

Knowledge

A survey of Nietzsche's published remarks on the problem of knowledge and the nature of truth reveals a superficial inconsistency. On the one hand, he often asserts that human beings are unable to obtain genuine knowledge, that we are condemned to illusions, lies, perspectives, and interpretations; on the other, there are many characteristic passages in which truths are spoken of as instruments for achieving human ends and in which knowing is defined as the actual process by which man makes his world habitable. Occasionally, both views are present in a single sentence, such as the following: "what then in the end are all of man's truths? They are only his *irrefutable* errors."[20]

The air of paradox surrounding Nietzsche's remarks on this subject is quickly dispelled by recognizing the simple, though implicit, distinction between two very different senses of "truth" and "knowledge." On the one hand, Nietzsche constantly presupposed, and thought that science presupposes, a rather literal correspondence model of knowledge and ideal of descriptive adequacy. When the knowledge that we actually think we possess is measured by such an ideal it invariably falls short of the expected standard of truth. On the other hand, Nietzsche did not fail to see that the distinction between truth and falsity lends itself to an altogether different interpretation to which ideal standards of perfectly adequate description are irrelevant. Understood in this second sense,

---

[20]*FW*, 307. Cf. the similar definition in *WM*, 493: "Truth is the kind of error without which a certain species of life could not live." A few representative passages in which Nietzsche argues for radical skepticism (thus presupposing the descriptivist ideal of truth) are: *GT*, 15; *MAMa*, 2; *M*, 243; *JGB*, 16; and *GM*, III, 12. Some passages in which he proposes an alternate, "instrumental" account of truth are: *UBb*, 10; *MAMa*, 31-2; and *JGB*, 4, 11, 34. (However, it should be noted that Nietzsche's proposals for interpreting truths in terms of their value for human life are almost invariably accompanied with some remark concerning the "illusory" or "fictional" character of such truths. These remarks are incomprehensible to those who fail to recognize Nietzsche's own deep and abiding commitment to the correspondence ideal which he criticized so mercilessly.)

knowing is not an attempt to mirror an independently real world, but rather a process of accommodating ourselves to the world in which we live and that world to us: truths are humanly constructed instruments designed to serve human purposes. These two views of the nature of truth and knowledge are encountered together in almost all of Nietzsche's writings; however, they receive their clearest exposition and are most explicitly related to each other in just those unpublished writings with which we are here concerned.

The prevailing epistemological mood of the notebooks of the early 1870's is one of profound nihilism, with respect both to the possibility of genuine knowledge ("Truth cannot be recognized. Everything which is knowable is illusion." *WL*, 187), and the value of seeking it ("Considered as an unconditional duty, truth stands in a hostile and destructive relationship to the world." *WL*, 176). But in these writings, Nietzsche not only gave eloquent expression to his doubts on the subject of knowledge, he connected these doubts with their theoretical presuppositions and consequences. That is to say, he developed an *analysis* of the nature of knowledge, which he conjoined with an *argument* designed to show how scepticism unavoidably follows from the naive pursuit of truth ("theoretical optimism"). On the basis of this analysis and argument, Nietzsche made the first of his many attempts to *evaluate* the significance of the demand for truth.

According to *WL*, 1, the typical "knower," or "lover of truth" is a man who fancies himself confronted with an independently real world, which it is his task to examine, using his senses and his reason, so that he may finally succeed in throwing off illusion and in knowing the world just as it is. This point will be reached when his representations correspond exactly and in every detail to the "things themselves," when "designations" coincide with "things," thus guaranteeing "the adequate expression of an object in the subject." That such "correspondence" or "coincidence" is possible is a tacit *presupposition* of his quest for truths which are "really and universally valid apart from man."

As an *ideal*, Nietzsche believes that this theoretical model is almost universally presupposed in the modern, "enlightened" world; indeed, he himself presupposes it insofar as he endorses the skepticism to which it inevitably leads.[21] The reason that this descriptivist ideal leads to skepti-

---

[21]To the extent that Nietzsche subscribed to the correspondence ideal he held that the world has a "true nature," which is unknowable. However critical he may later have become of the distinction between "reality" and "appearance" (see, e.g. the section entitled "How the True World finally became a Fable" in *GD*), it *is* presupposed in his earlier writings, including *GT* and the notes translated in this volume. He seems to have thought of the metaphysically real world as a primal, unformed choas, a world (uncoincidentally) related to our world of knowledge

cism is that it is unsatisfiable in principle as well as in practice. Further-more, we can become aware that our own ideal of absolute knowledge is "a contradictory impossibility" (*WL*, 1). We can do this by reflection upon the character of human knowing and its incompatibility with our implicit ideal of truth. Put most starkly, the ideal demands a relation between knower and known so immediate as to require virtual identity—a re-quirement which conflicts with the difference and mediation ingredient in all real knowing. Thus, "absolute and unconditional knowledge is the desire to know without knowledge" (*P*, 114).

Philosophers have used a variety of images to characterize the relation between the knower and the known. To take two examples which are also used by Nietzsche, this relation has been compared to the relation between an original and a copy, or the relation between an object and its reflection in a mirror. However, Nietzsche favors a more original system of imagery, one obviously inspired by his philological background. Knowing always involves the kind of creative transference of meaning which we associate with *metaphors*; indeed, it "is nothing but working with the favorite metaphors . . ." (*P*, 149). What Nietzsche means by the puzzl-ing assertion that all knowledge involves metaphor is suggested by the etymology of the Greek word itself, which is derived from a verb mean-ing "to carry over," "to carry across," or "to transfer."[22] The reason that all knowledge involves metaphor is that knowing is supposed to be "the adequate expression of an object in the subject." And since the "subject" and the "object," the "knower" and the "known," are imagined to be radically independent of each other, knowing always demands a "trans-fer" or "carry-over" from the one sphere into the other. When he exam-ined actual cases of knowledge, Nietzsche concluded that the process involved in bridging the gap between subject and object bears a much closer resemblance to the process of metaphor formation than to any kind of "picturing" or "mirroring." He discovered a physical illustration of what he called the process of metaphor formation in the acoustical experiments of Chladni, in which sounds were "transferred" into sand patterns on a flat surface.[23]

Nietzsche found the parallel between knowing and metaphor forma-tion immensely suggestive, as well as less misleading and more widely applicable than alternative ways of interpreting the activity of knowing. His analysis of the "transferences" involved in simple perceptual judg-

---

and experience very much in the way that Schopenhauer's world of "will" is related to the world of "representation." (See below, *P*, 120, 123 and *PW*.)

[22] A key term in Nietzsche's own epistemological vocabulary is the German word, *übertragen*, which has almost exactly the same etymological meaning as the Greek verb. See below, *P*, n. 83.

[23] See below, *P*, n. 55.

ments is a good example of the way in which he elaborated this basic idea. First, there is the "purely physiological" transformation of a particular nerve stimulus into a particular image ("first metaphor").[24] Second, there is the translation of the perceived visual image into a sound, as occurs, for example, when I designate a particular visual image by saying "leaf." Third, the sound ("leaf") is detached from its original, particular relation to a particular image and allowed to serve as a metaphor for (i.e. to "refer to") an indefinitely large number of more or less similar images. Nietzsche calls this step "concept formation"; it is the one which most clearly reveals how knowing works to organize and master experience. (At the same time, of course, it is the step which most clearly shows why human knowing must always fall short of the previously mentioned correspondence ideal of descriptive adequacy.) It is also the step which most clearly indicates how closely Nietzsche's theory of knowledge is tied to a theory of *language*.

Though Michel Fouçault perhaps overstates matters when he contends that Nietzsche was "the first to reconcile the philosophical task with a radical reflection on language,"[25] it is certainly true that one of the most remarkable and significant features of Nietzsche's theory of knowledge is his grasp of the transcendental function of semantic unities and syntactical categories, their constitutive contributions to human understanding and the world we would understand. For Nietzsche language was much more than a neutral medium of expression or a natural phenomenon to be realistically described. "The spiritual activity of millenia is deposited in language" (*P*, 79); "the legislation of language likewise establishes the first laws of truth" (*WL*, 1). Philosophers, he thought, are guilty of ignoring the contribution which language makes to our world and our knowledge, and thus, without realizing it, they "struggle in the nets of language"—nets in which they, like everyone else, are caught in the end. Thus an essential ingredient in Nietzsche's analysis of knowledge, one which helps to enforce the conclusion that the kind of absolute truth demanded by the knowledge drive is not obtainable, is his very advanced appreciation of the extent to which we are all, philosophers included, "seduced" by words.[26]

---

[24]In several passages in these notebooks Nietzsche tried to develop a purely physiological account of consciousness and perception (see e.g. *P*, 64, 67, 97, and 122). Similar attempts may be found in Nietzsche's *Nachlass* from every stage of his career, and occasionally are hinted at in his published writings. I am convinced that Nietzsche always thought that consciousness has a physiological explanation, though his various attempts to provide such an explanation were never very successful. See below, *P*, n. 56 and n. 74.

[25]*Les mots et les choses* (Paris: Gallimard, 1966), p. 316.

[26]See below, *P*, 79; *WL*, 1; and *WWK*, p. 168. There are certain obvious similarities between this aspect of Nietzsche's theory of language and some well-known theses of contemporary "ordinary language philosophy." (Additional

Because of the role which syntactical categories play in structuring our thought and which semantic unities (concepts) play in constructing our world, Nietzsche concluded that knowledge could never be any more purely descriptive than language itself. And for him, the fundamental character of language is far more clearly revealed in the self-consciously creative use which the artist makes of language than by the putatively objective and literal propositions of natural science: language *is* rhetoric. It is not a transparent, neutral medium for the communication of timeless truths or the reflection of "things in themselves." In concepts and words men construct a second, more human, nature for themselves—an artfully constructed world which is the greatest testimony to the fundamental human power of imagination (or, as Nietzsche called it, "the drive toward the formation of metaphors").[27] Knowing is therefore founded upon operations which are usually dismissed as mere rhetorical tropes: upon transferring things from one sphere to an entirely different one (metaphor): upon confusing a thing with its properties (metonymy); upon taking a part for a whole (synecdoche); and upon illicit generalizations and abrupt shifts from one subject to another (metastasis). Science is fully as dependent upon such human, all-too-human building materials as are common understanding and art.

What then is truth? a movable host of metaphors, metonymies, and anthropomorphisms: in short, a sum of human relations which have been poetically and rhetorically intensified, transferred, and embellished, and

---

points of resemblance include his analysis of meaning in terms of use and his "family resemblance" interpretation of names.) But the *differences* between Nietzsche and most contemporary philosophers interested in language are even more striking than the similarities. The outstanding epistemological feature of Nietzsche's account of language—a feature notably absent from most contemporary discussions of the subject—is his constant *critical* intent. He wished to *expose* the unsuspected role which language has played in forming our thoughts and our conception of reality in order to try to *escape* its transcendental distortions.

[27]According to *WL*, 2, this drive toward the formation of metaphors "is the fundamental human drive, which one cannot for a single instant dispense with in thought, for one would thereby dispense with man himself." It is thus the same fundamental human drive which underlies language, ordinary understanding, science, myth, and art. Indeed, in some of the notes of this period (e.g. *P*, 52, 110) Nietzsche even suggests that this fundamental creative power is not limited to man, but is present everywhere in nature. (This idea, which has certain affinities with some of Nietzsche's later views concerning the "Will to Power," seems to have been suggested to him by his reading of Zöllner during the fall of 1872. See below, *PB*, n. 58.) Valuable material concerning Nietzsche's understanding of the fundamentally *rhetorical* and *metaphorical* character of language is contained in the lectures on rhetoric he delivered at the University of Basel. These lectures have only recently been published, along with an English translation, in *Friedrich Nietzsche on Rhetoric and Language*, ed. and trans. Sander L. Gilman, Carole Blair, and David J. Parent (New York: Oxford University Press, 1989).

which, after long usage, seem to a people to be fixed, canonical, and binding. Truths are illusions which we have forgotten are illusions; they are metaphors that have become worn out and have been drained of sensuous force, coins which have lost their embossing and are now considered as metal and no longer as coins.[28]

But how far such humanly attainable "truths" are from eternally valid descriptions of independently real things! If we are to retain our original epistemological ideal, then we must conclude that the only genuine truths which we can obtain are formal tautologies, mere "empty husks" of knowledge.[29] As for those human truths which we obtain from the exercise of our power of knowing—i.e. our power of metaphor formation—they clearly do *not* touch the heart of any independent reality, and since "knowing is nothing but working with the favorite metaphors," then "naturally, it cannot penetrate the realm of truth" (*P*, 149). Nor can we claim that our intellect copies or mirrors things, for we occupy no privileged standpoint from which we might be able to compare the "original" with the "copy"; if our intellect is a mirror, it is not one that we stand before. We *are* the mirror in this case, and our understanding is necessarily superficial, for we have no criteria for evaluating our "representations" apart from our own, always anthropomorphic standards of measurement and evaluation.[30]

If, despite the foregoing analysis of knowledge, we wish to make some sense of the ordinary distinction between "truths" and "lies" (or "illusions") we can only do so by proposing another account of the nature of truth, one radically different from the previously presupposed ideal. This is, of course, just what Nietzsche attempted to do: to complement his own skeptical analysis of knowledge with a theory of "truth and lies in a nonmoral sense." Judged by the ideal criterion of perfect descriptive adequacy, "truths" (in this second sense) will be just as illusory and false as "lies"; but judged by the more naturalistic criterion of utility for human life, some products of the intellect are more valuable ("truer") than others.

Stated very briefly, Nietzsche admitted two fundamental life-preserving functions of the previously analyzed process of knowing, and thus two ways in which truths might be distinguished from lies as instruments of essential human purposes. First of all, conventional designations are essential if there is to be any social life, and thus any culture or genuinely "human" form of life at all. One function then of the purely conventional distinction between "truth" and "falsity" (i.e., customary and non-customary designations for things) is to facilitate social life.

---

[28]*WL*, 1. See also below *P*, 91, 133, 140-2, 144, 148, 152.
[29]See below, *WL*, 1; *P*, 54, 150, and n. 46.
[30]See below *P*, 54, 84, 99, 101, 102, 114.

Secondly, the process of knowing is man's way of giving human form to a hostile world—a way of measuring the world by human standards and thus an essential step toward gaining mastery over the world. Thus the very features of knowledge and truth which were previously grounds for skepticism become, in the new account, foundations of the very possibility of truth. It is because knowledge is thoroughly "anthropomorphic" that it can minister to genuine human needs. It is because man has the capacity for metaphor formation that he can survive without sharp teeth or swift limbs.

Both the "ideal" and the "naturalistic" definitions of truth seem to be presupposed in the modern world, but the demands for the two different types of "truth" contradict each other. There is a manifest incompatibility between the desire to free oneself of all illusions, to settle for nothing less than ideal certainty in questions of truth, and the need for life-preserving fictions, which apparently must be believed to be true if they are to serve their intended function. For truths of this latter, instrumental type are only human creations, demanding for their production the identification of things which are *not* equal and requiring unacknowledged transferences from one sphere to another: in short, such "truths" are nothing but "lies" and "illusions."[31]

Consequently, Nietzsche's distinction between two kinds of truth points toward a more fundamental *value* distinction. Analysis of the conditions and character of knowledge is therefore only half of Nietzsche's "theory of knowledge." Left to be answered is the question of the relative significance and value of the conflicting demands uncovered by Nietzsche's analysis. In particular, Nietzsche took as his task the problem of the meaning and value of the demand for absolute truth, which proscribes illusion and seems to lead to the most desperate epistemological nihilism. Over and over again in the *Nachlass* of the early 1870's he

---

[31]See below *P*, 47, 50-2, 126; and *WL*, 1-2. Granted the apparent inutility of the demand for pure or "absolute" truth, it is not easy to imagine how the drive for such an impossible ideal could have ever arisen in the first place. The notebooks of the early 1870's contain many passages dealing with this problem and setting forth Nietzsche's theory concerning the origin of the knowledge drive. (See especially *WL*, but also *P*, 47, 70, 71, 91, 130, 131, 134, and 143.) The explanation advanced in these early writings is essentially the same as the one to be found in Nietzsche's later published writings (e.g. *FW*, 344): the pure truth drive originated from a social—i.e. moral—imperative not to deceive others. By gradual metastasis this drive has acquired a significance independent of social exigency; it has been transformed into a "theoretical drive" for pure knowledge, while, at the same time, truthfulness itself has been transferred from man to the world—which is now expected to be "true." (Of course, in addition to this general account of the origin of the knowledge drive, Nietzsche recognized a variety of *individual* motives for the pursuit of truth. (See, e.g. *UBc*, 6.)

returned to the problem of the *meaning* of "the knowledge drive," the *significance* of "the pathos of truth." The selections translated below contain Nietzsche's most important meditations on epistemological problems, but one misses the point of these passages unless one remembers that Nietzsche wished to find out what knowledge *is* primarily in order to be able to find out what it is *worth*. He described his intention in these words: "I would like to treat the question of the value of knowledge as it would be treated by a cold angel who sees through the whole shabby farce" (*P*, 164).

With this we return to our original theme of the crisis of modernity and the problem of a "scientific culture." For science, whatever its actual practice may suggest, is clearly committed to the correspondence ideal of truth; indeed, it is the very avatar of the knowledge drive. It follows that, to the extent that human existence in general and all culture in particular depend upon illusion for their very possibility, a purely scientific culture is an impossibility. First of all, because science lacks that ability to determine value and to command obedience which characterizes the genuine cultural force. For the pure knowledge drive is intrinsically unselective; it recognizes nothing "great" or "small" and thus is incapable of providing any unifying mastery. The only criterion it recognizes is the purely formal one of certainty, to which all other considerations—value for human life included—are irrelevant. Secondly, science is incapable of serving as the foundation of culture because of the general antipathy between illusion and the pure knowledge drive. Rather than a possible foundation for culture, knowing appears to be a substitute for it (*P*, 73 and 88). Finally, science cannot serve as a foundation for anything, not only because it opposes human needs and values, but because it stands in opposition to itself: the assiduous pursuit of absolute knowledge will turn into absolute nihilism. This happens when the critique of knowing turns into a self-critique, and science turns into philosophy.

Thus in his unpublished writings of the early 1870's, Nietzsche had already clearly grasped the basically nihilistic character of the demand for pure knowledge, an insight which appeared in print only many years later in the great works of his maturity, such as Book Five of *The Gay Science* and the Third Essay of *The Geneology of Morals*. But the secret concerning "scientific Socraticism" was out: it leads toward decline.[32]

---

[32]See below, *P*, 124, 125, 137; and *PW*. (Nietzsche employed the expression "scientific Socraticism" in *GT* to designate the intellectual movement inspired by the pure knowledge drive.) As early as 1870 he had arrived at the conclusion that "the goal of science is the destruction of the world" (see below, VII, n. 9), but it was only in the years immediately following the summer of 1872 that he tried to expand and pursue this insight. Indeed, the central thesis of the most detailed study of Nietzsche's *Nachlass* of the 1870's (Schlechta/Anders, *Friedrich Nietzsche:*

Philosophy

When Nietzsche's analysis of the knowledge drive is combined with his analysis of culture, when the demand for truth is juxtaposed with the necessity of illusion, there results what he called (in *WL*, 176) "the tragic conflict": "There can be neither society nor culture without untruth.... Everything which is good and beautiful depends upon illusion: truth kills—it even kills itself (insofar as it realizes that error is its foundation)."

Is there any way in which the unchained knowledge drive can be mastered and controlled? It appears to have gained the victory over all opponents. The basic thesis of "scientific Socraticism"—that illusion is intolerable, that man can replace lies with truths—is presupposed on every side, and even the proponents of art and religion feel impelled to *argue* their cases before the bar of rational self-consciousness. Modern consciousness is scientific consciousness. Theoretical optimism appears to have made itself invulnerable against external assault; therefore, if it is to be overturned it will have to be an "inside job." The only effective criticism of science is self-criticism, and according to Nietzsche the self-criticism of science is ultimately inevitable, because science demands truth everywhere—including the truth about knowledge and the will to truth. In *The Birth of Tragedy* he gave the following dramatic description of what happens when science becomes self-conscious about itself and its own presuppositions:

> But science, spurred by its powerful illusion, speeds irresistibly toward its limits where its optimism, concealed in the essence of logic, suffers shipwreck. For the periphery of the circle of science has an infinite number of points; and while there is no telling how this circle could ever be surveyed completely, noble and gifted men nevertheless reach, "e'er half their time" and inevitably, such boundary points on the periphery from which one gazes into what defies illumination. When they see to their horror how logic coils up at these boundaries and finally bites its own tail — suddenly the new form of insight breaks through, *tragic insight* which, merely to be endured, needs art as a protection and remedy.[33]

Von den verborgenen Anfängen seines Philosophierens) is that Nietzsche's insight into the nihilistic character of knowledge dates from the early 1870's and is the main theme of the notebooks of this period. Schlechta and Anders argue further that Nietzsche had also already grasped the necessity of relating the problem of the character of knowledge to the problem of the knowledge drive itself, and that he was interested in the history of Greek science and philosophy primarily because it provided neat historical illustrations of his independently developed theoretical arguments and conclusions concerning the meaning of the knowledge drive and the fate of theoretical optimism.

[33]*GT*, 15 (Kaufmann's translation). On Kant and Schopenhauer's victory over logical optimism, see *GT*, 18 and 19.

The name which Nietzsche gave to this ultimate, self-referential application of the knowledge drive is "philosophy." Furthermore, he thought
that the inevitable self-critique of knowing had already been largely
accomplished, namely in the epistemological writings of Kant and
Schopenhauer, whom he credited with the victory over logical optimism.
Not that Nietzsche ever identified philosophy with the critique of knowledge. On the contrary, he was very critical of attempts to reduce philosophy to epistemology. However, it is because philosophy *includes* a
critique of science and the unlimited knowledge drive that Nietzsche was
attracted toward an investigation of its cultural significance. The question is whether or not the critique of knowing leads inevitably to despair.
Could it instead serve to strengthen the affirmative cultural forces (like
religion and art)? Is philosophy itself such an affirmative force? Are
philosophers, who are in many ways the purest type of theoretical men,[34]
capable of *mastering* as well as of criticizing the knowledge drive? These
are the questions which inspired Nietzsche's historical and theoretical
investigations of philosophy and its relation to culture, investigations
which constitute a very large part of the *Nachlass* of the early 1870's.

Readers acquainted with Nietzsche's published remarks on philosophy
and philosophers are aware of a certain ambiguity in his views: on the
one hand (e.g. *GD*, II and III) he treats philosophers as the most ridicul-
ously self-deluded and decadent "lovers of truth"; on the other (e.g.
JGB, 211-3), he exalts them as almost superhuman creators of value and
cultural legislators. In the notes we will be considering this same tension,
as present in the distinction between "the philosopher of desperate
knowledge" and "the philosopher of tragic knowledge" (*P*, 37). However, it is clear from these notes that the distinction indicates no ambiguity in Nietzsche's view of philosophy, but instead refers to two different kinds of philosophers, who warrant two very different conclusions concerning the general value and cultural significance of philosophy.

On the one hand, the critic of knowledge can continue to cling to his
drive for truth, even after he has shown that his own goal cannot be
reached. He can turn into a "fanatic of distrust" whose insistence upon
self-conscious certainty maroons him on a barren reef of absolute skepticism. A philosopher whose devotion to "blind science," to "knowledge at
any price" has led him to this juncture is what Nietzsche means by a
"philosopher of desperate knowledge." It is easy to see that such a
philosopher taken by himself possesses no positive cultural significance:

---

[34]"I want to depict and empathize with the *prodigious development* of the *one*
philosopher who desires knowledge, the philosopher of mankind. . . . The one
philosopher is here identical with all scientific endeavor; for all the sciences rest
upon the philosopher's general foundation." *P*, 119.

he simply magnifies the deficiencies and vices of the drive to pure knowledge. He is the absolute scientist.

Very different is the "philosopher of tragic knowledge," but what distinguishes him is not any lack of interest in or appreciation of the epistemological critique elaborated by the philosopher of desperate knowledge. On the contrary, both philosophers accept the same analysis of knowledge and truth; they are both skeptics. What distinguishes the philosopher of tragic knowledge is that he does not remain a skeptic—which is to say, that he is a more radical skeptic, one who is skeptical about skepticism and the quest for ideal certainty. This is what gives philosophy its cultural significance: it uses knowledge to master the knowledge drive. It does this in both a negative and positive fashion. Negatively, the philosopher's chief function is to break the hegemony of pure knowing, not from without, but from within. Thus "he cultivates a *new* life; he returns to art its rights" (*P*, 37). The way he returns to art its rights is by re-establishing the legitimacy of illusion, by making possible once again that "good will toward appearance" (*FW*, 107) which is characteristic of art, but which has been denigrated by science.

But in order to achieve the mastery of the knowledge drive which his critique has made possible, the philosopher of tragic knowledge must move beyond the negative and destructive standpoint of criticism. "We must get beyond this skepticism," and how shall we do this? "Our salvation lies not in *knowing* but in *creating*!" (*P*, 84). Thus, in order for philosophy to make the greatest contribution to culture possible, the philosopher must become more than a "knower"; he must become a "creator" as well, a "totally new type of philosopher-artist" (*P*, 44). Hence the "philosopher of tragic knowledge" is only another name for that ideal embodiment of a synthesis between knowing and creating (an "artistic Socrates") which Nietzsche had already called for in *The Birth of Tragedy*. We have some idea by now of what Nietzsche understood "knowing" to mean. But before we can proceed any further in analyzing the positive value of philosophy, it will be necessary to summarize very briefly what "art" signified for him.

Nietzsche's view of art was undergoing rapid and profound change during the early 1870's; indeed, his views on the nature and general importance of art never ceased to develop and change. It is not surprising, therefore, that the passages in the *Nachlass* which are concerned with art and its relation to science, philosophy, and culture are somewhat confused and betray a more than superficial conflict in Nietzsche's own thoughts on this subject. Nevertheless, to the extent that it is possible to draw some general conclusions regarding art from Nietzsche's notebooks of the early 1870's, one finds in them an interpretation of the nature and significance of art which bears a closer resemblance to certain remarks about the wisdom of appearances in his last writings than to either the "artist's metaphysics" of *The Birth of Tragedy* or the tough-minded criticisms of artistic illusion characteristic of the published writings of the late 1870's.[35]

The aspect of art which most deeply intrigued Nietzsche was its constructive and almost self-conscious use of illusions. This is precisely what distinguishes art from lying: it "includes the delight of awakening belief by means of surfaces. But one is not really deceived!" If one is deceived, then it is not art, for "art treats *illusion as illusion*; therefore it does not wish to deceive; it *is true*" (*WL*, 184). Thus, unlike myth, for example, art shares science's commitment to *honesty*. Indeed, in the light of our foregoing analysis of the illusions implicit in the demand for absolute truth it would appear that art is the *more* honest of the two, that "it alone is now honest" (*P*, 73). Art is more honest than science because art recognizes and accepts the ultimacy of illusion, and, by treating illusions as illusions it can deal creatively with them—evaluating them by an essentially *aesthetic* criterion of value. Nietzsche clearly employs the word "art" in the broadest possible sense, synonymous with creative activity and thought in general. What he means by such an activity is perhaps best illustrated by *play*.[36] But play can be serious, and art has to assume the immense task of teaching mankind how to stand on its own, with no support from other realms—i.e. without recourse to lies and self-deception.

The critique of knowledge can chasten the pure knowledge drive, but this drive can be mastered only by goals and ideals. In a post-Enlightenment world, such ideals cannot be "truths" in the previously desired sense, nor can they be lies which are taken to be true. They can only be beautiful illusions consciously affirmed as such, deceptions which do not deceive us; in other words, they can only be works of art. For "the only criterion that counts for us" — the only criterion that *can* count at this

---

[35]The passages in Nietzsche's late writings to which I am referring are those in which he explains the wisdom contained in the cult of appearances and praises the profundity of a conscious clinging to the surface. An excellent example of this is the beautiful passage in section 4 of the 1886 preface to *FW*, a passage which Nietzsche reprinted in the epilogue to *NCW*. The two attitudes toward art with which such a view is contrasted are: first, the theory (presupposed in *GT*) that art is a kind of intuitive knowledge, which penetrates reality more deeply than does science; and secondly, the rather cynical dismissal of any claims by the artist to wisdom (an attitude most characteristic of *MAMa, b,* and *c*). In *MAMa* 27 and 222 Nietzsche even went so far as to claim that art has value only as a means for facilitating the transition from art to science!

[36]This is the sense in which play was interpreted by Schiller in his *Letters on the Aesthetic Education of Man*. Eugen Fink, in *Nietzsches Philosophie*, and Jean Granier, in *La problème de la vérité dans la philosophie de Nietzsche*, have both used the concept of play as a central device for interpreting Nietzsche's philosophy.

point—"is the aesthetic criterion."[37] Therefore, when Nietzsche concludes that "culture can emanate only from the centralizing significance of an art or work of art," he is not simply giving hyperbolic expression to his private preference for art over science. He is, instead, drawing the logical conclusion from his analyses of culture and knowledge, which is why the passage just quoted continues: "Philosophy will unintentionally pave the way for such a world view" (*PAK*, 175).

Philosophy paves the way for culture insofar as sustained epistemological reflection inevitably (as Nietzsche thought) reveals the inobtainability of truth and the utter necessity of illusion. Thus even philosophers like Kant, who perhaps have no intention of doing so, serve to clear the ground for cultural renaissance by disputing science's exclusive claim to the serious attention of modern men, and by waging this dispute with science's own tools. Philosophy in this sense "can *create* no culture; but it can prepare it and remove restraints on it ..." (*PAK*, 170). Yet such philosophy is still of primarily negative value and, by itself, tends to degenerate into a sterile skepticism, a mere intellectual border patrolling, which is not without its own specific dangers for life and culture.[38]

Whether philosophy can have any further, more positive, cultural significance depends upon how closely it is related to art. Until now we have been considering a type of philosophy which can only refute the claims of knowledge to rule over life, a kind of philosophy which can, at most, recognize what is needed, which it must then leave it to the artist to provide (*P*, 27). But Nietzsche also envisages another kind of philosophy, a philosophy which would be art as well as knowledge.[39] This is what he is imagining when he says of philosophy: "Both in its purposes and in its results it is an art. But it uses the same means as science—conceptual representation. Philosophy is a form of artistic invention" (*P*, 53). But to this definition honesty compels him to add, that "there is no appropriate category for philosophy; consequently, we must make up and characterize a species [for it]." And of course it was Nietzsche

---

[37]*P*, 41 (cf. *P*, 37 and 43). These remarks might be helpful for interpreting the famous claim in *GT* that the world is justified "only as an *aesthetic* phenomenon."

[38]See below, *P*, 41; *PAK*, 171; and *PB*, 56 and 58.

[39]*P*, 38, 60, and 61. Note that Nietzsche decisively rejected the suggestion that there might be a special kind of "philosophical knowledge" (a Schopenhauerian notion of which there are vestiges in *GT*). Insofar as philosophy seeks and can provide knowledge, it is simply a form of science; the only kind of knowledge is scientific knowledge. What distinguishes the philosopher from the scientist (in addition to the more radical character of the former's will to truth) has to be his willingness to go beyond knowledge and take responsibility for this step from "knowing" to "creating." If philosophy masters the knowledge drive, then philosophy is more than knowledge. Otherwise, it can only be a mediating link between art and science.

himself who worked the hardest to "make up and characterize" this "philosopher of the future," this "artistic Socrates," who really would be able to serve as the founder and supreme judge of a new culture. Such a philosopher would be able to occupy the place vacated by myth and able to control science, not because of his additional *knowledge* so much as because of his self-confident creativity. He will be an artist of values, who measures life by the (essentially aesthetic) concept of "greatness." What will distinguish such a philosopher-artist from all previous founders of culture is his lack of naiveté: he will understand both that his illusions are illusions and why they are justified.[40]

Few contemporary readers of Nietzsche probably think that he ever succeeded in making this ideal seem plausible. I am not even sure if Nietzsche himself ever really found it plausible. But he did devote a considerable amount of his energy and imagination to the task of exploring the nature and possibility of such a philosopher-artist, as many of the notes translated below testify. Still, most of us will probably find sufficiently ambitious the more moderate statement of purpose in *WWK*, 193: "My general task: to show how life, philosophy, and art can have a more profound and congenial relationship to each other, in such a way that philosophy is not superficial and the life of the philosopher does not become mendacious."

A striking feature of Nietzsche's notebooks of the early 1870's is the complex interconnection between the various topics which are discussed and examined, as should be apparent from the preceding survey of some of these topics. The connection between Nietzsche's theories of culture, of knowledge, of language, of science, of philosophy, and of art is by no means merely external: it really does, as Nietzsche said it did, "all hang together." Nietzsche might have decided to organize his presentation of all of these topics around a discussion of any one of them, or he might have tried to organize such a presentation by connecting one of them discursively to the next, like points on the rim of a wheel. Instead, however, he intended to adopt a very different format for the presentation of his thoughts; he planned to connect them to each other in the way that the spokes of a wheel are connected to a common hub. The various topics were to be related to each other by discussing each of them in the context of the general problem of early Greek antiquity.

The Greeks

Nietzsche's first book was about art and science and about the general problem of modern culture. It was at the same time a book about the Greeks of the sixth and fifth centuries B.C., specifically, about the history of Greek drama. We know that the unwritten *Philosophenbuch* was meant

---

[40]See below, *P*, 24, 28, 34, 48, 59, 60-1.

to be a "companion piece" to *The Birth of Tragedy*. We can never be sure exactly what Nietzsche may have meant by this expression, but his notes for the unwritten book suggest one obvious similarity between it and *The Birth of Tragedy*: as in the earlier book, Nietzsche here intended to examine a specific set of theoretical and practical problems with constant reference to Greek antiquity, though this time the emphasis was to be upon the Greek philosophers rather than the Greek tragedians.

The Greeks always held an interest for Nietzsche which cannot be accounted for merely in terms of his own professional training as a classical philologist. Even the lectures and courses which Nietzsche gave at Basel—not to mention the passages on the Greeks which appear in all of his writings—betray an interest in Greek culture, art, and philosophy which is not of a primarily historical or philological character. One explanation for the frequent references to the Greeks in his writings, is suggested by Nietzsche himself in *MAMb*, 218, a section entitled "The Greeks as interpreters":

> When we speak about the Greeks, we involuntarily speak of today and yesterday: their universally known history is a polished mirror which always reflects something which is not in the mirror itself. We take advantage of the freedom to speak about them in order to be able to be silent about other things—so that these Greeks might themselves whisper something into the ear of the thoughtful reader. Thus for the modern man the Greeks facilitate the communication of many things which are difficult or hazardous to communicate.

Yet much the same thing might be said of Roman antiquity or Biblical history. What else is there which might particularly recommend the ancient Greeks to the attention of modern men?

To begin with, there is the dependence of all subsequent Western culture upon the culture of the ancient Greeks. Thus in order to understand ourselves we have to understand the Greeks, for what we are is largely determined by what they were. Thus, any analysis or critique of modern culture will be superficial unless it succeeds in tracing the roots of our present crisis all the way back to certain features in the very foundation of our culture—all the way back to Greek antiquity.[41]

But this general consideration is not sufficient to explain Nietzsche's very specific interest in a certain portion of Greek history, the sixth and early fifth centuries, particularly the period just before and after the Persian wars. The answer, which is fully developed in *The Birth of Tragedy*, is that Nietzsche considered this "tragic age of the Greeks" to be humanity's finest hour, the great age of genius in comparison with which

---

[41]See below, *WWK*, 191. For Nietzsche's most explicit discussion of this theme, see *Wir Philologen*, in certain passages of which Nietzsche even blames Greek antiquity for having made Christianity possible. See *WP*, 18, 158, and 159.

all other ages appeared to him to be pale copies and impure imitations.[42] The very name which Nietzsche gave to this era reveals why he considered it to possess such supreme and universal significance: it was the age which produced the ancient Greek tragedy, still the most profound and universal art form.

The Greeks of this period were therefore of very considerable importance for Nietzsche as a constant source of *inspiration*. He unquestionably held a rather idealized notion of them, which served him as something of a personal refuge from the spiritual poverty of the present. This, for example, is the way he defended his high evaluation of the significance of art: "The Greeks show us what art is capable of. If we did not have them our faith would be chimerical" (*P*, 39). Consequently, it is hardly surprising that when Nietzsche turned his attention to philosophy he attached special importance to determining the nature of philosophy during the tragic age of the Greeks.

Part of Nietzsche's interest in the Pre-Platonic philosophers was a simple corollary of his high regard for Greek culture and art of the sixth and fifth centuries. For, after all, if it is part of the task of philosophy to pass judgment upon life, then it is obviously of some importance to become acquainted with any rare periods of relative perfection which history might make available to us. This is why "the ancient Greek philosophers' judgment concerning the value of existence is so much more meaningful than a modern judgment, because they had life itself in such sumptuous perfection before and around them, and because among them, unlike among us, the sentiment of the thinker is not entangled in the split between the desire for freedom, beauty, and greatness of life and the drive for truth, which asks only 'what is life as such worth?' "[43] In addition to this, Nietzsche thought that the philosophers of the tragic age were naturally more likely than the thinkers of any other age to have developed the kind of "tragic knowledge" which he had already mentioned and called for in *The Birth of Tragedy*.[44]

---

[42]See below, *WWK*, 199 and *P*, 79.

[43]*UBc*, 3. (There is an almost identical passage in *PtZG*, 1.) See also the many similar passages in the notebooks below, e.g. *P*, 18. Note that Nietzsche later rejected the idea that it is philosophy's task to judge life; indeed, he came to see this presumption as an indication of the spirit of revenge against the world. This change in Nietzsche's views is perhaps not unrelated to a remarkable change in his view of the ancient philosophers as expressed in his last published writings. In section X of *Twilight of the Idols*, for example, he characterizes the Greek philosophers as the decadents of Greek culture, claims that philosophy is something essentially Post-Socratic, and expresses his admiration for Thucydides over any of the Greek Philosophers!

[44]In a characteristically candid autobiographical note from the period between 1876 and 1879, Nietzsche commented as follows on this expectation:

When he turned from a general consideration of their age to a consideration of the Pre-Platonic philosophers themselves several additional factors recommended a study of these thinkers to Nietzsche. There is for example, the question of the philosopher's relation to culture. Here the ancient philosophers would seem to have much to teach us, for unlike modern philosophers, they had a flourishing and healthy culture to which they were able to relate their philosophizing. Furthermore, they lived in an age before overt hostility between philosophy and culture had arisen;[45] indeed, philosophy was an important part of general Hellenic culture.

Not only can a study of the Pre-Platonic philosophers illuminate the relation between philosophy and culture, it can also answer the question "what is philosophy?" For according to Nietzsche the line of thinkers from Thales to Socrates included all the possible *pure types*, both of philosophers (i.e. philosophical personalities and ways of living) and of philosophies. They invented or discovered all the original philosophical ideas, and all later philosophies are simply mixed types, usually inferior to these grand originals.[46] Thus Nietzsche, whose acquaintance with the history of philosophy from Plato to Kant was less than nodding, really believed that one could learn all one needed to know about the nature of philosophical thinking and philosophical systems from the Pre-Platonic philosophers. It would be hard to overemphasize the originality and novelty of such an emphasis on the contemporary importance of these ancient thinkers as *philosophers*, and not merely as antiquated figures in the history of philosophy. Nietzsche was one of the few philosophers since Aristotle actually to try to *learn* anything *from* the Pre-Socratic Greek philosophers.

As for the actual *content* of Pre-Platonic philosophy, Nietzsche clearly indicated what he took to be the three main problems of Pre-Platonic philosophy (and therefore, presumably, of philosophy as such) in a passage from his introductory lecture on these philosophers:

> The liberated intellect contemplates things; and now, for the first time, the *most ordinary things appear noteworthy, as a problem*. This is the true distin-

---

When I listened to the total sound of the early Greek philosophers, I thought that I perceived those tones which I was accustomed to hearing in Greek art, more precisely, in tragedy. I cannot yet say with certainty to what extent this lay in the Greeks and to what extent it only lay in my ears (the ears of a man with a great need for art). (*MA*, XXI, p. 68 = *GOA*, XI, p. 118.)

[45]". . .overt hostility against culture—negation—begins with Plato. But I want to know how philosophy behaves toward a presently existing or developing culture which is not the enemy." *PAK*, 175. See also *PtZG*, 2 and below, *P*, 32 and *PAK*, 173.

[46]See Nietzsche's "Introduction" to his lectures on Pre-Platonic philosophy, *MA*, IV, pp. 248-50 = *GOA*, XIX, pp. 127-9. Also see below, *P*, 79.

guishing mark of the philosophical drive: wonder concerning what is lying in front of everyone's nose. The most ordinary phenomenon is becoming, and with it Ionian philosophy begins. This problem reappears in an infinitely intensified form in the Eleatics: they observed that our intellect does not comprehend becoming at all, and from this they inferred the existence of a metaphysical world. All subsequent philosophies struggle against Eleaticism. This struggle ends in skepticism. Another problem is the problem of purposiveness in nature. With this problem the opposition between spirit and body is brought into philosophy for the first time. A third problem is the problem of the value of knowledge. Becoming, purpose, and knowledge: this is the content of Pre-Platonic philosophy.[47]

It is, I believe, this third problem, the problem of the value of knowledge, which most deeply interested Nietzsche and which figures most prominently in his own manuscripts on philosophy during this period. It was also a problem which he emphasized in his various presentations of the history of Greek philosophy. This point deserves emphasis, for it is seldom realized how tightly Nietzsche's interest in the Pre-Platonic philosophers focused on the problem of knowledge. The published text of his lectures, as well as the notebooks translated below, show the extent to which he tried to relate Greek science and philosophy to modern science and the epistemological themes so central to modern philosophy. They furthermore demonstrate that he wished to use the history of Greek philosophy from Thales to Socrates to illustrate his own theoretical conclusions concerning the anthropomorphic character of all knowing and the ultimately nihilistic tendency of the knowledge drive.[48]

Nietzsche, therefore, had good personal, historical, and theoretical reasons for his interest in Greek antiquity. Not only does it contain the highest examples and historical foundations of what we call culture, art, and philosophy; it is also a lens through which we can, perhaps for the first time, understand the culture, art, and philosophy of the present. The history of Pre-Platonic philosophy not only served as one of Nietzsche's main sources of knowledge about philosophy, it also served as a proving ground for his own analyses of knowledge, the pathos of truth, and the complex interrelations between philosophy, science, culture, and art. There is no mystery in Nietzsche's decision to integrate his

---

[47]*MA*, IV, p. 252 = *GOA*, XIX, p. 131. The published text of these lectures is assembled from Nietzsche's own lecture notes from 1872, 1873, and 1876.

[48]As Nietzsche wrote in 1870: "The goal of science is the destruction of the world. . . . It can be shown that this process has already been carried out in miniature in Greece. . . ." See below, VII, n. 9. The claim that Nietzsche's interest in the Pre-Platonic philosophers was largely epistemological—i.e. set in the context of his own inquiries into the nature and value of truth—is elaborately defended by Karl Schlechta and Anni Anders. See Schlechta/Anders, pp. 61-2, 40-1, and 99.

"theoretical" studies of these topics with an "historical" presentation of Pre-Platonic philosophy; the mystery is why he allowed this project, upon which he worked so long and so hard, to remain unfinished.

Some Conclusions

Nietzsche's unpublished notebooks of the years 1872-1876 are important, and in some respects essential, documents for understanding his intellectual development and his thoughts on several topics of central interest to philosophers. The grounds for this claim have been set forth in the preceding partial survey of the contents of these notebooks and can be very briefly restated.

These notebooks clearly show that no dramatic "break" occurred in Nietzsche's spiritual and intellectual development during the early 1870's, and thus they support Nietzsche's own later claims concerning the continuity of his thought. To be sure, there was a dramatic change in Nietzsche's public persona between *Richard Wagner in Bayreuth (UBd)* and the first part of *Human, All-too-Human*; but it is no more dramatic than the distance (in mood and content) separating his published writings of the early 1870's from his unpublished notebooks of the same period. The continuity in subject and direction between these notebooks and Nietzsche's later published writings is sufficient to warrant Karl Schlechta's conclusion, that "the break which one speaks of as lying between the four *Untimely Meditations* and *Human, All-too-Human* seems ... to be based more upon a break in our understanding of Nietzsche than in the matter itself."[49] But this break in our understanding of Nietzsche can be remedied by an acquaintance with the texts translated in this volume.

For anyone interested in the genesis and development of Nietzsche's thought, his early unpublished notebooks will be fascinating documents of central significance. Included in the notes of this period are the first sketches of many ideas which only appeared in Nietzsche's published writings many years later. A few examples of such ideas are: the "social" account of the origin and utility of the distinction between truth and lies; the "perspectival" analysis of knowing; the interpretation of art as "conscious illusion" and of the philosopher as a possible ally of the artist; the recognition of the constitutive contribution of language to thought and reality; and the uncovering of the life-denying tendency of the demand for absolute truth.

In the notebooks one can not only observe the birth of these characteristically "Nietzschean" ideas; one can also see how very closely the various strands of Nietzsche's thought are interwoven. Indeed, the interconnection between Nietzsche's basic ideas is more readily apparent in

---

[49]Schlechta/Anders, p. 18.

his unpublished notebooks than in his published and polished literary efforts. It seems to have been one of Nietzsche's stylistic aims to obscure the close connections between his various themes, to present his thoughts on various subjects as if they were independent of each other, for the purpose of forcing the reader to make the connections—and thus to do the thinking—for himself. But if one wishes to know how these themes and subjects actually came together in Nietzsche's own intellectual experience and desires to see how one question led to another and how each new insight was assimilated into the slowly developing totality of his thought, then one will turn again and again to his unpublished notebooks.

But the early *Nachlass* is just as important for the information it provides concerning *what* Nietzsche actually thought about certain subjects as for showing us *how* he came to think what he did about others. This is especially the case concerning Nietzsche's "theory of knowledge" and his answers to a broad range of epistemological questions. For it is not only true that, as Arthur Danto has contended, Nietzsche never modified "in any essential respect" the theory of truth which he advanced in his unpublished writings of the early 1870's,[50] but it is also true that these same writings contain by far his most explicit, detailed, and sustained treatments of basic epistemological issues. Not only are most of his later published remarks on this subject compatible with these early discussions, they actually seem in some cases to *presuppose* them. Perhaps it is possible to base an adequate and coherent account of Nietzsche's theory of knowledge and truth solely on his published writings, but I doubt that it can be done. In any case, no one remotely interested in this question can afford to ignore the material translated in this volume. These notes are particularly useful for clarifying the relationship between (1) Nietzsche's analysis of the correspondence ideal of "absolute truth" and the radical skepticism to which this leads; (2) his analysis of truths as instrumental fictions; (3) his analysis of the nature of language; and (4) his analysis of the nihilism implicit in the pure will to truth.

There are many additional special subjects treated in these notebooks, and many questions considered which will be of special interest to some readers. Examples of some of the questions considered explicitly and at length are: What is philosophy, and in what relation does the philosopher stand to the scientist and the artist? What constitutes "culture," and what is the cultural significance of philosophy? What meaning do Greek culture and Greek philosophy have in the modern world? Still, the passages in the notebooks discussing questions like these are more

---

[50]*Nietzsche as Philosopher* (New York: Macmillan, 1965), p. 38. Danto is referring specifically to *WL*, which is the only part of the early *Nachlass* with which he seems to be acquainted.

clearly *supplementary* to Nietzsche's published views on such topics than is the case with the passages dealing with truth and knowledge.

By this time it should be clear what kind of contribution the study of Nietzsche's unpublished writings can make to our understanding of his philosophy. Particularly when one pays special attention to the notebooks of the early 1870's, the thesis that the *Nachlass* can contribute nothing new to one's understanding of Nietzsche has to be rejected as unduly restrictive and general. I believe that the selections from Nietzsche's *Nachlass* which are translated in this volume demonstrate the untenability of the view that "Nietzsche said everything that he wanted to say or had to say in the writings which he himself published or specified for publication."[51]

We can conclude with the question raised at the end of the previous section: if these writings contain material of such importance, then why did Nietzsche allow them to remain unpublished? Why did he not, in the more than a dozen years that elapsed between the period of their composition and the conclusion of his career, carry through with his plan to work them into publishable form? And why should not his failure to do so be taken as evidence that he repudiated or outgrew the ideas expressed in these early writings?

All that is needed in order to dismiss the suggestion that Nietzsche did not prepare these notes for final publication because he had altered his views on the questions there discussed is a comparison of the notes in question with the books he later published. Of course there is evidence of some changes over the years, but the similarity between the contents of these notebooks and Nietzsche's later explicit and implicit views on the same topics is very striking indeed. But if Nietzsche's failure to complete his long-projected *Philosophenbuch* is not to be explained by later changes in his views on particular issues, how is it to be explained?

Perhaps Nietzsche's decision to abandon his projected study of philosophy and the Greeks had more to do with the form than with the content

---

[51]This is the opinion of Karl Schlechta, who is the best-known exponent of the view that, though the *Nachlass* may be of some interest to specialists in Nietzsche, it contains "no *new* central thought." See *Der Fall Nietzsche* (München: Hanser, 1959), p. 90 and Schlechta's *Nachwort* to Vol. III of his influential edition of Nietzsche's *Werke in drei Bänden* (München: Hanser, 1956), p. 1433. I am not sure what Schlechta means by a "new central thought," but it is surely insufficient to call the detailed discussions of knowledge, language, philosophy, and truthfulness which one finds in the unpublished writings of the early 1870's mere "variations" on Nietzsche's published remarks on these subjects. Indeed, Schlechta himself, in his 1962 collaboration with Anni Anders, emphasized the special significance of the early *Nachlass* (Schlechta/Anders, pp. 33-4); their entire book testifies to the importance of these notebooks and the unique contribution they make to our understanding of Nietzsche's thought.

of the unwritten book. As the notes make clear, the book that Nietzsche
had intended to write would be a "companion piece" to *The Birth of
Tragedy* in style and format as well as in subject matter; it was to be
another long, continuously argued treatise combining historical exposition, theoretical analysis, and cultural criticism of the present. A book
like *The Birth of Tragedy* could hardly be called "scholarly" in conception
and format; nevertheless, like the projected *Philosophenbuch*, there was
still something vaguely academic about this first book, in the discursive
continuity of its argument and narrative flow perhaps, or in its insistence
upon correcting our mistaken view about the nature of antiquity and its
straightforward defense of a "new theory" of Greek drama. In any case,
the format and style of *The Birth of Tragedy* are of an entirely different
order from the format and style of books like *Human, All-too-Human*,
Thus Spoke Zarathustra, and *Twilight of the Idols*. As it happened, however,
Nietzsche was making the first deliberate moves toward his new, more
authentic and personal, public voice during the very years that he was
working on the notes for the *Philosophenbuch*. If he had only begun work
on this project a year or two earlier, in the spring of 1871 for example,
then I consider it probable that he would have been able to complete and
publish it. But by the time that he was ready to start working his notes for
this project into publishable form he had already begun the series of
"Untimely Meditations," those polemical and retrospective steps toward
public self-definition which were, in turn, abandoned for the much more
radical and risky format of *Human, All-too-Human* and the works which
followed. Once Nietzsche was securely on the "path toward himself" he
sacrificed everything toward his new goal. Among the things sacrificed
were his plans for a book which would discuss general questions concerning the nature of knowledge and philosophy within the context of an
historical presentation of the Pre-Platonic philosophers. The publication
of such a relatively "safe" and traditionally structured book was impossible after the publication of *Human, All-too-Human*, which Nietzsche himself would have been the first to recognize.

Of course the notes assembled for the unwritten book can hardly be
said to have gone to waste! We have already seen how many characteristically "Nietzschean" ideas received their first development in the notes
for the *Philosophenbuch*, and when Nietzsche abandoned his plans to
publish a work of the kind he had originally envisioned he tried to
salvage as much usable material as he was able from the manuscript
material he had compiled for the unwritten book.[52] Like Robinson

---

[52] In this respect the numerous outlines and plans included below (see especially section VII) are of special interest, for they show how Nietzsche tried to
recast the material assembled for the *Philosophenbuch* in a variety of new forms
more in keeping with his changing perception of himself and his task as a writer.

Crusoe supplying himself from the wreck of his ship, Nietzsche appears to have turned again and again over the years to his notebooks of the early 1870's, returning as it were to the original source of many of his thoughts and the original exposition of many of his themes. Though he never wrote the book for which these notes were intended, they laid the foundations for the books that he did eventually write.[53]

[53]Cf. the comment of the editors of the original edition of the notes for the *Philosophenbuch*: "these philosophers never let him go; through the later books, up until the 'Revaluation,' visible threads still run back to this unwritten book." *GOA*, X, *Nachbericht* I, p. 509 (second edition).

Note on the Texts,
Translation, and Annotation

Not one of the writings translated in this volume was published by Nietzsche himself or intended by him for publication in the form here presented. All of them, the relatively polished little essays like *PW* and the first two sections of *WL*, as well as the editorial compilations of rough notes like *P* and *PB*, are translated from posthumously published texts which are themselves based upon handwritten drafts and notes found among Nietzsche's very extensive literary remains or *Nachlass*. All of the writings included in this volume date from the early 1870's, and most of them are to be found, intermixed with notes on other topics, in the large bound notebooks in which Nietzsche customarily composed.

The history of the editing and publication of Nietzsche's *Nachlass*—a history which begins with his collapse in the early days of 1889—is an interesting and complicated one.[1] The principal published text of Nietzsche's *Nachlass*, and the basis for almost all later editions, has been and remains volumes IX through XVI of the second edition of Nietzsche's complete writings in the so-called *Grossoktavausgabe* (*GOA*; 1901-11).[2] The policy followed by the editors of *GOA* was not to publish the *Nachlass* in its entirety nor in the chaotic state in which it was left by Nietzsche, but rather to impose some systematic order upon the material. The resulting order was often quite external and was achieved at the cost of considerable editorial liberty. In practice this meant that the

---

[1]In addition to the *Nachberichten* to the individual volumes of *GOA* and *MA*, see Richard Oehler *"Die bisherige herausgeberische Tätigkeit des Nietzsche-Archivs,"* in vol. I of the *Historisch-Kritische Gesamtausgabe* of Nietzsche's *Werke* (Munich: Beck, 1933), pp. xvii-xxx, as well as Karl Schlechta's *"Philologischer Nachbericht"* to vol. III of his edition of Nietzsche's *Werke in drei Bänden*, pp. 1382-1432. The best account of this controversial editorial history available in English is in Kaufmann's *Nietzsche*.

[2]*GOA* also included three volumes of *Philologica* in vols. XVII-XIX. The contents of vols. IX-XVI of *GOA* are identical to vols. IX-XVI of the *Kleinoktavausgabe* (1899-1912), which may thus also be consulted for all references to *GOA* included in this volume. (Only the pagination of the *Nachberichten* differs in the two editions.)

relatively finished drafts and manuscripts which were found in the *Nachlass* were published in their original form and that the rest of the notes were abridged and arranged by date and subject matter. Wherever it was possible, the editors made what seems to have been a sincere attempt to organize the notes according to plans or outlines which were made by Nietzsche himself and which were included in the *Nachlass*. This is how the famous non-book, *The Will to Power* was constructed by Nietzsche's editors. However, since the *Nachlass* contains an enormous number of such plans, there still remained plenty of room for editorial decision in choosing which particular plan to follow, and even more in "filling out" the chosen plan with passages from the notebooks.

It is by now the scholarly consensus that the only satisfactory way of publishing Nietzsche's *Nachlass* is to publish it in its entirety and in a form which resembles as closely as possible the form of the manuscripts themselves. This was the editorial principle applied in the ambitious *Historisch-Kritische Gesamtausgabe* (1933-42), only a few volumes of which ever appeared. It is also being applied in the new *Kritische Gesamtausgabe* (*WKG*, 1967ff.), edited by G. Colli and M. Montinari. This impressive edition is well under way and when it is completed will certainly render all previous editions obsolete. However, most of the *Nachlass* included in the present translation has not yet appeared in *WKG*.

Most of the notes here translated were first published in the second edition of Vol. X of *GOA*, edited by Ernst Holzer and August Horneffer (1903). This edition was used as the basis for yet another "complete edition" of Nietzsche's works published between 1920 and 1929. This so-called *Musarionausgabe* (*MA*) improves upon *GOA* in two ways: it does not separate published and unpublished writings, but arranges everything chronologically; and it includes a few items (e.g. *PW*) which were not included in the earlier edition. Nevertheless, in most cases the editors of *MA* (Max and Richard Oehler and F. Würzbach) simply reproduced the various "texts" assembled from the *Nachlass* notes by the editors of *GOA*. They did, however, omit the section numbers which the earlier editors had added to Nietzsche's notes.

In all cases the primary printed text upon which my translations are based is the one found in *MA*. I have, however, compared the *MA* text with the *GOA* and, in the only case in which it is possible (viz. *WWK*) compared these texts with the original notebook as published in *WKG*, indicating and translating all variant and omitted passages. Departing from the editorial principles of *MA*, I have decided to reinsert the section numbers from *GOA*. The argument against the use of these numbers is that they give the texts a deceptively "finished" look, more specifically, a look closer to that of certain "aphoristic" books actually published by Nietzsche. On the other hand, they undeniably facilitate cross reference and make it much easier to consult various versions of the German text. Thus, so long as one carefully guards against the illusion of actually reading a "book" of Nietzsche's, there seems to be no good reason not to use the section numbers. Keep in mind that the numbers are not found in Nietzsche's manuscripts themselves; they do not designate separate "aphorisms" nor do they necessarily indicate sequences of thoughts or natural divisions of an argument. The section numbers are convenient indexing devices added by later editors, and the individual texts themselves, for all the genuine importance and interest which they possess, are on the whole mere editorial selections from and rearrangements of material contained in Nietzsche's notebooks of the early 1870's.

The Individual Texts[3]

I. *The Philosopher: Reflections on the Struggle between Art and Knowledge*. During the summer, fall, and winter of 1872, Nietzsche was fully occupied with his study of Pre-Platonic philosophy. During this period he compiled a large collection of notes and drafts for a projected book dealing with certain basic philosophical problems and illustrated by frequent references to the ancient Greek philosophers. He had already prepared a continuous historical exposition of Pre-Platonic philosophy in conjunction with his lectures on the topic during the summer semester of 1872.[4] But it was during the fall and winter of 1872 that he filled over 100 pages of a large bound notebook (P I 20) with fascinating notes, which, though they contain many references to the Pre-Platonic philosophers, are of a more obviously and purely "theoretical" character than any of his earlier extended studies of philosophy and philosophers. A large proportion of these notes are concerned with quite general

---

[3]Sources for the information utilized below are: (1) the editorial *Nachberichten* of *GOA*, vols. IX-X and *MA*, vols. IV, VI, and VII; (2) H.J. Mette's *"Sachlicher Vorbericht"* to vol. I of the *Historisch-Kritische Gesamtausgabe*, pp. xxi-cxxvi; (3) Schlechta/Anders; [(4) manuscript source information from *WKG*].

[4]Nietzsche first lectured in the Pre-Platonic philosophers in the winter semester of 1869-70, but no information concerning these lectures has survived. His real enthusiasm for the ancient philosophers first becomes apparent in conjunction with the lectures on the Pre-Platonic philosophers which he gave in the summer semester of 1872. He devoted great care to the preparation of this course of lectures and offered it again, with revisions, in the summer semesters of 1873 and 1876. The printed text of these lectures (*MA*, IV, pp. 245-364 = *GOA*, XIX, pp. 125-234) is actually a compilation of material from the different versions of the course. Nietzsche's well-known "book" on the Pre-Platonic philosophers (*PtZG*) is an unfinished though polished text written in the spring of 1873 and based upon the texts of his lectures. In the spring of 1874 Nietzsche had a fair copy of this draft made by a student, Adolf Baumgartner, and in 1879 he made a few minor corrections in the manuscript and dictated the brief second preface. Nevertheless, *PtZG* was not published by Nietzsche himself.

epistemological problems. In separate letters to Edwin Rohde of
November 21 and December 7, Nietzsche variously referred to the above
project by the names "The Philosopher" and "The Last Philosopher."
Accordingly, the editors of *GOA*, X printed their quite extensive selection of passages from this notebook under the double title: *Der letzte
Philosoph. Der Philosoph: Betrachtungen über den Kampf von Kunst und Erkenntniss (P)*. Under this title they included most of Nietzsche's
philosophical notes from P I 20, though not all of them. They omitted
certain notes, for example those which were obviously early versions of
material later worked into a more complete form in *PW* and *WL*. And
they did not hesitate to rearrange the notes that they did publish. How
important are the omissions? In their 1962 book, *Friedrich Nietzsche. Von
den verborgenen Anfängen seines Philosophierens*, Karl Schlechta and Anni
Anders compared the published text of *P* with Nietzsche's original
notebook (which is preserved in the Goethe-Schiller Archives in
Weimar) and concluded that the editors of *GOA* had systematically omitted many passages which conflicted with their own preconceived ideas
concerning Nietzsche's purposes and intentions regarding his book on
philosophy. In particular, they had omitted many of the notes in which
Nietzsche poses most sharply the problem of the value of truth (which
Schlechta and Anders take to be *the* theme of these notes). The published
text of *P* consequently gives undue prominence to the *cultural* significance of the Pre-Platonic philosophers and unduely obscures the
explicitly epistemological orientation of Nietzsche's dialogue with ancient philosophy.[5] In order to prove their point Schlechta and Anders
include in their book a number of important passages from P I 20 which
were not printed in the text of *P* included in *GOA* and *MA*. The reader
may make up his own mind on this question: I have translated the
complete text of *P* as published in *MA* (reinstating the section numbers
from *GOA*), plus, as an appendix to *P*, a selection of representative
passages from those published in Schlechta/Anders. The outline, "The
Last Philosopher," with which the published text of *P* concludes, has
been translated in section VII of this volume.

P = *MA*, VI, pp. 3-62 = *GOA*, X, pp. 108-177 [= *WKG*, III, 4, pp.
6-86 and 153-4]. The texts translated in the "Appendix" are from
Schlechta/Anders, pp. 38-9, 43-6, and 116 [= *WKG*, III, 4, pp. 27-8, 37,
34-5, 76-7, 70, 62-3, 82, 86, 58, and 80].

---

[5]Schlechta has correctly observed even the rather innocent editorial decision to omit from the published text of *P* those passages which are obviously only
preliminary versions of passages found in *WL* creates a misleading picture of
Nietzsche's thoughts during the period 1872–3. In particular, it obscures the
close connection between his studies of philosophy and the Greek philosophers
and his studies of science and the theory of knowledge. In other words, it makes
it more difficult to observe the genuine continuity of thought between *P*, *PW*,
PAK, and *WL*. See Schlechta/Anders, pp. 34–6.

(The manuscript source is P I 20b [summer 1872-beginning of 1873], except for P 155, which is included in Mp XII 4 (winter 1872-3).

II. *On the Pathos of Truth.* For Christmas 1872, Nietzsche presented Cosima Wagner with a handwritten manuscript entitled "Five Prefaces to Five Unwritten Books" (to which he added in the letter which accompanied his gift—"and not to be written"). The first of these five miniature essays—and the one which Nietzsche himself, in a letter to Rohde, January 31, 1873, called the "main section"—was entitled *Über das Pathos der Wahrheit (PW).*[6] Of the five "prefaces," *PW* is obviously the one most closely related to Nietzsche's own studies of the fall and winter; indeed, certain passages in *PW* are clearly revisions of notes found in *P*. Nietzsche himself was so pleased with this little essay that he incorporated many long passages from it in later manuscripts: in *PtZG,* in *WL,* and in *UBb,* 2. Both Schlechta and the editors of *MA* consider it a "preliminary version" of *WL*—though the theme of the philosopher's pride and love of fame finds no correlate in *WL*. Because so much of its contents was later employed elsewhere, the editors of *GOA* omitted *PW* altogether from their edition. It was however included in *MA* on the grounds of its "special urgency," and the charm of its "stylistic polish," and because "it is such a characteristic example of Nietzsche's manner of drawing *his own* nourishment from this pre-occupation with the Greek philosophers...."[7]

PW = *MA,* IV, pp. 141-7 = *WKG,* III, 2, pp. 249-54. (The manuscript source is U I 7 [Christmas 1872].)

III. *The Philosopher as Cultural Physician.* During the early weeks of 1873 Nietzsche was largely occupied with his contributions to the Wagnerian "cause," but he soon returned to what he called—in a letter to Rohde, March 22, 1873—his "very slowly gestating book" on Greek philosophy, which he now refers to under a new name, *Der Philosoph als Arzt der Kultur (PAK).* Under this title the editors of *GOA* published the new material compiled on the topic during the spring of 1873, consisting mainly of several long outlines and plans for rearranging the material included in *P*.

PAK = *MA,* VI, pp. 65-73 = *GOA,* X, pp. 180-8 [= *WKG,* III, 4, pp. 136-55 and 221-3]. (The manuscript source is Mp XII 4 [winter 1872-3], except *PAK* 170 and 172, which are included in Mp XIII 1 [spring-fall 1873]).

---

[6]The remaining four "prefaces" are: *Gedanken über die Zukunft unserer Bildungsanstalten; Der griechische Staat (GS); Das Verhältniss der Schopenhauerischen Philosophie zu einer deutschen Kultur (VSP);* and *Homers Wettkampf (HW).*

[7]Editors' *Nachbericht* to *MA,* IV, p. 454.

IV. *On Truth and Lies in a Nonmoral Sense.* In the summer semester of
1873 Nietzsche again offered his course of lectures on the Pre-Platonic
philosophers. At the same time he returned to his projected book on
philosophy and philosophers. However, by this time the accumulated
thoughts and manuscripts were becoming difficult to work into the general form of the long-projected book on Greek philosophy. Accordingly,
during this summer Nietzsche began a new manuscript, which takes up
many of the problems treated in *P*, but in a fresh form. He seems to have
been undecided whether or not this new manuscript was to be a part of
the earlier project or was to be a relatively independent treatment of the
problem of truth. In any case, these new drafts and notes were published
in *GOA* under the general title *Erkenntnisstheoretische Einleitung,* though
they are generally referred to by the title of the fragmentary essay with
which the notebook begins: *Über Wahrheit und Lüge im aussermoralischen
Sinne (WL).* The manuscript consists of a polished fair copy of sections 1
and 2 of *WL* (dictated by Nietzsche to his friend, von Gersdorff, and
corrected in Nietzsche's own hand), followed by brief notes outlining the
contents of the unwritten sections. The rest of the notebook consists of
miscellaneous notes on a variety of related topics, a selection of which
were numbered and published in *GOA* as "drafts for a continuation" of
WL.

WL = *MA*, VI, pp. 75-99 = *GOA*, X, pp. 189-215 = *WKG*, III, 2, pp.
369-84 (sections 1 and 2 only) and *WKG*, III, 4, pp. 309 and 230-41. (The
manuscript source of the fragments following section 2 is U II 2
[summer-fall 1873].)

V. *Philosophy in Hard Times.* The first "Untimely Meditation" was
written in the spring of 1873. Quickly thereafter Nietzsche set about
revising many of his earlier plans and reworking the manuscripts into
the new format. In the fall of 1873 he apparently attempted such a
revision of his thoughts on philosophy and began assembling notes for
an "Untimely Meditation" to be entitled *Die Philosophie in Bedrängniss
(PB).* The projected "Untimely Meditation" on philosophy was never
written; instead, Nietzsche turned his immediate attention to history and
the historians and composed *UBb.* Some of the material assembled for
the "Untimely Meditation" on philosophy was eventually incorporated in
the book on Schopenhauer, *UBc,* which was written in the spring and
summer of 1874. A selection from the remaining material (i.e. from the
notes not directly utilized in later projects) was published by the editors
of *GOA* under the title *PB.* The printed text was assembled from passages excerpted from a variety of different sources, and even the editors
of *GOA* were sensitive to the lack of coherent organization and unity in
the resulting collection. Nevertheless, *PB* contains some very interesting
passages which show how Nietzsche once more tried to use the history of

Greek philosophy as an armature for supporting and arranging his own thoughts on philosophy.

PB = *MA*, VII, pp. 11-33 = *GOA*, X, pp. 287-313 [= *WKG*, III, 4, pp. 230-331, 341-54, 359-64, and 431-2]. (The manuscript source is U II 2, U II 3, Mp XIII 5, and Mp XIII 3 [summer 1873-summer 1874].)

VI. *The Struggle between Science and Wisdom.* Near the end of the year 1875 Nietzsche returned, for what proved to be the last time, to his long-projected book on philosophy and the Greeks. This time he put aside all his previously assembled notes and drafts and attempted a fresh approach to the entire subject, an approach which, like that of *PB*, tended to emphasize the cultural question over the epistemological problems which had featured so prominently in the earlier notes. Under the title *Wissenschaft und Weisheit im Kampfe (WWK)* the editors of *GOA* published practically the entire contents of the notebook in which Nietzsche jotted down his new thoughts on this old topic. In this case alone the complete text of the original notebook has been published in *WKG*, and though the differences between the two texts are not great, I have compared them and have indicated and translated all the passages which were omitted in the earlier editions of *WWK*.

WWK = *MA*, VI, pp. 100-19 = *GOA*, X, pp. 216-37 = *WKG*, IV, 1 pp. 173-90. (The manuscript source is notebook U II 8c [end of 1875].)

VII. *Additional Plans and Outlines.* Nietzsche was extraordinarily fond of planning future projects and drawing up detailed outlines of unwritten books. His *Nachlass* contains hundreds of such plans. I have translated a *selection* of plans and outlines from the years 1872-6. These provide important information concerning Nietzsche's own (changing) intentions regarding the arrangement and publication of his notebook material on knowledge, philosophy, and the Greek philosophers. Thus they are useful guides for interpreting the various "texts" assembled and translated in this volume. But these plans and outlines (which have been rather arbitrarily arranged in four sets) should be supplemented by the many outlines and plans which are included elsewhere in the other selections in this volume. The selection, arrangement, and numbering of these plans and outlines are my own.

A. *Plans from the Summer of 1872.* From *MA*, IV, pp. 238-43 = *GOA*, X, pp. 101-6 [= *WKG*, III, 4, pp. 143-4, 117, 119-22]. (The manuscript source is U I 4b and Mp XII 4 [summer 1872-summer 1872-3].)

B. *Plans from Winter 1872-Spring 1873.* No. 1 is from *MA*, VI, pp. 63-4 = *GOA*, X, pp. 178-9 [= *WKG*, III, 4, pp. 104-6]. (The manuscript source is P I 20b [summer 1872-beginning of 1873].) Nos. 2–5 are published in Schlechta/Anders, pp. 40, 45-6, and 57 [= *WKG*, III, 4, pp. 50-1, 84-5, and 107]. (The manuscript source is P I 20b [summer 1872-beginning of

1873].) Nos. 6-7 are from *MA*, VI, pp. 73-4 = *GOA*, X, *Nachbericht* I, pp. 507-8 [= *WKG*, III, 4, pp. 63-4 and 24]. (The manuscript source is P I 20b [summer 1872-beginning of 1873].) Nos. 8-9 are published in Schlechta/Anders, pp. 95 and 91-2 [= *WKG*, III, 4, pp. 142 and 173-4]. (The manuscript source is Mp XII 4 and U I 5b [winter-spring 1872-3].)

C. *Two Plans from the Summer of 1873.* From *MA*, VI, *Nachbericht*, pp. 346-7 = *GOA*, X, *Nachbericht* I, pp. 513-4 [= *WKG*, III, 4, pp. 242-3]. (The manuscript source is U II 2 [summer-fall 1873].)

D. *Plans for the "Untimely Meditations."* From *MA*, VI, pp. 123-7 = *GOA*, X, pp. 473-7 [= *WKG*, III, 4, pp. 108, 354-5, 307-8, 330-1, 369 and IV, 2, p. 385]. (The manuscript source is P I 20b, U II 3, U II 2, U II 5a [summer 1872-spring 1874] and N II 1 [1876].)

Nietzsche is widely and rightfully regarded as one of the foremost German prose stylists. Yet no one knew better than he the cost of cultivating a superior style—a cost calculated in terms of revision, reorganization, self-sacrifice, and sheer effort. With one or two exceptions, none of the texts here translated show Nietzsche at his stylistic best.[8] These are, after all, excerpts from notebooks and unpublished papers, and though we can never be sure how Nietzsche himself might have finally revised and reorganized these notes if he had ever succeeded in publishing the book for which they were all, in one way or another, intended to be preliminary studies, we can be quite certain of one thing: scarcely a single sentence would have survived the transformation from notebook to printed page without meticulous stylistic revision and integration into a carefully constructed whole. In contrast with his published writings, Nietzsche's notebooks (unsurprisingly) contain careless ambiguities, obvious grammatical and stylistic errors, infelicitous choices of words, and occasional clauses or sentences which are hardly coherent. On the other hand, there are also many passages of striking brilliance and originality, passages which convey something of that atmosphere of breathless exhilaration which surrounds a thinker when he believes himself to be closest to his deepest and most valuable thoughts and can hardly move his pen fast enough to capture the ideas which crowd in upon him, one

---

[8]The exceptions are *PW* and the first two long sections of *WL*. Unlike the rest of the material in this volume, both of these selections are obviously polished literary accomplishments and not mere first drafts.

[9]In the poignant final section of *JGB* Nietzsche laments the necessity with which written thoughts seem to lose their original life and the fact that when we have found adequate expression for a thought it is already on the verge of withering and losing its fragrance. It seems to me that these selections from Nietzsche's notebooks, for all of their impetuosity and occasional inadequacy of expression—indeed, perhaps in part *because* of their unfinished form—do convey a peculiar sense of living thought and have a fragrance all their own.

after another. Consequently there is an ingenuous urgency to many of these notes which gives them a certain artless but real elegance.[9]

The special, unfinished nature of this material in some ways lightens the task of a translator and in others makes it more difficult. For though one is not faced with the perhaps insuperable problem of finding an adequate English approximation to Nietzsche's perfected German prose style, one does have to engage to an uncomfortable extent in guessing at the relation between clauses and in filling in missing words and punctuation. As always, the main desideratum is fidelity to the original texts, and in the present case this is best insured by a rather literal style of translation (as is not always true in translating Nietzsche's published writings, where a too-literal translation sometimes destroys the very important tone of the original).

As a general rule I have translated these selections as literally as possible, not hesitating to leave ambiguous, awkward, or unclear those passages which are so in the original. On the other hand, like most notebook writers, Nietzsche sometimes made careless but easily recognizable slips without correcting them and employed a few private conventions, abbreviating and omitting articles and connectives. I have not hesitated to correct obvious grammatical mistakes or to supply obviously necessary missing words (like "is" or "the"). But where there is any doubt about the correct reading of a passage, I have indicated my editorial interpolation by placing it within square brackets. I have also followed the standard practice of sometimes breaking long German sentences into several shorter English ones and of substituting nouns for pronouns as required for definiteness of reference. I have followed English rather than German conventions for the use of quotation marks and punctuation—though I have preserved Nietzsche's sometimes puzzling use of underlining (italics) for special emphasis. As previously explained, most of the section numbers within the various texts are later editorial additions and do not appear in the original notebooks.

Nietzsche took a certain amount of pride in not using any technical "philosophical" vocabulary, even in his discussions of clearly and rather narrowly philosophical questions, like the nature of truth or the character and reliability of perception. Like the Pre-Socratics and like Hegel, he uses ordinary words in even the most abstruse contexts; but in order to do this he sometimes uses the ordinary words in rather extraordinary ways, almost metaphorically at times.[10] He takes full advantage of peripheral and connotative meanings of words, which makes it extraordinarily difficult to find a single English word with which to translate

---

[10]Of course, according to the theory of language and concept formation developed below in *WL*, the distinction between "literal" and "metaphorical" usage is entirely relative—a difference in degree rather than kind.

every occurrence of a particular German word. And though I have tried
not to use the same English word (or words) to translate more than one
German word, I have not always succeeded. In lieu of a general glossary
of German words and English translations I have included remarks on
translation in the footnotes to the appropriate passages.

With two exceptions (viz., *PW* and the first two sections of *WL*), all of the
selections included in this volume are here translated into English for the
first time.[11]

The Annotation

The only justification for the extensive annotation which accompanies
this translation is to make it as accessible as possible to its intended
audience: serious readers and students of Nietzsche who are unable or
unwilling to read him in his own language. The notes are of several
different types. In addition to comments on matters of translation from
German into English, I have provided translations of all the non-
German words and phrases which occur in Nietzsche's manuscripts.
There are also many notes identifying persons, places, books, and events
to which Nietzsche alludes. Other notes relate a particular passage in
these notebooks to other passages in Nietzsche's writings, particularly in
his published writings, which bear on that passage. Finally, brief inter-
pretive commentary is appended to particularly significant or prob-
lematic passages.

There is an unavoidable element of arbitrariness involved in selecting
passages for comment and words or names for identification. Accordingly, I have had to rely upon my own presentiments in this matter,
upon my suspicion, for example, that the typical reader of these translations will not need to be told who Kant or Solon is, but might well
appreciate a brief note identifying Trendelenburg or Gracian. But since
no reader is really "typical," there will inevitably be too many notes for
some and not enough for others.

As a rule, Nietzsche's writings are referred to by abbreviations of their
German titles, followed by *section* number. All of his published writings
are divided into convenient sections (and sometimes subsections). Some

---

[11]An accurate English translation by David S. Thatcher of *On the Pathos of Truth* was
published in a special Nietzsche issue of *The Malhat Review*, No. 24 (October 1972),
pp. 134-8. The first two sections of *WL* were translated under the title "On Truth and
Falsity in the Extramoral Sense" in 1911 by Maximillan A. Mügge in *Early Greek
Philosophy and Other Essays* (vol. II of the Oscar Levy edition of "The Complete Works
of Friedrich Nietzsche"). But like many other translations in the Levy edition,
Mügge's translation of *WL* is inconsistent in its translation of certain key terms and
inadequate for serious students of Nietzsche. *Selections* from the first section of *WL*
(constituting altogether less than one-third of the section) are available in a good
translation by Walter Kaufmann in *The Portable Nietzsche* (New York: Viking, 1954),
pp. 42-7.

of the shorter unpublished pieces have no internal divisions, and in some cases the section numbers for the unpublished material were added by later editors. I have retained these numbers and have followed the general practice of referring to all of Nietzsche's writings by section numbers in order to facilitate the use of various editions and translations. A list of Nietzsche's writings with a key to the abbreviations follows.

List of Nietzsche's Writings
and
Key to Abbreviations

I. Collected editions of Nietzsche's writings.

   GOA = *Nietzsches Werke (Grossoktavausgabe)*. Revised edition. Leipzig: Kröner, 1901-1913.

   MA = *Nietzsches Gesammelte Werke (Musarionausgabe)*. München: Musarion, 1920-1929.

   WKG = *Nietzsches Werke (Kritische Gesamtausgabe)*. Berlin: de Gruyter, 1967ff. (in progress).

II. Selections included in this volume.

   PW = *Über das Pathos der Wahrheit* ("On the Pathos of Truth"), 1872.

   P = *Der letzte Philosoph. Der Philosoph. Betrachtungen über den Kampf von Kunst und Erkenntniss* ("The Last Philosopher. The Philosopher. Reflections on the Struggle between Art and Knowledge"), 1872.

   PAK = *Der Philosoph als Arzt der Kultur* ("The Philosopher as Cultural Physician"), 1873.

   WL = *Über Wahrheit und Lüge im aussermoralischen Sinne* ("On Truth and Lies in a Nonmoral Sense"), 1873.

   PB = *Gedanken zu der Betrachtung: Die Philosophie in Bedrängniss* ("Thoughts on the Meditation: Philosophy in Hard Times"), 1873.

   WWK = *Wissenschaft und Weisheit im Kampfe* ("The Struggle between Science and Wisdom"), 1875.

III. Books published or prepared for publication by Nietzsche.

   GT = *Die Geburt der Tragödie* ("The Birth of Tragedy"), 1872; second slightly altered ed., 1874; third ed., with new preface, 1886.

UBa = *Unzeitgemässe Betrachtungen. Erstes Stück: David Strauss, der Bekenner und der Schrifsteller* ("Untimely Meditations. First Part: David Strauss, the Writer and the Confessor"). 1873.

UBb = _____ . *Zweites Stück: Vom Nutzen und Nachteil der Historie für das Leben* ("Second Part: On the Use and Disadvantage of History for Life"), 1874.

UBc = _____ . *Drittes Stück: Schopenhauer als Erzieher* ("Third Part: Schopenhauer as Educator"), 1874.

UBd = _____ . *Viertes Stück: Richard Wagner in Bayreuth* ("Fourth Part: Richard Wagner in Bayreuth"), 1876.

MAMa = *Menschliches, Allzumenschliches. Erster Band* ("Human, All-too-Human. Volume One"), 1878; second ed. with a new preface, 1886.

MAMb = _____ . *Zweiter Band: Erste Abteilung: Vermischte Meinungen und Sprüche* ("Volume Two. First Section: Assorted Opinions and Sayings"), 1879; second ed., with *MAMc* and a new preface, 1886.

MAMc = _____ . *Zweiter Band. Zweite Abteilung: Der Wanderer und sein Schatten* ("Volume Two. Second Section: The Wanderer and his Shadow"), 1880; second ed., with *MAMb* and a new preface, 1886.

M = *Morgenröte* ("Dawn"), 1881; second ed. with a new preface, 1887.

FW = *Die fröhliche Wissenschaft* ("The Gay Science"), 1882; second ed. with substantial additions and a new preface, 1887.

Z = *Also sprach Zarathustra* ("Thus Spoke Zarathustra"), Part One, 1883; Part Two, 1883; Part Three, 1884; Part Four, privately published, 1885.

JGB = *Jenseits von Gut und Böse* ("Beyond Good and Evil"), 1886.

GM = *Zur Genealogie der Moral* ("On the Genealogy of Morals"), 1887.

W = *Der Fall Wagner* ("The Case of Wagner"), 1888.

GD = *Götzen-Dammerung* ("Twilight of the Idols"), prepared for publication, 1888; first ed., 1889.

NCW = *Nietzsche contra Wagner* ("Nietzsche contra Wagner"), prepared for publication, 1888; printed, but withdrawn before publication, 1889; published 1895.

A   = *Der Antichrist* ("The Antichrist"), prepared for publication, 1888; first ed., 1895.

EH   = *Ecce Homo* ("Ecce Homo"), prepared for publication, 1888; first ed., 1908.

IV. Miscellaneous writings and collections not published by Nietzsche.

MW   = *Über Musik und Wort* ("On Music and Words"), 1871.

GS   = *Der griechische Staat* ("The Greek State"), 1871.

ZB   = *Über die Zukunft unserer Bildungs-Anstalten* ("On the Future of our Educational Institutions"), 1872.

HW   = *Homers Wettkampf* ("Homer's Contest"), 1872.

VSP   = *Das Verhältnis der Schopenhauerschen Philosophie zu einer deutschen Kultur* ("The Relation of Schopenhauerian Philosophy to German Culture"), 1872.

PtZG   = *Die Philosophie im tragischen Zeitalter der Griechen* ("Philosophy in the Tragic Age of the Greeks"), 1873.

WP   = *Wir Philologen* ("We Philologists"), 1874/75.

WM   = *Der Wille zur Macht* ("The Will to Power"), a selection of excerpts from Nietzsche's notebooks of the 1880's; first published in 1901; second, greatly expanded edition, 1906.

V.   A note on English translations.

All the published and unpublished writings in categories III and IV are presently available in reliable English translations. Students of Nietzsche are fortunate indeed that all the works in category III, except *UBa-d*, *MAMa-c*, and *M*, are available in uniformly excellent translations by Walter Kaufmann, as is *WM*. (*Z*, *GD*, *NCW*, and *A* are published by Viking/Penguin; the rest are published by Random House/Vintage.) Good translations by R.J. Hollingdale of the remaining works (*UBa-d*, *MAMa-c*, and *M*) have recently been published by Cambridge University Press. (Hollingdale's translations of most of Nietzsche's other writings are published by Penguin Books.) *PtZG* is available in a translation by Marianne Cowan (Henry Regnery Books). A translation by Sander L. Gilman, Carole Blair, and David J. Parent of Nietzsche's unpublished 1872/73 lectures on rhetoric is included in *Friedrich Nietzsche on Rhetoric and Language* (Oxford University Press), which also includes translations of several other short, unpublished texts from the years 1869-1875.

The Philosopher:
Reflections on the Struggle Between
Art and Knowledge

1872

I
The Philosopher: Reflections on the Struggle Between Art and Knowledge[1]

16
[Seen] from the right height everything comes together: the thoughts of the philosopher, the work of the artist, and good deeds.

17
What must be shown is the way in which the entire life of a people reflects in an unclear and confused manner the image[2] offered by their highest geniuses. These geniuses are not the product of the masses, but the masses show their effects.

What is the relationship between the people and the genius otherwise?

There is an invisible bridge from genius to genius which constitutes the genuinely real "history" of a people. Everything else amounts to shadowy, infinite variations in an inferior material, copies made by unskilled hands.[3]

---

[1]This is one of a number of titles which Nietzsche was considering during the early 1870's for a book for which many of these notes were apparently intended. Another projected title was *The Last Philosopher*. Accordingly, the editors of *GOA*, X and *MA*, VI assigned to this collection of notes the double title, *The Last Philosopher. The Philosopher: Reflections on the Struggle between Art and Knowledge*. I have retained the section numbers (added by the editors of *GOA*, X and removed in *MA*, VI) because they facilitate reference. It must, however, be remembered that these numbers are mere indexing devices, editorial additions with little or no basis in the manuscripts themselves. (*P* begins with section 16; sections 1-15 are "Notes for a Continuation of *Pt/G*.")

[2]*Bild*. This important term in Nietzsche's rather loose perceptual vocabulary is usually translated here as "image" and sometimes as "picture" or "portrait."

[3]The nature of the relationship between "culture," the "people," and the highly gifted creative individual (the "genius") is one of the major themes of inquiry in all of Nietzsche's early published and unpublished writings. As many passages in the present collection make clear, Nietzsche's interest in the Greeks was largely motivated by the belief that they could cast some light upon this ques-

3

18

How did they philosophize in the splendid world of art?[4] Does philosophizing cease when life achieves perfection? No, true philosophizing begins now for the first time. Its judgment *concerning existence means more*, because it has before it this relative perfection and all the veils of art and illusions.

19

In the world of art and philosophy man cultivates an "immortality of the intellect."

The will alone is immortal;[5] that immortality of the intellect which is achieved through education and which presupposes human brains looks miserable in comparison. One can see the natural lineage to which such immortality belongs.

But how can the genius be the highest goal of nature as well? *Living on by means of history* and living on by means of *procreation*.

This is where Plato's "procreating upon the beautiful" belongs:[6] thus the birth of the genius requires that history be overcome. It must be immersed and eternalized in beauty.

Against *iconic historiography!*[7] It contains within itself a barbarizing element.

---

tion. His conclusion is that each individual person has value only as a tool of the genius—who, in turn, has value only insofar as he "justifies existence" by his creative production. (See the "Translator's Introduction," as well as Nietzsche's other writings of the period, especially *GS*, the little essay on the Greek state.)

The image of a "bridge" or "spiritual mountain range" of superior individuals is derived from Schopenhauer's idea of a "republic of genius" and occurs frequently in Nietzsche's early writings. Cf. e.g. *UBb*, 9; *Pt/G*, 1; and (below) *P*, 34.

[4]I.e. in Greece during the so-called "tragic age" between Homer and Plato. This note helps to explain Nietzsche's unusual interest in Pre-Platonic philosophy: the question is whether or not there existed a "tragic philosophy" paralleling "tragic art," a philosophy, which like that art, could affirm life and suffering. For a more general discussion of Nietzsche's interest in the Greeks and their philosophers, see the "Translator's Introduction" and below, *P*, 57; *PAK*, 173, 175; and *WWK*, 191, 199. (Cf. also *Pt/G*, 1 and *UBc*, 3.)

[5]This is, of course, a fundamental Schopenhauerian tenet. One of the minor pleasures to be gained from a reading of the notes translated in this volume is observing the young Nietzsche as he slowly formulates for himself his theoretical and practical differences with Schopenhauerianism and, tentatively at first and then more resolutely, begins to make his decisive break from his great "educator." See below, *WL*, n. 9.

[6]The allusion is to Diotoma's definition of love as a "procreating upon the beautiful" in *Symposium*, 206 b.

[7]"Iconic" is a word derived from the Greek *eikonikos*, meaning "copied from

History should speak only of what is great and unique, of exemplary models.

With this one lays hold of the task facing the new philosophical generation.

None of the great Greeks of the age of tragedy have anything of the historian about them.

20

The *unselective* knowledge drive[8] resembles the indiscriminate sexual drive—signs of *vulgarity*!

21

The philosopher does not stand so completely apart from the people as an exception: the will desires something from him too. The intention is the same as in the case of art—the glorification and deliverance of the will itself. From one rung to the next the will strives for *purity and ennoblement.*

22

The drives which distinguish the Greeks from other people are expressed in their philosophy. But these are precisely their *classical* drives.

Their way of dealing with history is significant.

The gradual degeneration in antiquity of the concept of the historian: its dissolution into mere curiosity and the pretense of knowing everything.

---

life." "Iconic historiography" cherishes a literalist ideal of history as "value-free science," a neutral record of "what happened." Nietzsche devoted the second of his *Untimely Meditations* (*UBb*, 1874) to the problem of the relationship between history and the needs of human life. The three types of history with which *UBb* is mainly concerned—namely, "monumental," "antiquarian," and "critical" history—are all types of non-iconic history. The demand that history become an objective science is denounced as the cause of its inutility or even harmfulness to human life (see especially *UBb*, 4). Yet Nietzsche was far from wishing to reject historical investigation altogether. On the contrary, his own later "genealogical method" is an excellent example of the kind of "history in the service of life" which he meditated upon in the early 1870's.

[8]*Erkenntnistrieb. Trieb*, a word which occurs very frequently in these notes, means "driving force," "impetus," or "inclination"; "instinct" would be a good translation in many contexts. Because of its importance I have (almost) always translated it as "drive." Thus, though *Erkenntnistrieb* might plausibly be rendered as "instinct for knowledge," it is translated here as "knowledge drive"—as is *Wissenstrieb*, another term which Nietzsche uses less frequently than *Erkenntnistrieb* but with exactly the same meaning.

23

Task: to recognize the *teleology* of the philosophical genius. Is he really nothing but a wanderer who appears accidentally? In any case, if he is a genuine philosopher he has nothing to do with the accidental political situation of a people; in contrast to his people, he is *timeless*. But this does not mean that his connection with his people is merely accidental. What is unique in a people here comes to light in an individual; the drive of the people is interpreted as a *universal drive* and is employed to solve the riddle of the universe. By *separating* them, nature will one day succeed in contemplating its drives clearly. The philosopher is a means for finding repose in the restless current, for becoming conscious of the enduring types by disdaining multiplicity.[9]

24

The philosopher is a self-revelation of nature's workshop; the philosopher and the artist tell the trade secrets of nature.

The sphere of the philosopher and the artist exists above the tumult of contemporary history, beyond necessity.

The philosopher as *brakeshoe on the wheel of time.*

Philosophers appear during those times of great danger, when the wheel of time is turning faster and faster. Together with art, they step into the place vacated by myth. But they are far ahead of their time, since the attention of their contemporaries only turns toward them very slowly.

A people which is becoming conscious of its dangers produces a genius.

25

After Socrates it is no longer possible to preserve the commonweal: hence that individualizing ethics which seeks to preserve the individual.

---

[9]Regarding the philospher as nature's own means of becoming self-conscious ("the teleology of the philosopher"), see *UBc*, 5. What Nietzsche is trying to do in this note is to provide a "metaphysical justification" of philosophy similar to the justification of the artist already propounded in *GT*. Nietzsche's view of the connection between the philosopher and his particular time and place underwent a slow and interesting evolution. The present passage and many others in these notes imply that the philosopher always bears a necessary relation to his people. According to a passage in *PtZG*, 1, on the other hand, it is only among the ancient Greeks that the philosopher has such a relation to his people; everywhere else he is a chance wanderer. Then, in *UBc*, 7, it is implied that the philosopher is always merely a chance wanderer in his time and place. Finally, in *JGB*, 212, Nietzsche argues that the philosopher must *necessarily* stand in contradiction to his time and its values.

The unmeasured and indiscriminate knowledge drive is, along with its historical background, a sign that life has grown old. There is great danger that individuals are becoming inferior; therefore, their interests are powerfully captivated by objects of knowledge, no matter which. The universal drives have become so feeble that they are no longer able to hold the individual in check.

The Teuton used the sciences to transfigure all of his limitations at the same time that he transmitted them: fidelity, modesty, self-restraint, diligence, cleanliness, love of order—the familial virtues. But also formlessness, the complete lack of any vivacity in life, and pettiness. His unlimited knowledge drive is the consequence of an impoverished life. Without this drive he would be petty and spiteful—which he often is despite it.[10]

Today we are presented with a higher form of life, against a background of art: and now likewise, the immediate consequence is [the development of] a selective knowledge drive, i.e. *philosophy.*[11]

Terrible danger: the fusion of the American kind of political agitation with the rootless culture of the scholars.[12]

26

With the selective knowledge drive *beauty* again emerges as power.
It is most remarkable that Schopenhauer *writes well*! His life too has

---

[10]Cf. the following similar passage from *VSP* (1872):

"Even the celebrated German science, in which a number of the most useful domestic and familiar virtues—fidelity, self-restraint, diligence, modesty, and cleanliness—appear to have been removed into a clearer atmosphere and, as it were, transfigured, is nevertheless, by no means the consequence of these virtues. Considered closely, that motive which in Germany impels one toward restricted knowing appears to bear a closer resemblance to a flaw, defect, or lack, than to a superabundance of strength. It almost seems like the consequence of an impoverished, formless, lifeless life, and even like an escape from the moral pettiness and spite to which the German is subjected without such diversions—and which breaks through despite science, and indeed, still more frequently within science." (*MA*, VI, p. 4)

[11]This "higher form of life" is, of course, imagined by the young Nietzsche to be presented by Wagner and his "cause." See the last half of *GT* for Nietzsche's impassioned panegyric of Wagner's art, as well as his attempt to convince himself that this new art form signals a rebirth of philosophy as well—a rebirth already begun in Kant and Schopenhauer, who, along with Wagner, are the harbingers of a rebirth of tragedy. The "likewise" refers to the union of art and philosophy among the Greeks during their "tragic age."

[12]*Gelehrtenkultur. Gelehrten* means "those who have been educated," "learned persons." I have usually translated it "scholars," though it has a rather broader connotation than the English word. (The adjective *gelehrten* has been translated as "scholarly" or "learned.")

more style than that of a university teacher—but he had a stunted environment.

No one today knows what a good book looks like; one must show them. They do not understand composition; more and more the press is ruining the feeling for it.

Oh, to be able to hold fast to the sublime!

27

Enormous *artistic* powers[13] are required in opposition to iconic historiography and natural science.

What should the philosopher do? In the midst of this ant-like swarming he must emphasize the problem of existence, all the eternal problems.

The philosopher should *recognize what is needed,* and the artist should *create* it. The philosopher should empathize to the utmost with the universal suffering, just as each of the ancient Greek philosophers expresses a need and erects his system in the vacant space indicated by that need. Within this space he constructs his world.

28

The difference between the effect of philosophy and that of science[14] must be made clear, and likewise, their different origins.

It is not a question of annihilating science, but of *controlling* it. Science is totally dependent upon philosophical opinions for all of its goals and methods, though it easily forgets this. *But that philosophy which gains control also has to consider the problem of the level to which science should be permitted to develop: it has to determine value.*[15]

---

[13]*Kräfte* (singular *Kraft*). I have translated this frequently occurring term as "force," "strength," or "power." (The term *Macht* = "power," which is familiar to readers of Nietzsche's later writings, is used infrequently in these early notebooks. And of course, Nietzsche had no conception of the "will to power" at this early date—though many of the steps toward this later formulation are already taken in these notes.)

[14]*Wissenschaft.* This word has to be translated as "science," but it is important to remember that "science" in German refers to rigorous, systematic, disciplined inquiry as such, and is by no means synonymous with "natural science." Mathematics, history, and philosophy are all "sciences" in the fullest sense of the German word.

[15]This paragraph introduces one of the major themes to be investigated in the notes which follow, viz. the problem of *controlling* science by determining the value and goal of its knowing. Of course, to the extent that it is the philosopher who is entrusted with this task, then he is more than a "scientist." It is worth comparing this picture of the relation between the man of science and the

29

Proof of the *barbarizing* effects of science: it easily looses itself in the service of "practical interests."

Schopenhauer is valuable, because he calls to mind the memory of *naive, universal* truths. He dares to articulate beautifully so-called "trivialities."

We have no noble popular philosophy, because we have no noble concept of *peuple (publicum)*.[16] Our popular philosophy is for the *peuple*, not for the public.

30

If we are ever to achieve a culture, unheard-of artistic powers will be needed in order to break the unlimited knowledge drive, in order to produce unity once again. *Philosophy reveals its highest worth when it concentrates the unlimited knowledge drive and subdues*[17] *it to unity.*

31

This is the way in which the earlier Greek philosophers are to be understood: they master the knowledge drive. How did it happen that they gradually lost this mastery after Socrates? To begin with *Socrates and his school* showed the same tendency: the knowledge drive should be restrained out of *individual* concern for *living happily*. This is a final, inferior phase. Previously, it was not a question of *individuals*, but of the *Hellenes*.

32

The great ancient philosophers are part of *general Hellenic life; after Socrates* philosophers formed *sects*. Gradually philosophy let the reins of science drop from its hands.

In the middle ages these reins were picked up by theology. Now is the dangerous age of emancipation.

---

philosopher with the very similar picture painted fourteen years later in *JGB*, 204-13.

[16]*Peuple,* is the ordinary French word for "people," in the sense of "everybody." *Publicum* is a Latin word usually used to designate the property of the state, but here used in the sense of "commonwealth" or "public weal."

[17]*bändigen* (noun, *Bändigung*). This is one of the central terms in the analysis of knowledge which follows. It means "to restrain," "to subjugate," "to master," or "to subdue," and is often used to express the kind of subjugation which occurs when an animal is "tamed" or "broken in." I have occasionally translated it "subdue," but usually as "master" (noun: "subjugation," "mastery.").

The general welfare again desires a *mastery* and thereby at the same time elevation and concentration.

The *"laisser aller"*[18] *of our science* resembles certain *dogmas of political economy*: one has faith in an absolutely beneficial result.

In a certain sense, *Kant's* influence was detrimental, because belief in metaphysics has been lost. No one would rely upon his "thing in itself" as if it were a principle which could master anything.

We can now comprehend what is remarkable about Schopenhauer: He assembles all the elements which are still of use for controlling science; he hits upon the most profound and primal problems of ethics and of art; he poses the question concerning the value of existence.

The marvelous unity of Wagner and Schopenhauer! They originate from the same drive. The deepest qualities of the Germanic spirit here prepare themselves for battle—as in the case of the Greeks.

Return of *circumspection.*

33
My task: to comprehend *the internal coherence and necessity of every true culture*; to comprehend a culture's preservatives and restoratives and their relationship to the genius of the people. A culture is the consequence of every great art world, but it often happens that—due to hostile countercurrents—this final resonance of a work of art remains unachieved.

34
Philosophy should hold fast to that *spiritual mountain range* which stretches across the centuries, and therewith, to the eternal fruitfulness of everything that is great.

For science there is nothing great and nothing small—but for philosophy! The value of science is measured in that sentence.

Holding fast to that which is sublime!

What an extraordinary *deficiency* there is in our age of books which breathe an heroic strength. Even Plutarch is no longer read!

35
Kant said (in the second Preface to the *Critique of Pure Reason*): *"I have therefore found it necessary to deny knowledge, in order to make room for faith."* The dogmatism of metaphysics, that is, the preconception that it is possible to make headway in metaphysics without a previous criticism of

---

[18]"let it go"; "leave it alone."

reason, is the source of all that unbelief, always very dogmatic, which wars against morality."[19] Very significant! Kant was impelled by a cultural need!

What a curious opposition, *"knowledge and faith"*! What would the Greeks have thought of this? Kant *was acquainted with no other opposition, but what about us*!

A cultural need impels Kant; he wishes to *preserve* a domain *from knowledge*: that is where the roots of all that is highest and deepest lie, of art and of ethics—Schopenhauer.

On the other side[20] he assembles everything which *has ever been worth knowing*—ethical, popular, and human wisdom (standpoint of the seven wise men, of the Greek popular philosophers).

He breaks this faith up into its elements and shows the insufficiency of the Christian faith for our deepest needs: question concerning the value of existence.

36

The struggle between knowledge and knowledge.

Schopenhauer calls attention to even that thinking and knowing of which we are *unconscious*.

The mastery of the knowledge drive: Does it work to the advantage of a religion? Or to the advantage of an artistic culture? The answer should now become evident; I favor the latter alternative.

To this I add the question concerning the *value* of historical, *iconic* knowing, as well as of *nature*.

In the case of the Greeks this mastery works to the advantage of an artistic culture (and religion?), the mastery which is intended to *prevent* a state of total release. We desire to regain mastery over that which has been totally released.[21]

37

The philosopher of tragic knowledge. He masters the uncontrolled knowledge drive,[22] though not by means of a new metaphysics. He establishes no new faith. He considers it *tragic* that the ground of metaphysics has been withdrawn,[23] and he will never permit himself to be satisfied with

---

[19]*Critique of Pure Reason,* B xxx. Quoted in the Kemp Smith translation.

[20]I.e. in the domain forbidden to knowledge and preserved for faith.

[21]*den ganz entfesselten.*

[22]*den entfesselten Wissenstrieb.*

[23]*Er empfindet den weggezogenen Boden der Metaphysik tragisch.* . . . Note that "tragic" has here a double sense: it is a "tragic thing" that the ground of metaphysics has been withdrawn; and this withdrawal is the occasion for the development of a "tragic" kind of philosophy—paralleling tragic art.

the motley whirling game of the sciences. He cultivates a new *life*; he returns to art its rights.

The philosopher of *desperate knowledge* will be absorbed in blind science: knowledge at any price.

For the tragic philosopher the appearance of the metaphysical as merely anthropomorphic completes the *picture of existence*. He is not a *skeptic*.

Here there is a concept which must be *created*, for skepticism is not the goal. When carried to its limits the knowledge drive turns against itself in order to proceed to the *critique of knowing*. Knowledge in the service of the best life. One must even *will illusion*—that is what is tragic.[24]

38

The last philosopher—this could be entire generations. He only has to assist *life*. Naturally, he is "the last" in a relative sense, "the last" for our world. He demonstrates the necessity of illusions, of art, and of that art which rules over life. It is not possible for us to produce again a series of philosophers like that of Greece during the age of tragedy. Their task is now accomplished by *art alone*. Such a system remains possible only as *art*. Judged from the standpoint of the present, an entire period of Greek philosophy simultaneously belongs within the realm of their art.

39

The mastery of science occurs now *only* by means of *art*. It is a question of *value judgments* concerning knowledge and polymathy.[25] How enormous is the task, and how worthy of it art is! It must create everything anew and, *all by itself, it must give birth anew to life*. The Greeks show us what art is capable of. If we did not have them, our faith would be chimerical.

---

[24]For a discussion of the origin and significance of what Nietzsche here calls "tragic knowledge," see *GT*, 7 and 15. "Tragic knowledge" is that knowledge which penetrates the illusions and the *principium individuationis* and thereby provides one with a vision of the suffering character of existence. For this reason it "kills action" and demands the new saving illusions of tragic art ("returns to art its rights"). The *general* problem indicated in the last sentence—viz. the problem of consciously willing illusion—is one central to all phases of Nietzsche's work. The problem remains long after Nietzsche has discarded the Schopenhauerian context in which he first poses it. (It is easy to find dozens of passages from every period of Nietzsche's career which deal with the necessity of illusion for life and the problem which this causes the "lover of truth." Perhaps the most poignant discussion on this topic, however, is found in the very important "Prefaces" which Nietzsche wrote in 1886 for most of his earlier books.)

[25]*Wissen und Vielwissen.*

Whether or not a religion is able to establish itself here within this vacuum depends upon its strength. *We* are committed to *culture*: the "German" as a *redeeming* force! In any case, that religion which would be able so to establish itself would have to possess an immense *power of love*—against which knowledge would shatter as it does against the language of art.

But might not art itself perhaps be capable of creating a religion, of giving birth to myth? This was the case among the Greeks.

40

Philosophies and theologies which have now been *demolished* still continue to operate in science. Even when the roots have died, the branches still live for a while. The *sense of history*[26] has been widely developed, especially as a counter-force against theological myth, but also against philosophy. In history and in mathematical natural science *absolute knowing* celebrates its Saturnalia. The smallest matter that can actually be *decided* in these realms is worth more than all the ideas of metaphysics. Value is here determined by the degree of *certainty,* not the degree of *indispensability* for men. It is the old struggle between *faith and knowledge*.

41

These are barbarian biases.

All that philosophy can do now is to emphasize the *relativity* and *anthropomorphic* character of all knowledge, as well as the all pervasive ruling power of *illusion*. By doing this philosophy is no longer able to check the uncontrolled knowledge drive, which *judges* more and more according to the degree of certainty and which seeks smaller and smaller objects. Whereas every man is glad when a day is over, the historian seeks to unearth and to reconstruct this day in order to save it from oblivion. Thus, what is *small* shall be eternal, *because it is knowable*.

The only criterion which counts for us is the aesthetic criterion.[27] What is *great* has a right to history, but not a history of the iconic sort; rather, it merits a *productive and stimulating canvas of historical events*. We leave the *graves undisturbed*; we take possession of what is eternally alive.

Pet topic of the present age: *the great effects of the smallest thing*. For example, historical grubbing, when taken as a whole contains an element of grandeur. It is similar to that stunted vegetation which gradually reduces the Alps to dust. We see a great drive which employs a *grand number* of small instruments.

---

[26]*Das Historische*.

[27]Cf. the repeated claim in *GT* the world is justified "only as an aesthetic phenomenon." *GT*, 5 and 24.

42

On the other hand, one could mention: *the small effects of what is great*, where greatness is represented by individuals. What is great is difficult to grasp; the tradition often dies away; hatred against it is universal; its value depends upon its quality, which always has few admirers.

Great things only have an effect upon great things, just as the signal flares in *Agamemnon* leap only from summit to summit.[28]

The task of *culture* is to see to it that what is great in a people does not appear among them as a hermit or exile.

This is the reason why we wish to relate what we perceive. It is not our business to wait until the valleys have been penetrated by the feeble reflection of what is already clear to me—namely, that in the final analysis the great effects of the smallest things are only aftereffects of *great things*. They have started an avalanche; now we are having trouble stopping it.

43

History[29] and the natural sciences were necessary to combat the middle ages: knowledge versus faith. We now oppose knowledge with *art*: return to life! Mastery of the knowledge drive! Strengthening of the moral and aesthetic instincts!

This seems to us to constitute the *salvation of the German spirit, so that that spirit might once again be a savior*.[30]

For us the essence of this spirit has been absorbed into *music*. Now we understand the way in which the *Greeks* made their culture dependent upon music.

44

In order to create a religion one would have to *awaken belief* in a mythical construction which one had erected in the vacuum[31]—which

---

[28] Allusion to the opening scene of Aeschylus' *Agamemnon*.

[29] *Das Historische.*

[30] The previous time when the "German spirit" was a "savior" was presumably the Lutheran reformation, which "saved" Christianity. Nietzsche's views on Germans in general and on the significance of the Protestant reformation in particular later underwent drastic change. See, e.g. his passionate indictment of the Germans as "delayers" (especially in their "reformation"): *FW*, 148; *W*, "postscript"; *A*, 61; and *EH*, III, "W," 2. As for the expression "the German spirit," one should compare the attitude expressed here with Nietzsche's view in 1888, that such an expression is a contradiction in terms: *GD*, I, 23 and letter to Georg Brandes, April 10, 1888.

[31] I.e. in the "vacuum" left by the destruction of myth. See above, *P*, 24 and 39.

would mean that this construction corresponds to an extraordinary need. It is *unlikely* that this will ever happen again after the *Critique of Pure Reason*. On the other hand, I can imagine a totally new type of *philosopher-artist* who fills the empty space with a *work of art*, possessing aesthetic value.[32]

How *creatively* the Greeks dealt with their gods!
We are all too familiar with the opposition between historical truth and untruth. It is strange that the Christian myths are said to be thoroughly *historical*!

45
Pity and being good are fortunately independent of the decay or the growth of any religion; good *deeds*, on the other hand are determined to a very large extent by religious imperative. By far the largest percentage of good, dutiful acts have no ethical value, rather, they have been performed under *compulsion*.[33]
Practical morality will suffer greatly from every breakdown of religion. The metaphysics of punishment and reward seems to be indispensable.
If one could create *customs*—strong *customs*—one would thereby have ethics as well.[34]
Customs, but customs which have been fashioned on the *example of powerful individual personalities*.
I do not expect an awakening of *goodness* among any substantial portion of the propertied classes, but one might be able to instill in them a *custom*, a duty toward tradition.
If mankind spent for education and schools what it has spent until now for the construction of churches! If it now directed the intelligence to education that it does to theology!

---

[32]The idea of a new type of "philosopher-artist" is a constant theme in all Nietzsche's writings, from the "Socrates who practices music" of *GT* to the creative affirmations of Zarathustra and beyond. The present collection of notes contains many interesting passages in which Nietzsche tries to work out and more sharply to delineate this ideal.
[33]The understanding of "ethical value" which underlies this passage is thoroughly Kantian: i.e. the only moral act is one performed on the basis of an autonomous moral imperative, independent of all external compulsions, including prudence and desire.
[34]The plausibility of this assertion is reinforced by the similarity between the German words *Sitte* (="customs," "mores") and *Sittlichkeit* ("ethics," "morals"). Nietzsche was not the first German philosopher to be intrigued by this connection (cf. e.g. Chapter VI of Hegel's *Phenomenology of Spirit*), but he perhaps is the one who made the most of it. See the discussion of the "morality of mores" in, e.g., *M*, 9.

46

The problem of *culture* is seldom grasped correctly. The goal of a culture is not the greatest possible *happiness* of a people, nor is it the unhindered development of *all* their talents; instead, culture shows itself in the correct *proportion* of these developments.[35] Its aim points beyond earthly happiness: the production of great works is the aim of culture.

In all the drives of the Greeks there is manifested a *mastering unity*—let us call it the "Hellenic *will*." Each of these drives by itself endeavors to exist to eternity. The ancient philosophers attempt to construct a world from these drives.

The *culture* of a people is manifest in the *unifying mastery* of *their drives*: philosophy masters the knowledge drive; art masters ecstasy and the formal drive; ἀγάπη masters ἔρως,[36] etc.

Knowledge *isolates*. The early philosophers represented in isolation things which Greek art allowed to appear together.

The contents are the same in art and in ancient philosophy, but in philosophy we observe the *isolated* elements of art employed in order to *master the knowledge drive*. This must also be demonstrable in the case of the Italians: individualism in life and art.[37]

47

The Greeks as discoverers, voyagers, and colonizers. They knew how to *learn*: an immense power of appropriation. Our age should not think that it stands so much higher in terms of its knowledge drive—except that in the case of the Greeks everything was *life*! With us it remains knowledge!

When one considers, on the other hand, the *value* of knowledge, and, on the other hand, a beautiful illusion which has exactly the same value as an item of knowledge—provided only that it is an illusion in which one believes—, then one realizes that life requires illusions, i.e. untruths which are taken to be truths. What life does require is belief in truth, but

---

[35]"Culture" is defined by Nietzsche as "above all, the unity of artistic style in all the expressions of a people's life." (*UBa*, 1) For a discussion of Nietzsche's understanding of culture and the significance of this understanding in his early writings, see the "Translator's Introduction."

[36]*Agape* means "love," especially the sort of "transcendant" love which is supposed to exist between family members and between man and God. *Eros* is also "love," generally of a sexual sort. Thus the contrast between *agape* and *eros* is often similar to the contrast between "spiritual" and "carnal" love.

[37]Nietzsche is presumably thinking of the Italians of the Renaissance (whom he always viewed through lenses ground by his esteemed colleague at Basel, Jakob Burckhardt).

illusion is sufficient for this. That is to say, "truths" do not establish themselves by means of logical proofs, but by means of their effects: proofs of strength.[38] The true and the effective are taken to be identical; here too one submits to force. How then is one to explain the fact that any logical demonstration of truth occurred at all? In the *struggle between "truth" and "truth"* both sides seek an alliance with reflection. *All actual striving for truth has come into the world through the struggle for a holy conviction*—through the πάθος [39] of the struggle. Otherwise men have no interest in the logical origin.

48

How does the philosophical genius relate to art? There is not much to be learned from his direct conduct. We must ask: "What is there of art in his philosophy? [In what respect is it] a work of art? What *remains* when his system has been destroyed as science?" But this left over element must be precisely the one which *masters* the knowledge drive;[40] therefore, it must be the artistic element in his philosophical system. Why is such a mastery necessary? For, considered scientifically, a philosophical system is an illusion, an untruth which deceives the drive to knowledge and satisfies it only temporarily. In such satisfaction, the value of philosophy does not lie in the sphere of knowledge, but in that of *life*. The *will to existence employs philosophy* for the purposes of a higher form of existence.

It is impossible for art and philosophy to *oppose* the will. Morality likewise is in its service. Omnipotence of the *will*. One of the most delicate forms of existence, relative nirvana.

49

The beauty and grandeur of an interpretation of the world[41] (*alias*

---

[38]A "proof of strength" is one which demonstrates the truth of a proposition or theory by the beneficial consequences of believing it to be true. (On the biblical and theological origin of this notion, see Walter Kaufmann's "note" to section 347 of his translation of *FW* [New York: Random House, 1974].) One should compare Nietzsche's remarks in these notebooks concerning the "proof of strength" with his many published and unpublished *criticisms* of "proofs" of this sort: they prove nothing regarding the truth of the views in question. In other words, Nietzsche is no pragmatist regarding truth. See e.g. *FW*, 347; *A*, 50; and *WP*, 171 and 452.

[39]*Pathos.* See *PW*, n. 1.

[40]The left-over element has to be the source of mastery, because it is the "unscientific" element in philosophy, and because what distinguishes science from philosophy is precisely the lack of mastery and unity in the former.

[41]*einer Weltkonstruktion.*

18

philosophy) is what is now decisive for its value, i.e. it is judged as *art*. Its form will probably change: The rigid mathematical formula (as in Spinoza) which had such a soothing influence on Goethe now remains justified only as an aesthetic means of expression.

50

This proposition must be established: We live only by means of illusions; our consciousness skims over the surface. Much is hidden from our view. Moreover, there is no danger that man will ever understand himself *completely*, that he will penetrate at every instant all the laws of leverage and mechanics and all the formulas of architecture and chemistry which his life requires. However, it is quite possible that the *schema* of everything might become known. That will change almost nothing regarding our lives. Besides, this is all nothing but formulas for absolutely unknowable forces.

51

Owing to the superficiality of our intellect we indeed live in an ongoing illusion, i.e. at every instant we need art in order to live. Our eyes detain us at the *forms*. But if we have gradually acquired such eyes for ourselves, then there is an *artistic power* which holds sway within us. Thus in nature itself we see mechanisms opposed to absolute *knowledge*: the philosopher *recognizes* the language of nature and says "we need art" and "we require only a portion of knowledge."

52

Every kind of *culture* begins by *veiling* a great number of things. Human progress depends upon this veiling: life in a pure and noble sphere separated from the more common attractions. The struggle against "sensuality" by means of virtue is an essentially aesthetic struggle. When we employ as our guiding stars *great* individuals, we veil over many things about them; indeed, we disguise all the circumstances and accidents which make possible their formation. In order that we may venerate them, we *isolate* them from themselves. Every religion contains such an element: the men who are under divine protection are considered infinitely important. Indeed, all ethics begins when the individual is taken to be of *infinite importance*—in contrast to nature, which behaves cruelly and playfully toward the individual. If we are better and more noble, it is because we have been made this way by those illusions which isolate us.

Natural science opposes this with the absolute truth of nature: advanced physiology will certainly comprehend the artistic powers already present in our development—and not only in human development, but also in that of the animals. Advanced physiology will declare that the *artistic* begins with the *organic*.

Perhaps the chemical transformations in inorganic nature should also be called artistic processes, mimic roles adopted by a particular force. But there are *several* roles which it can play!

53

Great dilemma: is philosophy an art or a science? Both in its purposes and its results it is an art. But it uses the same means as science—conceptual representation. Philosophy is a form of artistic invention.[42] There is no appropriate category for philosophy; consequently, we must make up and characterize a species [for it].

The natural history of the philosopher. He knows in that he invents, and he invents in that he knows.[43]

He does not grow: I mean, philosophy does not follow the course of the other sciences, even if certain of the philosopher's territories gradually fall into the hands of science. Heraclitus can never be obsolete. Philosophy is invention beyond the limits of experience; it is the continuation of the *mythical drive*. It is thus essentially pictorial.[44] Mathematical expression is not a part of the essence of philosophy.

Overcoming of knowledge by means of the powers that *fashion myths*. *Kant* is remarkable—knowledge and faith! Innermost kinship between *philosophers* and *founders of religion*.

Curious problem: the self-consumption of philosophical systems! This is equally unheard of in science and in art. Religion, however, is *similar* to philosophy in this respect: this is remarkable and significant.

54

Our understanding is a surface power; it is *superficial*. One also calls it "subjective." It understands things by means of *concepts*; i.e. our thinking is a process of categorizing[45] and naming. Thus thinking is something dependent upon human option and does not touch the thing itself. Man possesses absolute knowledge only while calculating and only in the forms of space; i.e. *quantities* are the ultimate boundaries of what is knowable. Man does not *understand* a single quality, but only quantity.

---

[42]*Dichtkunst.*

[43]*Er erkennt, indem er dichtet, und dichtet, indem er erkennt.* A *Dichter* is an author of creative fiction and poetry; *dichten* means to write poetry or fiction, but it also has the more general significance of "inventing" or "devising."

[44]*in Bildern*, i.e. philosophical thinking is a thinking by means of concrete images (*Bilder*); it is "picture thinking" (*Bilderdenken*). Cf. *P*, 63 (below).

[45]*ein Rubriciren. Rubriciren* is a verb meaning "to place in columns under headings." This term appears frequently in these notes and is always translated "categorize."

What can be the purpose of such a surface power?

To the concept there corresponds, in the first place, the image. Images are primitive thoughts, i.e. the surfaces of things combined in the mirror of the eye.

The *image* is one thing; the *calculation* is another.[46]

Images in the human eye! This governs all human nature: from the *eye* out! Subject! The *ear* hears sound; an entirely different and marvelous conception of the same world.

Art depends upon the *inexactitude* of *sight*.

Similarly in the case of the ear: art depends upon a similar inaccuracy regarding rhythm, temperament, etc.

55

There exists within us a power which permits the *major* features of the mirror image to be perceived with greater intensity, and again there is a power which emphasizes rhythmic similarity beyond the actual inexactitude. This must be an *artistic power*, because it is *creative*. Its chief creative means are *omitting, overlooking,* and *ignoring*. It is therefore an anti-scientific power, because it does not have the same degree of interest in everything that is perceived.

The word contains nothing but an image; from this comes the concept. Thinking thus calculates with artistic magnitudes.

All categorization is an attempt to arrive at images.

We relate superficially to every true *being*; we speak the language of symbol and image. Then, we artistically add something to this by reinforcing the main features and forgetting the secondary ones.

56

Art's apology. Our public, civic, and social life amounts to an equilib-

---

[46]*Das Bild ist das eine, das Rechenexempel das andre. Rechenexempel* literally means "calculated sum." Though the meaning of this sentence in the present context is obscure, it can be explained in terms of Nietzsche's general theory that all our knowledge is of two types: (1) conceptual knowledge, which is, according to Nietzsche's theory of concept formation, always based upon images, and (2) knowledge of numerical proportions. Knowledge of this second type is "absolute" knowledge—though it is only knowledge of abstract relations between things and not knowledge of the things themselves. Some traces of this distinction may be found in certain passages translated below (e.g. *P*, 150), but Nietzsche's clearest statement of the relationship between metaphors and numbers occurs in a note from the winter of 1872-3 occurs in a note from the winter of 1872-3, which is printed in Schlechta/Anders, p. 36 [= *WKG* III, 4, p. 154]:

"Our perception is already modified by concepts. Concepts are relations, not abstractions.

rium of self interests. It answers the question of how to achieve a mediocre existence lacking any power of love, merely as a result of the prudence of the self interests involved.

Our age hates art, as it does religion. It desires no reconciliation, neither by means of an allusion to the beyond, nor by means of an allusion to the transfiguration of the world of art. It considers this to be useless "poesy," amusement, etc. Our "poets" *conform* to this desire. But art as terrible seriousness! The new metaphysics as terrible seriousness! We want to so rearrange the world for you with images that you will shudder. And it is within our power to do this! Even if you stop up your ears, your eyes will see our myths. Our curses will fall upon you.

Science must now demonstrate its utility! It has become a source of nourishment for egoism. The state and society have drafted a science into their service in order to exploit it for *their* purposes.

The normal condition is that of *war*: we conclude *peace* only for specific periods of time.

57

I have to know how the Greeks philosophized in the age of their art. The *Socratic* schools sat in the middle of a sea of beauty: what does one see of this in their work? An immense expenditure is made in behalf of art, towards which the Socratics have either a hostile or a theoretical attitude.

The earlier philosophers, on the other hand, are governed in part by a drive similar to the one which created tragedy.

58

The concept of the philosopher and the types [of philosophers]. What do they all have in common?

---

1. Metaphors are based on activities.
2. They form a system among themselves; *numbers* form the fixed, basic skeleton.
3. The kernel of things, what is essential, expresses itself in the language of numbers.
4. Wherein lies the arbitrariness of metaphors?"

(This note is on a loose sheet in Mp XII 4, the same sheet from which *P*, 155 is drawn—the only passage in *P* which is not derived from notebook P I 20.) In an earlier note from 1870 Nietzsche sketched a similar contrast between the world of the will, the world of pleasure and displeasure, and the mathematical world of number, space, and logic, the world of absolute knowledge (*MA*, III, p. 207 = *GOA* IX, p. 73) [= *WKG*, III, 3, p. 67].) For further discussion of this distinction, see Schlechta/Anders, pp. 114-5.

The philosopher is either the product of his culture or else he is hostile towards it.

He is contemplative like the plastic artist, compassionate like the religious man, and, like the man of science, is concerned with causes. He tries to permit all the sounds of the world to resonate within himself and to present this total sound outside of himself by means of concepts: expanding himself to the macrocosm while, at the same time, maintaining reflective circumspection—like the actor or dramatic poet who transforms himself and at the same time retains his circumspection so that he can project himself outwards. Dialectical thinking is like a shower pouring over all of this.[47]

Plato is remarkable: an enthusiast of dialectic, i.e. of such circumspection.

59

The philosophers. Natural history of the philosopher. The philosopher alongside the man of science and the artist.

Mastery of the knowledge drive by means of art; mastery of the religious drive for unity by means of the concept.

The juxtaposition of conception and abstraction is curious.

The meaning for culture.

Metaphysics as a vacuum.

The philosopher of the future?[48] He must become the supreme tribunal of an artistic culture, the police force, as it were, against all transgressions.

60

Philosophical thinking can be detected in the midst of all scientific thinking, even in the case of conjectures.

It leaps ahead on nimble legs, while the understanding ponderously wheezes along behind and seeks sturdier legs when the tempting magical image has appeared to it.[49] An infinitely rapid flight through immense spaces! Is philosophical thinking only distinguished by its greater rapidity? No. It is the wingbeat of imagination, i.e. a repeated leaping from

---

[47]Cf. the similar passage at the end of *PtZG*, 3.

[48]Wagner was fond of calling his own art "music of the future" (*Zukunfstmusik*). Nietzsche's first book had been attacked in similar terms as "philology of the future" (*Zukunfstphilologie*) by Ulrich Wilamowitz-Moellendorff. (For a short history of the rather acrimonious controversy with Wilamowitz, see section 2 of Kaufmann's "Introduction" to his translation of *GT* [New York: Random House, 1967].)

[49]Cf. the similar passage in *PtZG*, 3.

possibility to possibility—possibilities which, for the time being, are accepted as certainties. Here and there, from a possibility to a certainty and then back to a possibility.

But what is a "possibility" of this sort? A sudden notion,[50] e.g.: "it might perhaps be possible." But how do such notions *occur*? Occasionally by external accident: a comparison takes place, the discovery of some sort of analogy. A process of *expansion* and *amplification* now begins. Imagination consists in the *quick observation of similarities*. Afterwards, reflection measures one concept by another and performs tests. *Similarity* will be replaced by *causality*.

Now then, is "scientific" thinking distinguished from "philosophical" thinking merely by the *dosage,* or perhaps by the *domain*?

61

There is no distinct philosophy separated from science: there they think in the same manner that we do here. The reason why *indemonstrable* philosophizing retains some value, and for the most part a higher value than a scientific proposition, lies in the *aesthetic* value of such philosophizing, in its beauty and sublimity. Even when it cannot prove itself as a scientific construction, it continues to exist as a *work of art.* But isn't it the same in the case of scientific matters? In other words, the *aesthetic* consideration is decisive, not the pure *knowledge drive.* The poorly demonstrated philosophy of Heraclitus possesses far more artistic value than do all the propositions of Aristotle.

Therefore, in the culture of a people, the knowledge drive is mastered by the imagination. This fills the philosopher with the highest *pathos of truth:*[51] the *value* of his knowledge vouches to him for its *truth.* All *fruitfulness* and all driving force are derived from these *prescient* glimpses.

62

Imaginative production may be observed in the eye. Similarity leads to the boldest further development. But so do entirely different relationships: contrasts lead unceasingly to contrasts. Here one can *see* the extraordinary productivity of the intellect. It is a life in images.[52]

63

In order to think, one must already possess in imagination that which

---

[50]*Einfall* means an idea which occurs all of a sudden; it connotes something similar to the English "bright idea."

[51]See *PW*, n. 1 for a discussion of this "pathos."

[52]*ein Bilderleben.*

one seeks, for only then can reflection judge it.[53] Reflection accomplishes this by measuring that which is to be judged against customary and time-tested standards.

What is really "logical" about picture-thinking.[54]

The sober man seldom uses and seldom *possesses* imagination.

In any case, this production of forms, by means of which the memory of something occurs, is something artistic. *It throws this form into relief* and strengthens it thereby. Thinking is a process of throwing into relief.

There are many more sets of images in the brain than are consumed in thinking. The intellect rapidly selects similar images; the image chosen gives rise, in turn, to a profusion of images; but again, the intellect quickly selects one among them, etc.

Conscious thinking is nothing but a process of selecting representations. It is a long way from this to abstraction.

(1) the power which produces the profusion of images; (2) the power which selects and emphasizes what is similar.

Feverish persons deal in the same way with walls and tapestries; the difference is that healthy persons project the tapestry as well.

64

There is a twofold artistic power here: that which produces images and that which chooses among them.

The correctness of this is proved by the dream world: in this world one does not proceed to abstraction, or: one is not guided and modified in this world by the images which pour in through the eyes.

When one considers this power more closely, it is obvious that here too there is no totally free artistic inventing—for that would be something arbitrary and hence impossible. Instead, these images are the finest emanations of nervous activity as it is viewed on a surface. The images are related to the underlying nervous activity which agitates them in the same way that Chladni's acoustical figures are to the sound itself.[55] The

---

[53]Thus, the ancient "problem of the criterion"—how can we "know before we know" (Plato, *Meno*, 80e)—was shifted in the nineteenth century, largely due to the influence of Kant's analysis of the role of productive and reproductive imagination in knowledge, to the *problem of* (conscious and unconscious) *creativity*: what are the sources and standards of imaginative production? Seen in this way Nietzsche's concern with the relation between art and knowledge is a part of a century-long effort to draw the consequences of Kantianism and not an arbitrarily constructed mixture of two different "interests" that he might have had.

[54]*Bilderdenken*.

[55]Ernst Florens Friedrich Chladni (1756-1827), German physicist, one of the founders of modern scientific acoustics. His "sound figures" (sometimes called "Chladni figures" or "sand figures") are patterns made on a sand-covered flat

most delicate oscillation and vibration! Considered physiologically, the artistic process is absolutely determined and necessary. On the surface all thinking appears to us to be voluntary and within our control. We do not notice the infinite activity.[56]

It is blatantly anthropopathic to imagine an *artistic process apart from a brain*: but the case is the same with "willing," "morality," etc.

Desire is therefore nothing but a physiological epi-activity which wants to discharge itself and which exerts pressure upon the brain.

65

Result: it is only a question of *degrees* and *quantities*. All men are artistic, philosophical, scientific, etc.

Our esteem depends upon quantities, not qualities. We admire what is *great*, which is, of course, also what is *not normal*.

For admiration for the grand effects of what is small is nothing but astonishment at the results and at the incongruity of the smallest cause. We have the impression of greatness only when we add together a great many effects and view them as a *unity*; i.e. by means of this unity *we produce* greatness.

But humanity grows only through admiration for what is *rare* and *great*. Even something which is merely imagined to be rare and great—a miracle, for example—has this effect. Fright is the best part of mankind.

Dreaming as the selective continuation of visual images.

In the realm of the intellect everything qualitative is merely *quantitative*. What leads us to qualities is the concept, the word.

66

Perhaps man is able to *forget* nothing. The operations of seeing and perceiving are much too complicated for it to be possible for them to be entirely effaced; i.e. all the forms which the brain and the nervous sys-

---

surface by the sonic vibrations produced by a string affixed below the plane. Nietzsche was greatly taken by this particular experimental device and frequently used it as a metaphor for perception.

[56]I.e. the nerve activity which takes place "below the surface" of consciousness and is physiologically determined. Despite the appearance of conflict with some of his other views Nietzsche often toyed with speculations about the physiological determinants of thought and behavior, though he had nothing very profound to say on this subject and most of these speculations remained in his notebooks. Nevertheless, this passage, along with others like it which appear later in *P*, do illuminate some of Nietzsche's published remarks on this topic, e.g. *M*, 119: "all our so-called 'consciousness' is a more or less imaginary commentary on an unconscious and perhaps unknowable, though felt, text." A similar theme is found in the discussion of the "great" and "small reason" in *Z*, I.

tem have once produced are often repeated in the same way from then on. The same nervous activity produces the same image again.

67

The most delicate sensations of pleasure and displeasure constitute the genuine raw material for all perceiving.[57] The real mystery concerns that surface upon which forms are sketched by the activity of the nerves in pleasure and pain: sensation immediately projects *forms,* which in turn produce new sensations.

It is the nature of sensations of pleasure and displeasure to express themselves through adequate motions. The sensing of the *image* arises from the fact that these appropriate motions in turn bring about sensations in other nerves.

Darwinism applies also to picture-thinking: the stronger image consumes the weaker one.

Whether thinking proceeds with pleasure or with displeasure is an essential distinction: the person who finds thinking to be genuinely difficult is certainly less likely to apply himself to it and will also probably not get as far. He *forces* himself, which is useless in this realm.

68

A result which has been obtained by leaps is sometimes immediately proved to be true and fruitful when considered from the standpoint of its consequences.

Is a scientific inquirer of genius guided by correct *presentiment?* Yes, what he sees are precisely *possibilities* which lack sufficient support. That he considers something like that to be possible betrays his genius. He rapidly passes over what he is more or less able to prove.

The misuse of knowledge: in the endless repetition of experiments and gathering of material, when the conclusion can be quickly established on the basis of a few instances. This even occurs in philology: in many cases the completeness of the materials is superfluous.[58]

69

Even that which is moral has the intellect as its sole source, but the effect of the binding chain of images is different in this case than in the cases of the artist and the thinker. Here it provokes an *act.* The sensing and identification of similar things is certainly a necessary prerequisite,

---

[57]See below, *P*, 97-8.

[58]For Nietzsche's full indictment of such a misuse of intelligence and knowledge, see *UBc*, 6.

followed by the recollection of one's own pain. Thus, "to be good" might mean "to identify *very easily* and *quickly*." There is a transformation here similar to that of an actor.

On the other hand, all righteousness and justice are derived from an *equilibrium of self-interests*: from reciprocal agreement not to harm each other; thus, from prudence. It appears differently, of course, in the form of fixed principles, as *firmness* of character. The opposition of love and justice, culminating in sacrifice for the sake of the world.

The action of the just man is determined by anticipation of possible feelings of displeasure: he knows empirically the consequences of injuring his neighbor—but also of injuring himself. The Christian ethic is the opposite of this: it is based upon identifying oneself with one's neighbor. Doing good unto another is here a good deed toward oneself; suffering with others is here the same as one's own suffering. Love is bound up with a desire for unity.

70

Man demands truth and fulfills this demand in moral intercourse with other men; this is the basis of all social life. One anticipates the unpleasant consequences of reciprocal lying. From this there arises the *duty of truth*.[59] We permit epic poets to *lie* because we expect no detrimental consequences in this case. Thus the lie is permitted where it is considered something pleasant. Assuming that it does no harm, the lie is beautiful and charming. Thus the priest invents myths for his gods which justify their sublimity. It is extraordinarily difficult to revive the mythical feeling of the free lie. Yet the great Greek philosophers dwell entirely within this justification of the lie.

Where one can know nothing that is true, there the lie is permitted.

Every man allows himself to be continually deceived in his dreams at night.[60]

-----

[59]This is one of Nietzsche's very earliest attempts to explore the origin of "truthfulness," of man's own sense of duty to tell the truth and not to deceive. The topic is one which assumes considerable importance in the notes which follow (especially, of course, in *WL*), but it is also one of the *constant* matters of inquiry in *all* of Nietzsche's published writings, where it is very often treated under the heading "intellectual conscience." A few representative passages are: 344, *MAMb*, 98; *MAMc*, 43; *M*, Pref., 4; *FW*, 110 and 344; *JGB*, 1; *GM*, III, 24-7.

[60]Compare this with Descartes' claim (which is often a target of ridicule for contemporary philosophers) that, "I have on many occasions in sleep been deceived by similar illusions, and in dwelling carefully on this reflection I see so manifestly that there are no certain indications by which we may clearly distinguish wakefulness from sleep that I am lost in amazement." *Meditations*, I. In, *Philosophical Works of Descartes*, trans. E.S. Haldane and G.R.T. Ross (New York: Dover, 1955), Vol. I, p. 146.

Mankind acquires the aspiration for truth with infinite slowness. Our feeling for history is something quite new in the world. It might be possible for this historical feeling to suppress art completely.

The utterance of the *truth at any price* is something *Socratic*.

71

Truth and lie physiologically considered.

Truth as moral commandment—the two sources of morality.

The essence of truth as judged according to its *effects*.

These effects tempt us to posit unproven "truths."

In the *struggle* between such truths which live by means of force the need to discover some other way becomes evident: either using it [i.e. the "truth"] to explain everything, or else arriving at it from examples and appearances.

The marvelous invention of logic.

Gradual predominance of the forces of logic and limitation of the field of *possible* knowledge.

Incessant reaction of the forces of art and limitation to the field of what is *worth* knowing (judged according to its *effect*).

72

The philosopher's inner struggle. His universal drive pushes him in the direction of poor thinking; the immense pathos of truth which is produced by his breadth of vision pushes him toward *communication* and this, in turn, toward logic.

On the one side there grows up an *optimistic metaphysics of logic*,[61] which gradually contaminates everything and covers it with lies. When logic is thought to be the sole ruler it leads to lies; for it *is* not the sole ruler.

The other sort of feeling for truth is one that grows out of *love*: proof of strength.

Uttering *blissful* truth out of *love*: this is based upon the kind of knowledge which the individual is not obliged to communicate, but which he is forced to communicate by an overflowing bliss.

73

Man's longing to be completely truthful in the midst of a mendacious natural order is something noble and heroic. But this is *possible* only in a *very relative sense*. That is tragic. That is *Kant's tragic problem*! Art now acquires an entirely *new* dignity. The sciences, in contrast, are *degraded* to a degree.

---

[61]See *GT*, 14-5 for a discussion of "logical optimism," and its representative figure, Socrates.

The truthfulness of art: it alone is now honest.[62]

Thus, after an immense detour, we again return to the *natural* condition (that of the Greeks). It has proven to be impossible to build a culture upon knowledge.

74

The great ethical strength of the Stoics may be seen in the fact that they violated their own principle on behalf of the freedom of the will.

On moral theory: In politics the statesman frequently anticipates his opponent's act and does it before him: "If I don't do it, he will." A sort of *self-defense* as the fundamental principle of politics. The standpoint of war.

75

The ancient Greeks lack a normative theology: everyone has the right to invent and to believe whatever he likes about it.

The enormous *quantity* of philosophical thinking among the Greeks (together with its continuation through the centuries as theology).

Their great powers of logic are revealed for instance in the organization of cults in the individual cities.

The Orphic phantasma are *stiff and poorly formed,* bordering on allegory.

The Stoic gods concern themselves only with what is great, neglecting what is small and individual.

76

Schopenhauer denies the moral efficacy of moral philosophy, just as artists do not create according to concepts. Interesting! It is true that every man is already an intelligible being (determined through countless generations!),[63] but these moral powers are *strengthened* by the more intense excitation of certain sensations by means of concepts. Such exci-

---

[62] For art alone is powerful enough to endure and to present the "truth" about the world. Again, it is in *GT*, 14 and 15 that Nietzsche explains the relation between the self-destruction of theoretical optimism and the justification of art which this makes possible. Here too, one should note that the "artistic metaphysics" which Nietzsche embraced during his early period (and later claimed to reject) is not *merely* evidence of his intoxication with Schopenhauer and Wagner. He has, in addition, a sound *theoretical* basis for his turn toward art.

[63] In the language of Kantian and Schopenhauerian moral philosophy an "intelligible being" is a noumenal, or non-phenomenal *moral* subject. Thus one can be "determined" as a phenomenal being, but "free" as an intelligible one.

tation creates nothing new, but it concentrates the creative energies on one side. For example, the categorical imperative has greatly strengthened the unselfish feeling of virtue.

Here likewise we see that the individual man of moral eminence casts an imitative spell. The philosopher is supposed to spread this spell. What is a law for the highest specimens must gradually be accepted as law as such, even if only as a *barrier* to the others.

77

The lawsuit of all religion, philosophy, and science vs. the world: it begins with the grossest anthropomorphisms and *unceasingly becomes more refined.*

The individual person considers even the celestial system to be serving him or in connection with him.

In their mythology the Greeks transformed all of nature into their own image. It was as if they regarded nature merely as a masquerade and a disguise for anthropomorphic gods. In this they showed themselves to be the opposite of all realists. There was within them a profound opposition between truth and appearance. Their metamorphoses are what distinguishes them.

78

Does intuition refer to the concept of the species or to the perfected *types?* But the concept of the species always falls far short of a good specimen, and the perfect type surpasses actuality.

Ethical anthropomorphisms.	Anaximander: justice.
	Heraclitus: law.
	Empedocles: love and hate.
Logical anthropomorphisms.	Parmenides: nothing but being.
	Anaxagoras: νους.[64]
	Pythagoras: everything is number.

79

The briefest version of world history is the one which is apportioned according to significant contributions to philosophical knowledge, omitting those periods which were hostile to philosophy. Among the *Greeks* we observe a sensitivity and creative power to be found nowhere else.

---

[64]The *noûs* of Anaxagoras is "intellect" or "mind," considered as the regulating principle of the universe.

They occupy the greatest space of time:[65] they really produced all the types.[66]

They are the inventors of *logic*.

Hasn't language already disclosed man's capacity for producing logic? It certainly includes the most admirable logical operations and distinctions. But language did not develop all at once; it is instead the logical conclusion of endlessly long spaces of time. Here the origination of the instincts must be considered: they have developed quite gradually.

The spiritual activity of millenia is deposited in language.

80

Only very slowly does man discover how infinitely complicated the world is. At first he consider it to be something quite simple, i.e. something as superficial as he himself is.

He starts from himself, from the most recent result of nature, and imagines that the forces—the primal forces—are similar to what enters his consciousness. He accepts the *operations of the most complicated mechanism*, the brain, as similar to the very earliest modes of operation. Since this complicated mechanism is able to produce something intelligible in a short time, he assumes that the existence of the world is very recent. He thinks that it cannot have taken the creator so very much time.

Thus he believes that something has been explained by the word "instinct," and indeed, he assigns an unconscious purposive activity to the original genesis of things.

Space, time, and the feeling of causality appear to have been given along with the first *sensation*.

Man is acquainted with the world to the extent that he is acquainted with himself; i.e. its depth is revealed to him to the extent that he is astonished by himself and his own complexity.

81

It is just as rational to take man's moral, artistic, and religious wants as the basis of the world as it is to take as its basis his mechanical wants: we are acquainted with neither impact nor gravity. (?)

---

[65] I.e. they occupy the greatest period in our abridged version of world history. Compare this passage to the opening sentences of *UBd*, 4.

[66] "That is to say, they discovered the *types of philosophical thinkers,* and all posterity has discovered nothing else which is essential." *PtZG*, 1; see also *MAMa*, 261.

82

We do not know the true nature of *a single causality*. Absolute skepticism: the necessity of art and illusion. Perhaps gravity is to be explained by the movement of the aether, which—along with the entire solar system—revolves around some immense heavenly body.

83

Neither the metaphysical, nor the ethical, nor the aesthetic meaning of existence can be *proven*.

The orderliness of the world—the most laboriously and slowly achieved result of terrible evolutions—grasped as the essence of the world: Heraclitus!

84

It has to be *proven* that all constructions of the world are anthropomorphic, indeed, if Kant is right, all sciences. There is, to be sure, a vicious circle here: if the sciences are right, then we are not supported by Kant's foundation; if Kant is right, then the sciences are wrong.[67]

Against Kant, it must always be further objected that, even if we grant all of his propositions, it still remains entirely *possible* that the world is as it appears to us to be. Furthermore, this entire position is useless from a personal point of view; no one can live in this skepticism.

We must get beyond this skepticism; we must *forget* it! How many things do we not have to forget in this world![68] (Art, ideal shape, temperament.)

---

[67]This is an exceptionally interesting note for anyone concerned with Nietzsche's understanding of Kant. It is clear that he considers Kant's theory of knowledge to have an undermining and skeptical effect on the sciences in general. This is why he talks elsewhere about Kant's ("heroic") contribution to the defeat of theoretical optimism. In order to see the "circular inference" (*Zirkelschluss*) which Nietzsche refers to, it must be remembered that the *Critique of Pure Reason* is not only about science (*Wissenschaft*) it is itself supposed to be a science, or at least "scientific." In any case, this is Nietzsche's interpretation of the matter. Most of Nietzsche's remarks about Kant and the Kantian philosophy are either incidental or polemical. He seems to have had no very profound firsthand acquaintance with the writings of the thinker whom he later called "the Chinaman of Königsberg"; indeed, he appears to have relied upon Schopenhauer's interpretation of Kant (in the appendix to Volume One of *The World as Will and Representation*) long after he had ceased to think of himself as a "Schopenhauerian." The other major source upon which Nietzsche based his understanding of Kant is Friederich Albert Lange's *History of Materialism*—a book which exercised a very great and long lasting influence upon Nietzsche, and especially upon the development of his epistemological views.

Our salvation lies not in *knowing*, but in *creating*! Our greatness lies in the highest illusions, in the noblest emotion. If the universe is of no concern to us, then we ought to have the right to despise it.

85

The terrible loneliness of the last philosopher! Nature towers rigidly around him; vultures hover above him. And so he cries out to nature, "Grant me forgetfulness! Forgetfulness!" *No, he endures suffering like a Titan until he is offered reconciliation in the highest tragic art.*

86

To consider the "spirit,"[69] which is a product of the brain, to be something supernatural! Even to deify it! What madness!

Among millions of decaying worlds, there is once in a while an acceptable one! It too decays! It was not the first!

87

Oedipus
Soliloquy of the Last Philosopher
(A fragment from the history of posterity)

"I call myself the last philosopher, because I am the last man. No one speaks with me but myself, and my voice comes to me like the voice of a dying man! Let me associate for but one hour more with you, dear voice, with you, the last trace of the memory of all human happiness. With you I escape loneliness through self-delusion and lie myself into multiplicity and love. For my heart resists the belief that love is dead. It cannot bear the shudder of the loneliest loneliness, and so it forces me to speak as if I were two persons.

"Do I still hear you, my voice? Are you whispering as you curse? And yet your curses should cause the bowels of this earth to burst open! But the world continues to live and only stares at me even more glitteringly and coldly with its pitiless stars. It continues to live as dumbly and blindly as ever, and only *one thing* dies—man.

"And yet, I still hear you, dear voice! *Something* else dies, something other than me, the last man in this universe. The last sigh, *your* sigh, dies

---

[68]The positive value of selective forgetfulness—indeed, its necessity for life and happiness—is often affirmed by Nietzsche in his published writings. See, e.g. *UBb*, 1; *MAMa*, 92; *MAMb*, 122; *MAMc*, 236; and *GM*, I, 1.

[69]*Geist*. I have always translated this term "spirit," though it has a strongly intellectual connotation which the English word does not always have. In many contexts, including the present, "mind" might be a more accurate translation.

with me. The drawn-out 'alas! alas!' sighed for me, Oedipus, the last miserable man."

88

We see in contemporary Germany that the blossom of science is possible in a barbarized culture; likewise, we see that utility has nothing to do with science (though it might seem that it does from the preference which is given to chemical and scientific institutions: mere chemists can even become famous "authorities").

The blossom of science has a vital atmosphere of its own. It is made impossible neither by a declining culture (like the Alexandrian)[70] nor by a non-culture (like our own). Knowing is probably even a substitute for culture.

89

Are periods of *eclipse*, as e.g. the middle ages, really periods of health, perhaps times of sleep for the intellectual genius of man?

Or are even these *eclipses* results of higher purposes? If books have their own fate, then the decline of a book is certainly also a *fatum*[71] with some purpose.

What *perplexes* us is the *purpose*.

90

In the philosopher, activities are carried out by means of metaphor. The striving for *uniform* control. Each thing gravitates towards a condition of immeasurability. In nature, the character of the individual is seldom something fixed; instead, it is always expanding. Whether this occurs *slowly* or *quickly* is a highly human question. Considered from the point of view of what is infinitely small, every development is always *infinitely quick*.

91

What does the truth matter to man? The highest and purest life is possible with the belief that one possesses truth. Man requires *belief in truth*.

Truth makes its appearance as a social necessity. Afterwards, by means of a metastasis, it is applied to everything, where it is not required.

All virtues arise from pressing needs. The necessity for truthfulness

---

[70]"Alexandrian" culture is Nietzsche's name for the kind of scholarly, theoretical culture typical of the Hellenistic age. See *GT*, 17-8 and *WP*, 40-1 and 145.
[71]"Destiny."

begins with society. Otherwise man dwells within eternal concealments. The establishment of states promotes truthfulness.

The drive toward knowledge has a *moral* origin.[72]

92

Memory has nothing to do with the nerves and brain. It is itself an original property, for man carries around within himself the memory of all previous generations. A remembered *image* is something very artificial and *rare*.

One can just as little speak of an unerring memory as of an absolutely purposive action of natural law.

93

Is there such a thing as an unconscious inference? Does matter *infer*? It has feelings and it strives for its individual being. "Will" is first manifest in *change*, i.e. there is a kind of *free will* which modifies a thing's essence on the basis of pleasure and the flight from displeasure. Matter has a number of *Protean* qualities which are, according to the nature of the attack, accented, reinforced, and instituted for the whole. Qualities seem to be nothing but specifically modified activities of a *single* matter, activities which are encountered according to proportions of degree and number.

94

We are acquainted with but *one* reality—the reality of *thoughts*. In what way? What if thought were the essence of things? What if memory and sensation were the *matter* of things?

95

Thought provides us with the concept of a totally new form of *reality*: a reality constructed from sensations and memory.

A man in the world might actually be able to comprehend himself as a character *in a dream* which is itself being dreamt at the same time.

96

The impact, the influence of one atom upon another is likewise something which presupposes *sensation*. Something which is intrinsically alien can have no effect upon anything else.

What is difficult is not awakening sensation, but awakening conscious-

---

[72]See *FW*, 344 for a full explanation of this claim (published in 1886—fourteen years after these first notes on the topic were jotted down).

ness in the world. Yet this is nevertheless explicable if everything is sensate.

If everything is sensate then there is a pell mell confusion of the smallest, the larger, and the largest centers of sensation. Whether larger or smaller, these sensation complexes would be called "will."

We free ourselves from *qualities* only with difficulty.

97

Sensation, reflex movements which occur very frequently and with the speed of lightning and which gradually become very familiar, produce the operation of inferring, i.e. the sense of causality. Space and time depend upon the sensation of causality.[73] Memory preserves the established reflex movements.

Consciousness begins with the sensation of causality, i.e. memory is older than consciousness. E.g. the mimosa tree has memory, but no consciousness. In the case of plants, this is naturally a memory without *images*.

But *memory* then must be part of the essence of *sensation*; thus it must be an original quality of things. But then reflex movement must also be an original quality of things.

The inviolability of the laws of nature surely means that sensation and memory are part of the essence of things. It is a matter of memory and sensation that when one substance comes into contact with another it decides in just *the way that it does*. At one time or another it *learned* to do so, i.e. the activities of the substance are *developed laws*. But then the decision must have been made by *pleasure* and *displeasure*.[74]

98

However, if pleasure, displeasure, sensation, memory, and reflex

---

[73]*Kausalitätsempfindung. Empfindung* is usually translated here as "sensation," though occasionally "feeling" is more appropriate. In some contexts, notably in those in which Nietzsche is discussing our sensory consciousness of images, *Empfindung* has been translated "perception."

[74]I.e. the decision concerning the particular way that a certain substance will react to another (will "determine itself"). The hypothesis is that laws of nature have their ground or sufficient reason in the specific feelings of pleasure and displeasure which are (by this hypothesis) found in all parts of matter. The speculations in this and the following notes concerning whether or not sensation is an original fact of all nature are undoubtedly based upon Nietzsche's reading of Zöllner and Spir. The primordial character of sensation is one of Spir's basic principles. The attribution of sensation to matter and the fundamental character of sensations of pleasure and pain are theses defended by Zöllner in *Über das Natur der Komenten*. See below, *PB*, n. 59.

movement are part of the essence of things, *then human knowledge penetrates far more deeply into the essence of things* [than otherwise].

The whole logic of nature then dissolves itself into a system of *pleasure* and *displeasure*. Everything snatches at pleasure and flees displeasure: that is the eternal law of nature.

99

All knowing is a process of measuring according to a criterion. Without a criterion, i.e. without any limitation, there is no knowing. It is the same in the realm of intellectual forms. For example, when I ask what might be the value of knowing as such, I have to adopt some higher position, or at least one that is *fixed*, so that it can serve as a criterion.

100

If we trace the entire intellectual world back to *stimulus* and *sensation*, this most paltry perception explains almost nothing.

The proposition, "there is no knowledge with a knower," or "no subject without an object and no object without a subject" is quite true, but it is extremely trivial.

101

We can say nothing about the thing in itself, for we have eliminated the standpoint of knowing, i.e. of measuring. A quality exists *for us*, i.e. it is measured by us. If we take away the measure, what remains of the quality?

What things are is something that can only be established by a measuring subject placed alongside them. The properties of things considered in themselves are no concern of ours; we are concerned with them only to the extent that they affect us.

Now the question is, how does such a measuring being originate? The plant too is a *measuring being*.

The overwhelming human consensus regarding things proves the complete homogeneity of men's perceptual apparati.

102

For the plant the world is thus and such; for us the world is thus and such. If we compare the two perceptual powers we consider our view of the world to be the more correct one, i.e. the one that corresponds more closely to the truth. Now man has evolved slowly, and knowledge is still evolving: his picture of the world thus becomes ever more true and complete. Naturally it is only a clearer and clearer *mirroring*. But the mirror itself is nothing entirely foreign and apart from the nature of things. On the contrary, it too slowly arose as [part of] the nature of things.[75] We observe an effort to make the mirror more and more adequate. The natural process is carried on by science. Thus the things mirror themselves every more clearly, gradually liberating themselves from what is all too anthropomorphic. For the plant, the whole world is a plant; for us, it is human.

103

The progress of philosophy: It was first thought that men were the authors of all things. Gradually one explained things to himself by analogy with particular human qualities. Finally one arrived at *sensation*. Great question: is sensation an original fact about all matter? Attraction and repulsion?

104

The historical knowledge drive: Its goal is to understand human development and to eliminate everything miraculous from this development. This drive deprives the drive for culture of its greatest strength. This knowing is a mere luxuriating, for contemporary culture is raised no higher by means of it.

105

Philosophy is to be considered like astrology: namely, as an attempt to bind the fate of the world to that of man, i.e. an attempt to regard the highest evolution of *man* as the highest evolution of the *world*.[76] All the sciences receive their nourishment from this philosophical drive. Mankind abolishes first religions and then science.

106

Even the Kantian theory of knowledge was immediately employed by man for his own self-glorification: the world has its reality only in man. It is tossed back and forth like a ball in the heads of men. In truth however this theory means only this: Though one might think that there exists both a work of art and a stupid man to contemplate it, of course the work exists as a cerebral phenomenon for this stupid man only to the extent that he is himself an artist as well and contributes the forms [to the

---

[75]. . *sondern selbst langsam entstanden als Wesen der Dinge gleichfalls.*

[76]Schopenhauer had used astrology as the prime example of man's "miserable subjectivity" (*Aphorismen zur Lebenswelt,* V, c, 26 [in Vol. I of *Parerga und Paralipomena*]). Nietzsche was fond of underscoring the anthropomorphic character of philosophy by comparing it to astrology. See *P* 77 and 151, as well as *MAMa,* 4.

work]. He could boldly assert, "the work of art has no reality outside of my brain."

The *forms* of the intellect have very gradually arisen out of the matter. It is plausible in itself that these forms are strictly adequate to the truth. For where is an apparatus which could invent something new supposed to have come from?[77]

107

It seems to me that the most important faculty is that of perceiving *shape*, i.e. a faculty based upon mirroring. Space and time are only things which have been measured according to some rhythm.[78]

108

You should not flee into some metaphysics, but should actively sacrifice yourself to the *culture which is developing*. For this reason I am strongly opposed to dreamy idealism.

109

All knowledge originates from separation, delimitation, and restriction; there is no absolute knowledge of a whole.

110

Are pleasure and displeasure universal feelings? I believe not.

But where does artistic power make its appearance? In the crystal certainly. The formation of *shape*.[79] Yet mustn't a perceiver be presupposed here?

---

[77]The point of this rather puzzling but interesting passage seems to be: intellectual forms must closely correspond to the essence of things, because the intellect itself is a natural phenomenon (cf. above, *P*, 102) and lacks the power of creative distortion. Its forms could fail to correspond to the essence of things only if the intellect were more creative than it in fact is. This thought is, of course, in striking contradiction to other thoughts which Nietzsche jotted down at about the same time (e.g. below, *P*, 149). Obviously one function of these notebooks for Nietzsche himself was to provide a place to work out his thoughts, to "try out" several solutions to a problem and various interpretations of a single matter.

[78]I.e., measured according to some interval which can serve as a criterion (see above, *P*, 99). The point here seems to be that we have knowledge of space and time only insofar as *we* measure them according to some standard (see below *P*, 121).

[79]*Die Bildung der Gestalt. Bildung*, which is an important term in some of the later notes in this collection, is a very difficult word to translate. As the present context makes clear, it often means "formation" or "shaping." Sometimes it re-

111

Music as a *supplement* to *language*: many stimuli and entire states of stimulation which cannot be expressed in language can be rendered in music.[80]

112

There is no *form* in nature, because there is no inner and no outer. All art depends upon the *mirror* of the eyes.

113

Human *sensory knowledge* certainly aims at beauty: it glorifies the world. Why should we snatch at anything else? Why do we seek to transcend our senses? Restless knowledge leads to bleakness and ugliness. Let us *be content* with the aesthetic view of the world!

114

As soon as one wishes to *know* the thing in itself, *it is precisely this world* [which one comes to know]. Knowing is only possible as a process of mirroring and measuring oneself against *one* standard (sensation).

We *know* what the world is: absolute and unconditional knowledge is the desire to know without knowledge.[81]

115

The so-called *unconscious inferences* can be traced back to the *all-preserving memory*, which presents us with experiences of a parallel sort and thus is *acquainted* in advance with the consequences of an action. It is not an anticipation of the effects; it is rather the feeling "similar causes, similar effects," which is generated by a remembered image.

---

fers to the "shape" or "structure" which results from such a process. Very often it means simply "education," the process of "cultivating" or "forming" human beings. I have translated it variously as "education," "formation," and "cultivation."

[80]Nietzsche's earliest published and unpublished writings are filled with speculations about the origin of language and its relation to music (or between two *kinds* of language—gesture and tone language). In *GT* and the important unpublished essay of 1871 on this topic (*MW*) he ascribes to what might be called the Schopenhauer-Wagner position, which exalts music as a metaphysically more fundamental kind of language than the language of mere words and concepts. Music is supposed to be able to express directly the primal reality and thereby facilitate genuine knowledge thereof.

[81]Cf. Nietzsche's later ridicule of the demand for "knowledge in itself," a non-perspectival perspective on things! See e.g. *JGB*, 16 and *GM*, III, 12.

116

Unconscious *inferences* set me to thinking: it is no doubt a process of passing from *image* to *image*. The image which is last attained then operates as a stimulus and motive. Unconscious thinking must take place apart from concepts: it must therefore occur in *perceptions*.[82]

But this is the way in which contemplative philosophers and artists infer. They do the same thing that everyone does regarding their personal psychological impulses, but transferred[83] into an impersonal world.

This kind of picture thinking is from the start not strictly logical, but still it is more or less logical. The philosopher then tries to replace this picture thinking with conceptual thinking. Instincts likewise appear to be a variety of picture thinking, which finally becomes a stimulus and motive.

117

We far too readily confuse *Kant's* "thing in itself" with the *Buddhists'* "true essence of things." On the one hand actuality exhibits nothing but *illusion*; on the other, it exhibits an *appearance which is totally adequate to the truth*.[84] Illusion as non-being is confused with the appearance of beings. All possible superstitions find a place in this vacuum.

---

[82]*Anschauungen.* This is the term which Kant had used (in the singular) to designate both our direct awareness of individual entities (a process which, for us, is always by means of passive sensibility) and the percepts of which we are thereby aware. This term is often translated into English as "intuition," but such a translation gives an inappropriate air of mystery to what is, after all, the utterly ordinary experience of perceiving something through the senses (with the emphasis upon the reception, rather than the recognition of the percept). I have usually translated it "perception." According to Anders (Schlechta/Anders, p. 125) the theory that perception is based upon unconscious inferences, i.e. acts of thought, was defended by Zöllner and Helmholtz.

[83]*übertragen.* This verb, with its noun form *Übertragung*, is an essential key to understanding the theory of knowledge and of language which Nietzsche develops in the notes that follow, through *WL*. It is, alas, very difficult to translate it by the same English word in every context. The root meaning, which is the same as the root meaning of the Greek verb μεταφέρω (from which "metaphor" is derived), is "to carry across" or "to carry over." Depending upon the context, it has the sense of the English words "transfer," "transmit," "translate," etc.; i.e. it designates the process of moving something from one sphere into another, though often in a highly figurative sense. A paradigm of *Übertragung* for Nietzsche is the process whereby a word which originally meant one thing comes to mean something else (metaphor formation). I have (almost) always translated the verb "transfer" and the noun "transference." See also the "Translator's Introduction."

[84]The difference here is between the view that we can learn something about

118

The philosopher caught in the nets of *language*.[85]

119

I wish to depict and to empathize with the *prodigious development* of the *one* philosopher who desires knowledge, the philosopher of mankind.

Most people are so entirely under the control of their drives that they hardly notice what happens. I want to tell what happens and to call attention to it.

The *one* philosopher is here identical with all scientific endeavor; for all the sciences rest upon the philosopher's general foundation. The prodigious *unity* of all the knowledge drives must be demonstrated: the fragmented scholar.

120

Infinity is the primary fact. All that has to be explained now is where the *finite* comes from. But the point of view of the finite is purely sensuous, i.e. deceptive.

How can anyone dare to speak of the earth's destination?

There are no goals in infinite time and space: *what is there is always there,* in whatever form. There is no way to figure out what kind of metaphysical world there is supposed to be.

Mankind must be able to stand on its own without leaning on anything: the enormous task of the artists.

121

Time in itself is nonsense; it exists only for a being capable of sensation. It is the same with space.

All *shape* appertains to the subject. It is the grasping of *surfaces* by means of mirrors. We must subtract all qualities.

---

the true essence of things by considering the world as the adequate expression or appearance (*Erscheinung*) of this essence (the Buddhist view) and the view that the world gives us no warrant for claiming any knowledge of the true essence of things, a view which forces us to conclude that the world of appearances is an illusion (*Schein*). This latter is supposed to be Kant's position—though this passage is much more valuable for what it tells us about Nietzsche than for what it might tell us about Kant.

[85]The reader who is familiar with contemporary philosophy cannot fail to be struck by the resemblance between this remark (and others like it which follow) and certain celebrated maxims and claims of recent "ordinary language philosophy." But Nietzsche's differences with this movement are just as striking. See the "Translator's Introduction."

We are not able to think things as they are, because we are not permitted to think them [at all].

Everything remains as it is; i.e. all qualities give evidence of an undefinable and absolute state of affairs.

122

The terrible consequence of Darwinism (which, by the way, I consider to be true)[86]: all of our admiration is related to qualities which we consider to be eternal—moral qualities, artistic qualities, religious qualities, etc.

One does not advance a single step toward explaining purposiveness when one attempts to do so in terms of instincts. For even these instincts are only products of processes which have been going on for an endlessly long time.

The will does not objectify itself *adequately,* as Schopenhauer said it did.[87] This becomes apparent when one begins with the most perfect forms.

Even this will is a highly complicated end product of nature. It presupposes *nerves*.

And even the force of gravity is no simple phenomenon, but is, in turn, an effect of the movement of a solar system, of the aether, etc.

And mechanical impact is also something complex.

The universal aether as the primal matter.

123

All knowing is a mirroring in quite specific forms which did not exist from the beginning. Nature is acquainted with neither *shape* nor *size*; only to the knower do things appear to be large or small. Nature's *infinity*: it has no boundaries anywhere. Only for us is anything finite. Time is *infinitely* divisible.

---

[86]The consequences are "terrible" because Darwinism is thought by Nietzsche to entail a morality of universal war and the privilege of strength (see *UBa*, 7). Nietzsche's relation to Darwin and Darwinism is frequently misrepresented. In order to obtain some idea of the complexity of the problem, compare this note with the almost uniformly *critical* mention of Darwin found in Nietzsche's later writings, e.g. *FW*, 349 and *GD*, IX, 14.

[87]Schopenhauer considered the apparent world of representations to be the "objectification" of the metaphysical or "real" world of the will. But these representations were themselves further divided into classes or types and arranged in a hierarchy according to how "adequately" they objectify the underlying will. Note that it was years before Nietzsche published any of the criticisms of Schopenhauer's philosophy which appear in these notebooks.

124

The objective value of knowledge: it does not *improve* anything. It has no final, universal goals. It originates accidentally. The value of truthfulness: it, on the other hand, improves things! Its goal is decline. It sacrifices. Our *art* is the reflection of desperate knowledge.

125

In knowledge mankind possesses a beautiful means of decline.

126

That man has developed in the way that he has and not in some other way is after all certainly his own accomplishment: it is his *nature* to be so immersed in illusion (dream) and dependent upon the surface (eye). Is it surprising that, in the end, his truth drives return to his fundamental nature?

127

We feel ourselves to be great when we hear of a man who would not lie even when his life depended upon it—even more so when a statesman out of truthfulness demolishes an empire.

128

By means of a free transference in the realm of duty, our habits become virtues, i.e. because we include inviolability within the concept [of our habits]. In other words, our habits become virtues because we consider their inviolability to be more important than our own particular welfare. Accordingly this occurs through a sacrifice of the individual, or at least the hovering possibility of such a sacrifice. The realm of the virtues and the arts—our metaphysical world—begins at that point where the individual starts to regard himself as unimportant. If there were *nothing* in the nature of things which *corresponded to what is moral*, then *duty* would be especially *pure*.

129

I do not inquire concerning the purpose of knowing: it originated accidentally, i.e. without any rationally intended purpose—as an extension or a solidification of a way of thinking and acting which was necessary in certain cases.

130

Man does not by nature exist in order to know: *truthfulness* (and *metaphor*) have produced the inclination for truth. Thus the intellectual drive is produced by an aesthetically generalized moral phenomenon.

131

Like recalls like and compares itself to it. That is what knowing consists in: the rapid classification of things that are similar to each other. Only like perceives like: a physiological process. The perception of something new is also the same as memory. It is not thought piled upon thought.

132

The world's value must be revealed by even its smallest fraction. Look at man and then you will know what opinion you must have of the world.

133

In some cases necessity produces truthfulness as a society's means of existence.

Through frequent practice this drive is reinforced and is now unjustifiably transmitted by means of metastasis. It becomes an inclination in itself. A quality [viz. truth] develops out of a practice [designed] for specific cases. Now we have the drive for knowledge.

This generalization takes place by means of an intervening *concept*. This quality commences with a *false* judgment: "to be true means to be true *always*." From this arises the inclination not to live in lies: elimination of all illusions.

But one is chased out of one net and into another.

134

The good man now wants to be the true man as well and believes in the truth of all things—not only things of society but also of the world. Consequently, he also believes in the possibility of getting to the bottom of things. For why should the world deceive him?

Thus he transfers his own inclination to the world and believes that the world *must* also be true to him.

135

I consider it false to speak of an unconscious goal of mankind. Unlike an anthill, mankind is not a whole. One can perhaps speak of the unconscious goal of a city or a people, but what does it mean to speak of the unconscious goal of *all the anthills* on earth?

136

Mankind propagates itself through impossibilities; these are its *virtues*. The categorical imperative, as well as the demand "children, love one another," are examples of such impossible demands.

Similarly, *pure logic* is the impossibility which supports science.

The philosopher is the rarest of the great, because knowledge came to man only incidentally and not as an original endowment. But for this reason the philosopher is also the highest type of great man.

137

In pursuing the goal of knowledge, our natural science is heading for *decline*.

Our historical education is heading for the death of all culture. It enters into battle against religions and incidentally destroys cultures.

This is an unnatural reaction against frightful religious pressure— now taking refuge in extremes. Lacking all measure.

138

A *negative* morality is the kind with the most grandeur, because it is wonderfully impossible. What does it signify if man says "No!" with full consciousness, while all his senses and nerves say "Yes!" and his every fiber and cell oppose his negation?

When I speak of the frightful possibility that knowledge promotes decline, the last thing I intend to do is to pay a compliment to the present generation: for it contains nothing of such tendencies. But when one observes the progress of science since the fifteenth century, then, to be sure, such a power and such a possibility are revealed.

139

The combination of a felt stimulus and a glance at a movement produces causality, first of all as an empirical principle. Two things, a particular sensation and a particular visual image, always appear together. That the one is the cause of the other is a *metaphor borrowed from will and act*: an analogical inference.

The only causal relation of which we are conscious is the one between willing and acting. We transfer this onto all things and explain to ourselves the relationship between two alterations which are always found together. The intention or willing yields the *nomina*;[88] the acting, the *verba*.[89]

The animal as willing—that is its essence.

From *quality and act*: One of our properties leads us to act, whereas it is in reality the case that we infer from actions to properties. Since we see actions of a particular kind we assume the existence of properties.

Thus, the *action* comes first; we connect it with a property.

The word for the action originates first; the word for the quality is

---

[88]nouns.
[89]verbs.

derived from it. When transferred to all things this relationship [between action and property] is *causality*.

"Seeing" comes first, and then "vision." "The one who sees" is taken to be the cause of "seeing." Between the sense and its function we feel that there is a regular relationship. Causality is the transfer of this relationship (of sense to sensory function) to all things.

It is a primal phenomenon to refer the stimulus which is felt in the eye to the eye itself, i.e. to refer a sensory excitation to the sense. In itself all that is given is a stimulus; it is a causal inference to feel this stimulus as an activity of the eye and to call it "seeing." The first causal sensation occurs when *a stimulus is felt as an activity*, when something passive is sensed as something active. I.e. the first sensation already generates the causal sensation. The inner connection of stimulus and activity is transferred to all things. *The eye acts upon a stimulus*, i.e. it sees. We explain the world to ourselves in terms of our sensory functions, i.e. we presuppose causality everywhere, because we ourselves *continually experience* alterations of this sort.

140

Time, space, and causality are only *metaphors* of knowledge,[90] with which we explain things to ourselves. Stimulus and activity are connected: how this is we do not know; we understand not a single causality, but we have immediate experience of them. Every affliction elicits an act; every act, an affliction. This most universal of all feelings is already a *metaphor*. The perceived manifold already presupposes space and time, succession and coexistence. Temporal coexistence produces the sensation of space.

The sensation of time is given along with the feeling of cause and effect, as an answer to the question concerning the speed of various causalities.

The sensation of space can only be metaphorically derived from the sensation of time, or is it vice versa?

Two causalities located side by side.

141

The only way to subdue the manifold is by constructing classes, e.g. by calling a large number of ways of acting "bold." We explain them to ourselves when we bring them under the category "bold." All explaining and knowing is actually nothing but categorizing. With a bold leap, the

---

[90]The sense in which knowledge involves "metaphor" is best explained by Nietzsche in *WL*. Indeed, this and many of the notes which immediately follow are best read in conjunction with this later, more finished essay, which deals with many of the same topics, but in a less elliptical manner.

multiplicity of things is now brought under a single heading when we treat them as though they were so many countless actions of a *single* quality, e.g. as actions of water, according to Thales. Here we have a transference: an abstraction holds together innumerable actions and is taken to be their cause. What is the abstraction (property) that holds together the multiplicity of all things? The quality "watery," "moist." The whole world is moist; *therefore, being moist is the whole world.* Metonymy, A false inference. A predicate is confused with a sum of predicates (definition).

142

Logical thinking was employed very little by the Ionians and developed quite slowly. But, false inferences are more correctly understood as metonymies, i.e. they are more correctly understood rhetorically and poetically.

All *rhetorical figures* (i.e. the essence of language)[91] are *logically invalid inferences*. This is the way that reason begins.

143

We see how philosophy is at first carried on in the same manner that *language originated*—i.e. illogically.

Now the pathos of *truth* and *truthfulness* is added. To begin with this has nothing to do with matters of logic, but signifies merely that *no conscious deception* is committed. But these deceptions contained in language and philosophy are unconscious at first, and it is very difficult to become conscious of them. But a peculiar struggle ensued from the coexistence of difference philosophies (or religious systems), each of which was propounded with the same pathos. The coexistence of mutually hostile religions caused each to promote itself by declaring the others to be untrue. The case was the same with [coexistent philosophical] systems.

This led some persons to skepticism. "Truth is very deep,"[92] they sighed.

With Socrates, truthfulness gains possession of logic. It notices the infinite difficulty of correct classification.

144

Our sense perceptions are based, not upon unconscious inferences,

---

[91]In his 1874 lectures on rhetoric, Nietzsche argued that rhetoric was inseparable from the essence of language itself: "Language is rhetoric, because it wishes to transmit δόξα [belief], not ἐπιστήμη [knowledge]." *MA,* V, p. 298.

[92]Literally: "the truth lies in the well."

but upon tropes. The primal procedure is to seek out some likeness between one thing and another, to identify like with like. *Memory* lives by means of this activity and practices it continually. *Confusion* [of one thing with another] is the primal phenomenon. This presupposes the *perception of shapes*.[93] The image in the eye sets the standard for our knowing, as rhythm does for our hearing. Using only the eye, we should *never* have arrived at the notion of time;[94] using only the ear, we should never have arrived at the notion of space. The sensation of causality corresponds to the sense of touch.

From the very beginning, we see the visual images only *within ourselves*; we hear the sound only *within ourselves*. It is a big step from this to the postulation of an external world. Plants, for example, sense no external world. The senses of touch and vision provide [us with] two coexisting sensations, and, since they always appear together, they arouse the idea[94] of a connection (by means of a *metaphor*—for all things which appear together are not connected).

An abstraction is a most important product. It is an enduring impression which is retained and solidified in the memory. It is compatible with very many appearances and is for this reason very rough and inadequate to each particular appearance.

145

Man's falsity toward himself and toward others: Ignorance presupposed as necessary for existence (alone—and in society). The deception of ideas appears in the *vacuum*. The dream. The traditional concepts (which, despite nature, dominate the old German painters) are different in every age. Metonymies. Stimuli, not complete knowledge. The eye provides shapes. We cling to the surface. The taste for what is beautiful. Logical deficiency, but metaphors. Religions, philosophies. *Imitation*.

146

Imitation[95] is a means employed by all culture. By this means instinct is gradually produced. *All comparison (primal thinking) is imitation*. Thus arise

---

[93]For in order to be confused about what one perceives, one must have some notion of form. Otherwise there would be no distinctions among things and thus no way of confusing one with another.

[94]*Zeitvorstellung. Vorstellung* is a very general term which applies to all objects of consciousness—thoughts, perceptions, etc. It has something of the sense which "idea" has in Descartes and Locke and which "perception of the mind" has in Hume. It is customary to translate *Vorstellung* into philosophical English by the rather awkward term "representation." I have translated *Vorstellung* sometimes as "idea," but more often as "notion."

[95]*Nachahmen* means "imitation," in the sense of the process of copying.

types, which strictly imitate the first, merely similar, specimens, i.e. what are copied are the greatest and most powerful specimens.[96] Inculcation of a *second nature* by means of imitation. Unconscious copying is most remarkable in procreation, by the means of which a second nature is reared.

147

Our senses imitate nature by copying it more and more.

Imitation presupposes first the reception of an image and then a continuous translation[97] of the received image into a thousand metaphors, all of which are efficacious. Analog.

148

What power forces us to engage in imitation? The appropriation of an unfamiliar impression by means of metaphors. Stimulus and recollected image bound together by means of metaphor (analogical inference). Result: similarities are discovered and reanimated. A stimulus which has been *repeated* occurs once again in a recollected image.

Stimulus perceived; now *repeated* in many metaphors, in the course of which related images from a variety of categories flock together. Every perception produces a manifold imitation of the stimulus, but transferred[97] into different territories.

A stimulus is felt; transmitted to related nerves; and there, in translation,[97] repeated, etc.

A translation of one sense impression into another occurs: many people see or taste something when they hear a particular sound. This is quite a general phenomenon.

149

Imitation is the opposite of *knowing,* to the extent that knowing certainly does not want to admit any transference, but wishes instead to cling to the impression without metaphor and apart from the consequences. The impression is petrified for this purpose; it is captured and stamped by means of concepts. Then it is killed, skinned, mummified, and preserved as a concept.

But there is no "real" expression and *no real knowing apart from metaphor.* But deception on this point remains, i.e. the *belief* in a *truth* of sense impressions. The most accustomed metaphors, the usual ones, now pass for truths and as standards for measuring the rarer ones. The

---

[96]*d.h. dem grössten und kräftigsten Exemplare es nachmachen.* This clause makes little sense in German. My translation is only a possible reading.

[97]*Übertragung.* See above, n. 83.

only intrinsic difference here is the difference between custom and novelty, frequency and rarity.

Knowing is nothing but working with the favorite metaphors, an imitating which is no longer felt to be an imitation. Naturally therefore, it cannot penetrate the realm of truth.[98]

The pathos of the truth drive presupposes the observation that the various metaphorical worlds are at variance and struggle with one another. E.g. the world of dreams, lies, etc. and the ordinary usual view of things: the first type of metaphorical world is rarer; the other is more frequent. Thus the rule struggles against the exception, the regular against the unaccustomed: hence the higher esteem for everyday reality than for the dream world.

Now however, what is rare and unaccustomed is *more attractive*: the lie is felt as a stimulus. Poetry.

150

All laws of nature are only relations between x, y, and z. We define laws of nature as relations to an x, y, and z—each of which we are in turn acquainted with only in relation to other x, y, and z's.

Knowledge, strictly speaking, has only the form of tautology and *is empty*. All the knowledge which is of assistance to us involves the *identification of things which are not the same*, of things which are only similar. In other words, such knowledge is essentially illogical.

Only in this way do we obtain a concept. Then afterwards we behave as if the concept, e.g. the concept "man," were something factual, whereas it is surely only something which we have constructed through a process of ignoring all individual features. We presuppose that nature behaves in accordance with such a concept. But in this case first nature and then the concept are anthropomorphic. The *omitting* of what is individual provides us with the concept, and with this our knowledge begins: in *categorizing*, in the establishment of *classes*. But the essence of things does not correspond to this: it is a process of knowledge which does not touch

---

[98]This exceptionally interesting passage sheds unusually direct light on several of Nietzsche's fundamental (and often undeclared) epistemological presuppositions: (1) There is no immediate knowing; knowledge always involves a transference (*Übertragung*) between the different spheres of subject and object, and is therefore always indirect or mediated. (2) Truth as an ideal requires an immediate and direct grasp of the object by the subject. (3) Consequently, the *truth* about things cannot be *known*, for this would require a self-contradictory mediated immediacy. (4) The only "truths" available to us are empty tautologies, which are true by definition (see above, *P*, 150). This chain of inferences is seldom articulated clearly by Nietzsche himself, but it underlies most of his striking utterances regarding knowledge and truth.

upon the essence of things. A thing is determined for us by many individual features, but not by all of them. The sameness of these features induces us to gather many things under a single concept.

We produce beings[99] as the *bearers of properties* and abstractions as the causes of these properties. That a unity, e.g. a tree, appears to us to be a multiplicity of properties and relations is something doubly anthropomorphic: in the first place, this delimited unity, "tree," does not exist; it is arbitrary to carve out a thing in this manner (according to the eye, according to the form). Furthermore, each relation is not the true, absolute relation, but is again anthropomorphically colored.

151

What the philosopher is seeking is not truth, but rather the metamorphosis of the world into men. He strives for an understanding of the world with self-consciousness. He strives for an *assimilation.* He is satisfied when he has explained something anthropomorphically. Just as the astrologer regards the world as serving the single individual, the philosopher regards the world as a human being.

152

The nature of definition: the pencil is an elongated, etc. body. A is B. In this case, that which is elongated is also colored. Properties only support relations. A particular body is the equivalent of so many relations.[100] Relations can never be the essence [of the thing], but only consequences of this essence. A synthetic judgment describes a thing according to its consequences, i.e. *essence* and *consequences* become *identified,* i.e. a *metonymy.*

Thus a *metonymy* lies at the essence of synthetic judgment; that is to say that it is a *false equation.* In other words, *synthetic inferences are illogical.* When we employ them we are presupposing the popular metaphysics, i.e. that metaphysics which regards effects as causes.

The concept "pencil" is confused with the "thing" pencil. The "is" in a synthetic judgment is false; it includes a transference. Two different spheres, between which there can never be an equation, are placed next to each other.

---

[99]*Wesen.* This word means "essence" or "nature," or sometimes, "being"—in the sense of underlying essential nature.

[100]According to Anders, this note on the nature of definition is very closely modeled on a similar passage in Afrikan Spir's *Forschung nach der Gewissheit in der Erkenntnis der Wirklichkeit* (1869). See Schlechta/Anders, p. 119 and below, *PB*, n. 59.

We live and think amid nothing but effects of what is *illogical*—in ignorance and false knowledge.[101]

153

Individuals are the bridges upon which becoming depends. All qualities are originally only *solitary activities,* which are then frequently repeated in similar situations and finally become habits. The entire being of an individual takes part in every activity, and a specific modification of the individual corresponds to a habit. Everything in an individual, right down to the smallest cells, is individual—which means that it has a part in all the individual's experiences and past. Hence the possibility of *procreation.*

154

Certain sets of concepts can become so vehement through isolation that they draw into themselves the strength of other drives. The knowledge drive is an example of this.

A nature which has been thus prepared, determined right down to the cell, now propagates itself in turn and becomes heredity, intensifying until its general energy is finally destroyed by its one-sided absorption.

155

The artist does not gaze upon "ideas":[102] he feels pleasure in numerical ratios.

All pleasure [depends upon][103] proportion; displeasure upon disproportion.

Concepts constructed according to numbers.

Perceptions which exhibit good numerical ratios are beautiful.

The man of science *calculates* the numbers of the laws of nature; the artist *gazes* at them. In the one case, conformity to law; in the other, beauty.

What the artist gazes upon is something entirely superficial; it is no "idea"! The most delicate shell surrounding beautiful numbers.

156

The relation between the work of art and nature is similar to the relation between the mathematical circle and the natural circle.

---

[101]*Nichtwissen und Falschwissen.*

[102]That the artist is one who gazes upon the eternal "ideas" is a central tenet of Schopenhauer's philosophy of art. See Book III of *Die Welt als Wille und Vorstellung.*

[103]*beruht.* This word was added by the editors of *GOA,* X.

* *
*

[Notes for the Preface]

157

Dedicated to the immortal Arthur Schopenhauer. Preface to
Schopenhauer: Entrance to the underworld. I have sacrificed many a
black sheep to you—about which the other sheep complain.[104]

158

In this book I do not take present-day scholars into account and thus
appear to be indifferent toward them. But if one desires to reflect peace-
fully on serious matters, he must not be disturbed by disgusting sights. I
now turn to them with reluctance in order to tell them that I am not
indifferent toward them, though I wish that I were.

159

I am trying to be useful to those who are worthy of being seriously and
opportunely introduced to philosophy. This attempt may or may not
succeed. I am only too well aware that it can be surpassed and I wish
nothing more than that I might be imitated and surpassed to the benefit
of this philosophy.

Persons such as those mentioned above are advised—with good
reason—to read Plato rather than to trust themselves to the guidance of
the popular academic professional philosophers.

Above all, they should unlearn all sorts of stupidities and become
simple and natural.[105]

The danger of falling into the wrong hands.

160

The philologists of the present age have proven themselves unworthy
of being permitted to consider me and my book as one of their own. It is
hardly necessary to affirm that, in this case as well, I leave it up to them

---

[104]This image of the entrance to the underworld and the sheep sacrificed to the
memory of the great thinker finally appeared in print in *MAMb*, 408—though
there the sheep are sacrificed not just to Schopenhauer, but to seven other
thinkers as well.

[105]The idea that a "natural" state of being is something which has to be deliberately achieved, a goal and not a lost, pre-existing condition of man, becomes
very important in Nietzsche's later writings. "I too speak of a 'return to nature,'
though this is really an *ascent* and not a going back." *GD*, IX, 48.

whether they want to learn anything or not. But I still do not feel in the least inclined to meet them half way.

May that which now calls itself "philology" (and which I designate only neutrally on purpose)[106] ignore my book this time as well. For this book has a manly temperament and is of no value for castrati. It is much more seemly for them to be seated at the loom of conjecture.

161

I have not made things easy for those who merely wish to get a *scholarly* satisfaction from it, for ultimately, I have not considered them at all. There are no quotations.

162

The age of the seven wise men was not very concerned about the attribution of wise sayings, but considered it very important when someone adopted a saying.

163

Write in a completely impersonal and cold manner.
Omit all "us," "we," and "I." Also limit the number of sentences with "that." So far as possible, avoid all technical terms.
Everything must be said as specifically as possible, and every technical term, including "will" must be left out.[107]

164

I would like to treat the question of the value of knowledge as it would be treated by a cold angel who sees through the whole shabby farce. Without anger, but without warmth.

---

[106]"designate neutrally," i.e. without either a masculine or feminine article. Nietzsche says simply *"Philologie,"* whereas one would ordinarily say *"die Philologie."* This entire note is inspired by the rejection of *GT* by Nietzsche's profession. (See above, *P*, n. 48. The most interesting document in this regard are the notes Nietzsche made for an "Untimely Meditation" dealing with professional philology—*WP*.)

[107]This passage shows how self-consciously Nietzsche worked at the development of his own literary style. The stylistic ideal sketched here is the antithesis of the Wagnerian-Schopenhauerian prose style.

Appendix:
Some Additional Passages from Notebook P I 20[108]

1

Illusion is a necessity of life for a sensate being.

Illusion is necessary for the advance of culture.

What does the insatiable knowledge drive desire?
In any case, it is hostile to culture.
Philosophy seeks to master this drive; it is an instrument of culture.

The early philosophers.

2

All natural science is nothing but an attempt to understand man and
what is anthropological; more correctly, it is an attempt to return continuously to man via the longest and most roundabout ways. Man's infla-
tion to a macrocosm, in order to be able to say in the end: "in the end you
are what you are."[109]

3

In its own way, philosophical thinking is as valid as scientific thinking,
but the former appeals to *great* things and concerns. Greatness, however,
is a changeable concept, partly aesthetic and partly moral. Philosophical

---

[108]The editors of *GOA* compiled the text of *P* from the partial contents of
Nietzsche's notebook P I 20, but they did not print all the passages even from the
pages and sections which they utilized. In the first *Nachbericht* to *GOA*, X the only
omissions which are mentioned are passages which were later used in *WL* and
some additional outlines and plans (p. 503). But when Karl Schlechta and Anni
Anders compared the published text of *P* with the notebook in the Goethe-
Schiller Archives in Weimar, they found that the editors of *GOA* had not only
rearranged passages arbitrarily, but had omitted many notes which conflicted
with their own interpretation of *P*—an interpretation guided largely by *PtZG*
and Nietzsche's later, more narrowly "cultural" interpretation of Greek philosophy. Some of Nietzsche's most interesting notes dealing with questions of truth
and knowledge had not been included in *P*. Schlechta and Anders published the
most important of these omitted passages in their 1962 book, *Friedrich Nietzsche:
Von den verborgenen Anfängen seines Philosophierens*. I have selected twelve of these
passages to translate as a sort of corrective appendix to *P*. The arrangement and
numbering of these notes are my own.

[109]*Faust*, 1. 1806.

thinking is a mastery of the knowledge drive. This is its significance for culture.

4

Culture is a unity. The philosopher only seems to stand outside of it. He addresses the most distant posterity—fame. It is remarkable that the Greeks philosophized.

The beautiful lie. But it is even more remarkable that *man* in general came upon the pathos of truth. The images within him are certainly much mightier than the nature around him—as in the case of those 18th century painters, who, despite the encompassing nature, depicted limbs in the spidery fashion dictated by the old pious tradition.

Plato desires a state governed by *dialectic*; he denies the culture of the beautiful lie.

5

The pathos of truth in a world of lies.

The world of lies [encountered] again in the highest peaks of philosophy.

The goal of these highest lies is mastery of the unlimited knowledge drive.

How is it that there is any pathos of truth in this world of lies?

From morality. The pathos of truth and logic.

Culture and the truth.

Every small bit of knowledge contains within itself a great satisfaction, though not as truth, but rather as the belief that one has discovered truth. What kind of satisfaction is this?

6

The instincts of morality: maternal love—gradually turning into love in general. Sexual love likewise. I recognize *transferences* everywhere.

7

The man who does not believe in the truthfulness of nature, but instead sees metamorphoses, disguises, and masquerades everywhere— the man who catches a glimpse of gods in stones, [illegible] in horses, and nymphs in trees: now when such a man sets up truthfulness as a law for himself, he also believes in the truthfulness of nature toward him.

8

Nature has cushioned man in sheer illusions: that is man's proper element. He sees forms and feels stimuli rather than truths. He dreams and imagines godlike men as nature.

Man has accidentally become a *knowing being* through the unintentional pairing of two qualities. At some time or other he will cease to exist and nothing will have happened.

9
Likewise the basic thought of science is that man is the measure of all things. Ultimately, every law of nature is a sum of anthropomorphic relations. Especially number: the breaking up of all laws into multiplicities, their expression in numerical formulas, is a $\mu\epsilon\tau\alpha\phi o\rho\acute{\alpha}$,[110] in the same way that someone who is unable to hear judges music and sound by Chladni's sound figures.

10
One shows confidence in a *truth* he has found by wishing to communicate it. One can then communicate it in two ways: in its effects, so that others are convinced by a backwards inference of the value of the foundation; or by demonstrating [its] generation from and logical interconnection with truths which are all certain and previously recognized. The interconnection consists in the correct subordination of special cases under general principles—it is pure categorization.

11
Abstractions are metonymies, i.e. substitutions of cause and effect. But every concept is a metonymy, and knowing takes place in concepts. "Truth" turns into a *power* when we have first isolated it as an abstraction.

12
But the impulse to be true, transferred onto *nature*, gives rise to the belief that nature must be true toward us. The knowledge drive depends upon this transference.

---

[110]"metaphor," "transference."

On The Pathos of Truth

1872

II
On the Pathos of Truth[1]

Is fame actually nothing but the tastiest morsel of our self-love? Yet the eager desire for it has been linked to the rarest of men and to their rarest moments. These are moments of sudden illumination, moments in which the person stretches out his commanding arm as if to create a universe, draws up light from within himself and shines forth. At such a moment he is pierced by a certainty which fills him with happiness, the certainty that that which exalted him and carried him into the farthest regions—and thus the height of this *unique* feeling—should not be allowed to remain withheld from all posterity. In the eternal need which all future generations have for these rarest illuminations such a person recognizes the necessity of his own fame. From now on humanity needs him. And since this moment of illumination is the epitome and embodiment of his inmost nature, he believes himself to be immortal as the man of this moment, while he casts from himself all the other moments of his life as dross, decay, vanity, brutishness, or pleonasm and hands them over to mortality.

We observe every passing away and perishing with dissatisfaction, often with astonishment, as if we witnessed therein something fundamentally impossible. We are displeased when a tall tree breaks, and a crumbling mountain distresses us. Every New Year's Eve enables us to feel the mysterious contradiction of being and becoming. But what offends the moral man most of all is the thought that an instant of supreme universal perfection should vanish like a gleam of light, as it were, with-

---

[1] The German word *Pathos* is much more common than its English cognate. In addition to the ordinary sense of the English word, it also means "vehemence," "ardor," "solemnity," and "fervor." Nietzsche often uses the word in a manner which recalls the original Greek contrast between *ethos* (the more permanent and active character of a person, the universal or objective elements in an experience or thing) and *pathos* (the more transitory and passive experiences, the personal or subjective elements of something). Thus an investigation of the "pathos of truth" is not an investigation of "truth itself," but is instead concerned with man's *feelings* about truth, more specifically, with his *pride* in the possession of the same.

out posterity and heirs. His imperative demands rather, that whatever once served to propagate more beautifully the concept "man" must be eternally present.[2] The fundamental idea of culture is that the great moments form a chain, like a chain of mountains which unites mankind across the centuries, that the greatest moment of a past age is still great for me, and that the prescient faith of those who desire fame will be fulfilled.

Terrible cultural struggle[3] is kindled by the demand that that which is great shall be eternal. For everything else that lives exclaims "No!". The customary, the small, and the common fill up all the crannies of the world like a heavy atmosphere which we are all condemned to breathe. Hindering, suffocating, choking, darkening, and deceiving: it billows around what is great and blocks the road which it must travel toward immortality. This road leads through human brains—through the brains of miserable, short-lived creatures who, ever at the mercy of their restricted needs, emerge again and again to the same trials and with difficulty avert their own destruction for a little time. They desire to live, to live a bit at any price. Who could perceive in them that difficult relay race by means of which only what is great survives? And yet again and again a few persons awaken who feel themselves blessed in regard to that which is great, as if human life were a glorious thing and as if the most beautiful fruit of this bitter plant is the knowledge that someone once walked proudly and stoically through this existence, while another walked through it in deep thoughtfulness and a third with compassion. But they all bequeathed *one* lesson: that the person who lives life most beautifully is the person who does not esteem it. Whereas the common man takes this span of being with such gloomy seriousness, those on their journey to immortality knew how to treat it with Olympian laughter, or at least with lofty disdain. Often they went to their graves ironically—for what was there in them to bury?

The boldest knights among these addicts of fame, those who believe that they will discover their coat of arms hanging on a constellation, must be sought among the *philosophers*. Their efforts are not dependent upon a "public," upon the excitation of the masses and the cheering applause of contemporaries.[4] It is their nature to wander the path alone. Their

---

[2]The passage beginning with this sentence and continuing through the last sentence of the next paragraph is almost identical to one in *UBb*, 2.

[3]*Kampf* (= "struggle," "battle," "fight"). This term occurs very frequently in Nietzsche's early writings, one of the most constant themes of which is that struggle may be understood as something positive and creative. For Nietzsche's most sustained explication of this idea, see *HW*.

[4]The passage beginning with this sentence and continuing through this and the following two paragraphs is almost identical to one in *PtZG*, 8.

talent is the rarest and in a certain respect most unnatural in nature,[5] even shutting itself off from and hostile towards similar talents. The wall of their self-sufficiency must be made of diamond if it is not to be demolished and shattered. For everything in man and nature is on the move against them. Their journey towards immortality is more difficult and impeded than any other, and yet no one can be more confident than the philosopher that he will reach his goal. Because the philosopher knows not where to stand, if not on the extended wings of all ages. For it is the nature of philosophical reflection to disregard the present and momentary. He possesses the truth: let the wheel of time roll where it will, it will never be able to escape from the truth.

It is important to discover that such men once lived, for one would never be able to imagine on his own, as an idle possibility, the pride of the wise Heraclitus (who may serve as our example). For by its nature every striving for knowledge seems intrinsically unsatisfied and unsatisfying. Therefore, unless he has been instructed to the contrary by history, no one will be able to imagine such regal self-esteem, such boundless conviction that one is the sole fortunate wooer of truth. Men of this sort live within their own solar system, and that is where they must be sought. Even a Pythagoras and an Empedocles treated themselves with superhuman respect, indeed, with an almost religious awe. But they were led back to other men and to their salvation by the bond of sympathy, coupled with the great conviction concerning the transmigration of souls and the unity of all living things. But only in the wildest mountain wasteland, while growing numb from the cold, can one surmise to some extent the feeling of loneliness which permeated the hermit of the Ephesian temple of Artemis.[6] No overwhelming feeling of sympathetic excitement emanates from him, no desire to help and to save. He is like a star without an atmosphere. His burning eye is directed inward; from without it looks dead and frigid, as if it looked outward merely for appearances' sake. On all sides the waves of illusion and folly beat directly against the fortress of his pride, while he turns away in disgust. But even tender hearted men shun such a tragic mask. Such a being might seem more comprehensible in a remote shrine, among im-

---

[5]See below *PB*, 46.

[6]The "hermit" referred to here is Heraclitus of Ephesus. Artemis was the Ephesian diety and her temple (the Artemison) was situated on a lonely plain some distance from the city itself. According to Diogenes Laertius, Heraclitus was requested by the Ephesians to provide them with laws, but "he scorned the request because the state was already in the grip of a bad constitution. He would retire to the temple of Artemis," until finally "he became a hater of his kind and wandered on the mountains, and there he continued to live, making his diet of grass and herbs." *Lives of Eminent Philosophers*, trans. R.D. Hicks (Cambridge: Harvard University Press, 1926), IX, 3.

ages of the gods and amidst cold, sublime architecture. As a man among
men Heraclitus was incredible. And if he was perhaps observed while
watching the games of noisy children,[7] he had in any case been ponder-
ing something never before pondered by a mortal on such an occasion,
viz., the play of the great world-child, Zeus, and the eternal game of
world destruction and origination. He had no need for men, not even
for the purposes of his knowledge. He was not at all concerned with
anything that one might perhaps ascertain from them or with what other
wise men before him struggled to ascertain. "It was myself which I
sought and explored,"[8] he said, using words which signified the fathom-
ing of an oracle—as if he and no one else were the true fulfiller and
accomplisher of the Delphic maxim, "know thyself."

But what he heard in this oracle he presented as immortal wisdom,
eternally worthy of interpretation in the sense in which the prophetic
speeches of the sibyl are immortal. It is sufficient for the most distant
generations: may they interpret it only as the sayings of an oracle—as
Heraclitus, as the Delphic god himself "neither speaks nor conceals."[9]
Although Heraclitus proclaims his wisdom "without laughter, without
ornaments and scented ointments," but rather, as it were, "with foaming
mouth," it *must* penetrate thousands of years into the future.[10] Since the
world forever requires truth, it requires Heraclitus forever, though he
does not require the world. What does his fame matter to *him*! "Fame
among mortals who are continually passing away!" as he scornfully proclaims.[11] Fame is something for minstrels and poets and for those who
were known as "wise" before him. Let them gulp down this tastiest

---

[7]Diogenes' story continues: "He would retire to the temple of Artemis and play
at knuckle-bones with the boys; and when the Ephesians stood round him and
looked on, 'Why, you rascals,' he said, 'are you astonished? Is it not better to do
this than to take part in your civil life?' " *Lives,* IX, 3. CF. also Frag. 52 of
Heraclitus: "Time is a child playing a game of draughts; the kingship is in the
hands of a child." Translation by Kathleen Freeman, *Ancilla to the Pre-Socratic
Philosophers* (Oxford: Blackwell, 1962), p. 31.

[8]"He was exceptional from his boyhood; for when a youth he used to say that
he knew nothing, although when he was grown up he claimed that he knew
everything. He was nobody's pupil, but he declared that he 'inquired of himself,'
and learned everything from himself." Diogenes Laertius, *Lives,* IX, 5. Cf. also
Frag. 101.

[9]"The lord whose oracle is that at Delphi neither speaks nor conceals, but
indicates." Heraclitus, Frag. 93.

[10]"The Sibyl with raving mouth uttering her unlaughing, unadorned, unin-
censed words reaches over a thousand years with her voice, through the (*inspiration of the*) god." Heraclitus, Frag. 92.

[11]Frag. 29.

morsel of their self-love; the fare is too common for him. His fame matters to men, not to him. His self-love is love of truth, and it is this truth which tells him that the immortality of humanity requires him, not that he requires the immortality of the man Heraclitus.

Truth! Rapturous illusion of a god! What does truth matter to men! And what was the Heraclitean "truth"!

And where has it gone! A vanished dream which has been erased from mankind's countenance by other dreams! It was hardly the first!

Regarding everything which we call by the proud metaphors "world history" and "truth" and "fame," a heartless spirit might have nothing to say except:

"Once upon a time, in some out of the way corner of that universe which is dispersed into numberless twinkling solar systems, there was a star upon which clever beasts invented knowing.[12] It was the most arrogant and mendacious minute of world history, but nevertheless only a minute. After nature had drawn a few breaths the star cooled and solidified, and the clever beasts had to die. The time had come too, for although they boasted of how much they had understood, in the end they discovered to their great annoyance that they had understood everything falsely. They died, and in dying they cursed truth. Such was the nature of these desperate beasts who had invented knowing."

This would be man's fate if he were nothing but a knowing animal. The truth would drive him to despair and destruction: the truth that he is eternally condemned to untruth. But all that is appropriate for man is belief in attainable truth, in the illusion which draws near to man and inspires him with confidence. Does he not actually live *by means of* a continual process of deception? Does nature not conceal most things from him, even the nearest things—his own body, for example, of which he has only a deceptive "consciousness"?[13] He is locked within this consciousness and nature threw away the key. Oh, the fatal curiosity of the philosopher, who longs, just once, to peer out and down through a crack in the chamber of consciousness. Perhaps he will then suspect the extent to which man, in the indifference of his ignorance, is sustained by what is greedy, insatiable, disgusting, pitiless, and murderous—as if he were hanging in dreams on the back of a tiger.

"Let him hang!" cries art. "Wake him up!" shouts the philosopher in the pathos of truth. Yet even while he believes himself to be shaking the sleeper, the philosopher himself is sinking into a still deeper magical

---

[12]This and the following two sentences are identical to the opening sentences of *WL*.

[13]The passage beginning with this sentence and continuing through the end of this paragraph is almost identical to one in the third paragraph of *WL*, 1.

slumber. Perhaps he then dreams of the "ideas" or of immortality. Art is more powerful than knowledge, because *it* desires life, whereas knowledge attains as its final goal only—annihilation.[14]

---

[14]Compare this conclusion concerning the ultimately nihilistic goal of pure knowledge with the more elaborate presentation of the same conclusion by Nietzsche fifteen years later in the Third Essay of *GM*.

The Philosopher as Cultural Physician

1873

III

The Philosopher as Cultural Physician[1]

166

Plan.	What is a philosopher?
	What is a philosopher's relation to culture?
	In particular, to tragic culture?
Preparatory.	When did the works disappear?
	The sources. (a) for the lives, (b) for the dogmas.
	Chronology. Confirmed by means of the systems.
Main Part.	The philosophers, with passages and excursuses.
Conclusion.	Philosophy's attitude toward culture.

167

What is the philosopher?

1. *Beyond the sciences*: dematerializing.

2. *On this side of religions*: de-deifying, disenchanting.[2]

---

[1]*Der Philosoph als Arzt der Kultur* (more literally, "The Philosopher as the Physician of Culture"). The idea that the philosopher is a kind of physician is one that recurs again and again throughout Nietzsche's writings (see e.g., the 1886 preface to *FW*); however, the best gloss on the meaning of the expression "philosopher as cultural physician" is to be found in *PB*, 77 and 78 (below). Though the problem with which they deal is a quite general one, these notes are in fact concerned almost exclusively with the relationship between Greek philosophy and culture. The explanation of this is provided by Nietzsche himself in *PtZG*, 1: "The popular physicians repudiate philosophy. Anyone who wishes to justify it must show for what purpose healthy peoples use and have used philosophy. . . . If philosophy ever showed itself to be helpful, redeeming, or sheltering, it did so among healthy people." And of course, for Nietzsche, the pre-Socratic Greeks provide the best example of a "healthy people."

[2]*Jenseits der Wissenschaften . . . Diesseits der Religionen.* There is a play on words here which helps to convey Nietzsche's point about the relationship between philosophy, science, and religion. One might attempt to render it into English by saying that philosophy is "further out" than science, but not as "far out" as religion.

69

3. Types: the cult of the intellect.
4. Anthropomorphic transferences.

What should philosophy do now?
1. The impossibility of metaphysics.
2. The possibility of the thing in itself. Beyond the sciences.
3. Science as deliverance from wonder.
4. Philosophy against the dogmatism of the sciences.
5. But only in the service of a culture.
6. Schopenhauer's simplifying.[3]
7. His popular and artistically possible metaphysics. The expected results of philosophy are reversed.
8. Against general education.[4]

168

Philosophy has no common denominator: it is sometimes science and sometimes art.

Empedocles and Anaxagoras: the first wants magic, the second wants enlightenment; the first opposes secularization, the second favors it.

The Pythagoreans and Democritus: strict natural science.

Socrates and the skepticism which is now required.

Heraclitus: Apollonian ideal; everything is illusion and play.

Parmenides: the way toward dialectic and scientific *organon*.[5]

Heraclitus is the only one who is at rest.

Thales, like Anaxagoras, Democritus, Parmenides' *organon*, and Socrates, wishes to proceed toward science. On the other hand, Anaximander, like Empedocles and Pythagoras, wishes to move away from science.

169

1. The essential *imperfection* of things:
   In regard to the consequences of a religion—namely, optimistic or pessimistic,
   In regard to the consequences of culture,

---

[3]The point of this reference becomes clear when it is compared to Nietzsche's discussion (in *UBd*, 4) of Wagner as a "simplifier of the world." There Nietzsche explains that the task of contemporary culture is the production of a generation of "anti-Alexanders," who will rebind the frayed strands of Greek culture by mastering the overwhelming contemporary diversity of detail and providing us with a simplified picture of the universe as a whole.

[4]*die allgemeine Bildung*. Re. *Bildung*, see above, *P*, n. 79.

[5]"instrument."

In regard to the consequences of the sciences.

2. The existence of preservatives which fight for a while against an age. Among these must be included *philosophy,* which has no existence at all of its own. It is colored and filled according to the age.[6]

3. Early Greek philosophy was opposed to myth and in favor of science, partially opposed to secularization.

In the age of tragedy: Pythagoras, Empedocles, and Anaximander in agreement [with tragedy]; Heraclitus' Apollinian hostility; dissolution of all art—Parmenides.

170

I. 1. *Introduction.* What is a philosopher capable of doing in regard to the culture of his people?

He seems to be

    (a) an indifferent hermit,

    (b) a teacher to the hundred most spirited and abstract minds,

    (c) or a hated destroyer of popular culture.

Concerning (b) his effect is only indirect, but nevertheless genuine, as in (c).

Concerning (a) it certainly appears that, owing to the lack of purposiveness in nature, he will remain a hermit. Yet his work remains for later ages. Nevertheless, it must be asked whether he was necessary for his own age.

Does the philosopher have a *necessary* relationship to the people? Is there a teleology of the philosopher?

In order to reply to this, one must know that which we call his "age": it can be a minor or a very great age.

Major proposition: He is able to *create* no culture; but he can prepare it and remove restraints on it, or he can moderate and thereby preserve it, or he can destroy it. } always only negatively

A philosopher's positive aspects have never drawn the people after him. For he dwells in the cult of the intellect.

He acts as a *solvent* and a *destroyer* regarding all that is positive in a culture or a religion (even when he seeks to be a *founder*).

---

[6]The *necessary* opposition between a philosopher and his age or times is a theme which always interested Nietzsche and helps to explain the title, "*Untimely Meditations.*" However, his most elaborate treatment of this topic, where he sketches a most interesting "dialectical" account of the changing relationship of the philosopher to his age, may be found in *JGB,* 212-3. (Cf. also the remark concerning the necessary opposition between the genius and his age in *WP,* 115.)

He is most useful when there is *a lot to be destroyed,* in times of chaos or degeneration.

Every flourishing culture tries to make the philosopher *unnecessary* (or else to isolate him completely). This isolation or atrophy of the philosopher can be explained in two ways:

(a) on the basis of the lack of purposiveness in nature (at times when the philosopher is needed);

(b) on the basis of the purposive foresight of nature (at times when the philosopher is not needed).

II. His destructive and curtailing effects—upon what?

III. Now, since there is no culture, what must he prepare (destroy)?

IV. The attack upon philosophy.

V. The philosophers [are] atrophied.

Both [IV and V] are consequences of the lack of purposiveness in nature, which ruins countless seeds.[7] Yet it nevertheless manages to produce a few great things: Kant and Schopenhauer.

VI. Kant and Schopenhauer. The step from the one to the other is a step toward a freer culture.

Schopenhauer's teleology in regard to a future culture.

His two-fold positive philosophy (it lacks a living nucleus)—a conflict only for those who no longer hope. How the future culture will overcome this conflict.

171

The *value* of philosophy:

Cleanses muddled and superstitious ideas.[8] Opposes scientific dogmatism.

Philosophy cleanses and clarifies to the extent that it is a science;[9] to the extent that it is anti-scientific it is religio-obscurant.

Eliminates the theory of the soul[10] and rational theology.

---

[7]See below, *PB*, 41.

[8]*Vorstellungen.* See above, *P*, n. 94.

[9]Once again, the term *Wissenschaft* has a much broader connotation than the English "science." Cf. below, *P*, n. 14. This remark of Nietzsche's should therefore not be taken to imply that he thought that philosophy should model itself on physics.

[10]*Seelenlehre,* an old term for psychology. What Nietzsche is referring to is that sort of *a priori* study of the nature of the mind which Kant rejected as "rational psychology."

Proof of what is absolutely anthropomorphic.[11]

Opposes the fixed value of ethical concepts.

Opposes hatred of the body.

The *harmfulness* of philosophy:
Dissolves the instinct,
                  cultures,
                  customary moralities.[12]

The special business of philosophy in the present.

The absence of a popular ethic.

The absence of any sense of the importance of knowing and discriminating.

The superficiality of reflection upon church, state, and society.

The mania for history.

The talk concerning art and the absence of any culture.

172

Everything which is of *general importance* in a science has either become *accidental* or is *absent altogether*. [For example:]

The study of language, without the art of composition and rhetoric.

Indian studies, without philosophy.

[The study of] classical antiquity, unrelated to any practical attempt to learn from it.

Natural science, lacking the healing and repose which Goethe found in it.

History, without enthusiasm.

In short, sciences without practical application. And therefore sciences pursued in a manner different from the manner in which they have been pursued by genuine men of culture. Science as a livelihood![13]

You pursue *philosophy* with young, inexperienced persons. Your old people turn to history. You have no popular philosophy at all; instead, you have insultingly uniform popular lectures. Universities propose "Schopenhauer" as a topic for their students' prize essays. Popular addresses on Schopenhauer! This is lacking in any dignity.

How science could have become what now it has become is something which can only be clarified on the basis of the development of religion.

---

[11]*Beweis des absolut Anthropomorphischen.* The sense of this expression is unclear. It probably means that philosophy teaches man the extent to which his world and ideas are involved in anthropomorphism.

[12]*Sittlichkeiten.* See *P*, n. 33.

[13]Reading *Broterwerb* for *Broderwerb*.

173

If they are abnormal, then surely they have nothing to do with the people? This is not the case: the people *need* the anomalies *even if the anomalies do not exist for the people's sake.*

The work of art provides evidence for this: the creator himself understands the work; nevertheless, it has a side which is turned toward the public.

We desire to become acquainted with this side of the philosopher—the side which is turned toward the public—and to leave undiscussed the question concerning his extraordinary [inner] nature (in other words, his real objective, the question "why"). This [public] side is difficult to recognize from the standpoint of our present age, because we possess no popular cultural unity of this sort. Hence the Greeks.

174

Philosophy is *not something for the people*; thus it is *not the basis of a culture*, but merely the tool of a culture.

(a) against scientific dogmatism;

(b) against the confusion of images in nature brought about by mythical religions;

(c) against the confusion of ethics by religions.

In conformity with these goals the essence of philosophy

(a) 1. is convinced of the anthropomorphic [element within experience]; is skeptical;

    2. possesses discrimination and greatness;

    3. skimming the idea of unity;

(b) is a healthy interpretation and simplification of nature; is proof;

(c) destroys the belief in the inviolability of such [ethical] laws.

Philosophy's helplessness apart from culture, illustrated by the present.

175

The Philosopher as Cultural Physician

For the general introduction: description of the seventh century: the preparation of culture, the confrontation of drives; the oriental element. The centralization of education, beginning with Homer.

I will speak of the Pre-Platonic philosophers, because overt hostility against culture—negation—begins with Plato. But I want to know how philosophy behaves toward a presently existing or developing culture which is not the enemy: the philosopher at this point is the poisoner of culture.

Philosophy and the people. None of the great Greek philosophers were leaders of the people: at most, there is the attempt made by Empedocles (after Pythagoras), though he did not attempt to lead the people with pure philosophy, but with a mythical vehicle of the latter. Others reject the people from the start (Heraclitus). Others have as their public a quite distinguished circle of educated persons (Anaxagoras). Socrates possesses the most democratic and demogogic tendency: the result is the foundation of sects, and thus is counterevidence. How could inferior philosophers hope to succeed where philosophers such as these could not? It is not possible to base a popular culture on philosophy. Thus, in relation to a culture, philosophy can always be of secondary, but never of primary, significance. What is this [significance]?

Mastery of the mythical: strengthening the sense of truth over against free fiction.[14] *Vis veritatis*,[15] or the strengthening of pure knowing (Thales, Democritus, Parmenides).

Mastery of the knowledge drive: or the strengthening of that which is mythical, mystical, and artistic. (Heraclitus, Empedocles, Anaximander.) Legislation by *greatness*.

The destruction of rigid dogmatism:

    (a) in religion

    (b) in mores,

    (c) in science.

The *skeptical* impulse.

Every force (religion, myth, knowledge drive) has barbarizing, immoral, and stultifying effects when it is taken to extremes as an inflexible master (Socrates).

The destruction of blind secularization (a substitute for religion) (Anaxagoras, Pericles). *The mythical impulse.*

Result: Philosophy can create no culture,

               but it can prepare it;

               or preserve it;

               or moderate it.

For us: For these reasons the philosopher is the supreme tribunal of the schools. Preparation of the genius: since we have no culture. A study of the symptoms of the age shows the task of the schools to be as follows:[16]

---

[14]*frein Dichtung*.

[15]"force of truth."

[16]It is often not realized how deeply Nietzsche concerned himself with the theory and practical details of education, especially during his first years of teaching at Basel. In this regard the series of public lectures delivered in early 1872 (*ZB*) are particularly important. In these lectures Nietzsche opposes both the attempt to extend education to the masses and the attempt to subordinate it to the interests of the state.

1. The destruction of secularization (absence of a popular philosophy);

2. The subjugation of the barbarizing effects of the knowledge drive. (Thereby abstaining from this fantasizing philosophy itself.)
Against "iconic" history.
Against scholarly "labor."[17]

Culture can emanate only from the centralizing significance of an art or work of art. Philosophy will unintentionally pave the way for such a world view.

[17]Re. the concept of "scholarly labor" and Nietzsche's critique of the same, see *UBa*, 8; *UBb*, 7; *UBc*, 8; *ZB*, 1; *MAMa*, 284; *MAMc*, 171; *FW*, 329; *JGB*, 211; *GM*, III, 23; and *EH*, III, "UB."

On Truth and Lies
In A Nonmoral Sense

1873

IV

On Truth and Lies in a Nonmoral Sense[1]

1

Once upon a time, in some out of the way corner of that universe which is dispersed into numberless twinkling solar systems, there was a star upon which clever beasts invented knowing. That was the most arrogant and mendacious minute of "world history," but nevertheless, it was only a minute. After nature had drawn a few breaths, the star cooled and congealed, and the clever beasts had to die.[2] —One might invent such a fable, and yet he still would not have adequately illustrated how miserable, how shadowy and transient, how aimless and arbitrary the human intellect looks within nature. There were eternities during which it did not exist. And when it is all over with the human intellect, nothing will have happened. For this intellect has no additional mission which would lead it beyond human life. Rather, it is human, and only its possessor and begetter takes it so solemnly—as though the world's axis turned within it. But if we could communicate with the gnat, we would learn that he likewise flies through the air with the same solemnity,[3] that he feels the flying center of the universe within himself. There is nothing so reprehensible and unimportant in nature that it would not immediately swell up like a balloon at the slightest puff of this power of knowing. And just as every porter wants to have an admirer, so even the proudest of men, the philosopher, supposes that he sees on all sides the eyes of the universe telescopically focused upon his action and thought.

It is remarkable that this was brought about by the intellect, which was certainly allotted to these most unfortunate, delicate, and ephemeral beings merely as a device for detaining them a minute within existence.

---

[1] A more literal, though less English, translation of *Über Wahrheit und Lüge im aussermoralischen Sinne* might be "On Truth and Lie in the Extramoral Sense." For a discussion of the relation between the relatively polished and finished sections of this essay and other material translated in this volume, see the "Introduction" and "Note on the Texts."

[2] Cf. the very similar passage in the antepenultimate paragraph of *PW*.

[3] *Pathos.*

For without this addition they would have every reason to flee this existence as quickly as Lessing's son.[4] The pride connected with knowing and sensing lies like a blinding fog over the eyes and senses of men, thus deceiving them concerning the value of existence. For this pride contains within itself the most flattering estimation of the value of knowing. Deception is the most general effect of such pride, but even its most particular effects contain within themselves something of the same deceitful character.

As a means for the preserving of the individual, the intellect unfolds its principle powers in dissimulation, which is the means by which weaker, less robust individuals preserve themselves—since they have been denied the chance to wage the battle for existence with horns or with the sharp teeth of beasts of prey. This art of dissimulation reaches its peak in man. Deception, flattering, lying, deluding, talking behind the back, putting up a false front, living in borrowed splendor, wearing a mask, hiding behind convention, playing a role for others and for oneself—in short, a continuous fluttering around the *solitary* flame of vanity—is so much the rule and the law among men that there is almost nothing which is less comprehensible than how an honest and pure drive for truth could have arisen among them. They are deeply immersed in illusions and in dream images; their eyes merely glide over the surface of things and see "forms." Their senses nowhere lead to truth; on the contrary, they are content to receive stimuli and, as it were, to engage in a groping game on the backs of things. Moreover, man permits himself to be deceived in his dreams every night of his life.[5] His moral sentiment does not even make an attempt to prevent this, whereas there are supposed to be men who have stopped snoring through sheer will power. What does man actually know about himself? Is he, indeed, ever able to perceive himself completely, as if laid out in a lighted display case? Does nature not conceal most things from him—even concerning his own body—in order to confine and lock him within a proud, deceptive consciousness, aloof from the coils of the bowels, the rapid flow of the blood stream, and the intricate quivering of the fibers! She threw away the key. And woe to that fatal curiosity which might one day have the power to peer out and down through a crack in the chamber of consciousness and then suspect that man is sustained in the indifference of his ignorance by that which is pitiless, greedy, insatiable, and murderous—as if hanging in dreams on the back of a tiger.[6] Given this situation, where in the world could the drive for truth have come from?

---

[4]A reference to the offspring of Lessing and Eva König, who died on the day of his birth.

[5]Cf. *P*, 70.

[6]Cf. the very similar passage in the penultimate paragraph of *PW*.

Insofar as the individual wants to maintain himself against other individuals, he will under natural circumstances employ the intellect mainly for dissimulation. But at the same time, from boredom and necessity, man wishes to exist socially and with the herd; therefore, he needs to make peace and strives accordingly to banish from his world at least the most flagrant *bellum omni contra omnes*.[7] This peace treaty brings in its wake something which appears to be the first step toward acquiring that puzzling truth drive: to wit, *that* which shall count as "truth" from now on is established. That is to say, a uniformly valid and binding designation is invented for things, and this legislation of language likewise establishes the first laws of truth. For the contrast between truth and lie arises here for the first time. The liar is a person who uses the valid designations, the words, in order to make something which is unreal appear to be real. He says, for example, "I am rich," when the proper designation for his condition would be "poor." He misuses fixed conventions by means of arbitrary substitutions or even reversals of names. If he does this in a selfish and moreover harmful manner, society will cease to trust him and will thereby exclude him. What men avoid by excluding the liar is not so much being defrauded as it is being harmed by means of fraud. Thus, even at this stage, what they hate is basically not deception itself, but rather the unpleasant, hated consequences of certain sorts of deception. It is in a similarly restricted sense that man now wants nothing but truth: he desires the pleasant, life-preserving consequences of truth. He is indifferent toward pure knowledge which has no consequences; toward those truths which are possibly harmful and destructive he is even hostilely inclined. And besides, what about these linguistic conventions themselves? Are they perhaps products of knowledge, that is, of the sense of truth? Are designations congruent with things? Is language the adequate expression of all realities?

It is only by means of forgetfulness that man can ever reach the point of fancying himself to possess a "truth" of the grade just indicated. If he will not be satisfied with truth in the form of tautology,[8] that is to say, if he will not be content with empty husks, then he will always exchange truths for illusions. What is a word? It is the copy in sound of a nerve stimulus. But the further inference from the nerve stimulus to a cause outside of us is already the result of a false and unjustifiable application of the principle of sufficient reason.[9] If truth alone had been the deciding factor in the genesis of language, and if the standpoint of certainty

---

[7]"War of each against all."

[8]See *P*, 150.

[9]Note that Nietzsche is here engaged in an implicit critique of Schopenhauer, who had been guilty of precisely this misapplication of the principle of sufficient reason in his first book, *The Fourfold Root of the Principle of Sufficient Reason*. It is

had been decisive for designations, then how could we still dare to say "the stone is hard," as if "hard" were something otherwise familiar to us, and not merely a totally subjective stimulation! We separate things according to gender, designating the tree as masculine and the plant as feminine. What arbitrary assignments![10] How far this oversteps the canons of certainty! We speak of a "snake": this designation touches only upon its ability to twist itself and could therefore also fit a worm.[11] What arbitrary differentiations! What one-sided preferences, first for this, then for that property of a thing! The various languages placed side by side show that with words it is never a question of truth, never a question of adequate expression; otherwise, there would not be so many languages.[12] The "thing in itself" (which is precisely what the pure truth, apart from any of its consequences, would be) is likewise something quite incomprehensible to the creator of language and something not in the least worth striving for. This creator only designates the relations of things to men, and for expressing these relations he lays hold of the boldest metaphors.[13] To begin with, a nerve stimulus is transferred into an image:[14] first metaphor. The image, in turn, is imitated in a sound: second metaphor. And each time there is a complete overleaping of one sphere, right into the middle of an entirely new and different one. One can imagine a man who is totally deaf and has never had a sensation of sound and music. Perhaps such a person will gaze with astonishment at Chladni's sound figures;[15] perhaps he will discover their causes in the vibrations of the string and will now swear that he must know what men mean by "sound." It is this way with all of us concerning language: we

---

quite wrong to think that Nietzsche was ever wholly uncritical of Schopenhauer's philosophy (see, for example, the little essay, *Kritik der Schopenhauerischen Philosophie* from 1867, in *MA*, I, pp. 392-401).

[10]*welche willkürlichen Übertragungen*. The specific sense of this passage depends upon the fact that all ordinary nouns in the German language are assigned a gender: the tree is *der Baum*; the plant is *die Pflanze*. This assignment of an original sexual property to all things is the "transference" in question. On the translation of the key term *Übertragung*, see the "Introduction" and *P*, n. 83.

[11]This passage depends upon the etymological relation between the German words *Schlange* (snake) and *schlingen* (to wind or twist), both of which are related to the old High German *slango*.

[12]What Nietzsche is rejecting here is the theory that there is a sort of "naturally appropriate" connection between certain words (or sounds) and things. Such a theory is defended by Socrates in Plato's *Cratylus*.

[13]On the significance of "metaphor" (which is closely related to *Übertragung*) for Nietzsche's theories of language and knowledge, see the "Introduction."

[14]*Ein Nervenreiz, zuerst übertragen in ein Bild*. The "image" in this case is the visual image, what we "see." Regarding the term *Bild*, see *P*, n. 2.

[15]See *P*, n. 55.

believe that we know something about the things themselves when we speak of trees, colors, snow, and flowers; and yet we possess nothing but metaphors for things—metaphors which correspond in no way to the original entities.[16] In the same way that the sound appears as a sand figure, so the mysterious X of the thing in itself first appears as a nerve stimulus, then as an image, and finally as a sound. Thus the genesis of language does not proceed logically in any case, and all the material within and with which the man of truth, the scientist, and the philosopher later work and build, if not derived from never-never land,[17] is at least not derived from the essence of things.

In particular, let us further consider the formation of concepts. Every word instantly becomes a concept precisely insofar as it is not supposed to serve as a reminder of the unique and entirely individual original experience to which it owes its origin; but rather, a word becomes a concept insofar as it simultaneously has to fit countless more or less similar cases—which means, purely and simply, cases which are never equal and thus altogether unequal. Every concept arises from the equation of unequal things. Just as it is certain that one leaf is never totally the same as another, so it is certain that the concept "leaf" is formed by arbitrarily discarding these individual differences and by forgetting the distinguishing aspects. This awakens the idea that, in addition to the leaves, there exists in nature the "leaf": the original model according to which all the leaves were perhaps woven, sketched, measured, colored, curled, and painted—but by incompetent hands, so that no specimen has turned out to be a correct, trustworthy, and faithful likeness of the original model. We call a person "honest," and then we ask "why has he behaved so honestly today?" Our usual answer is, "on account of his honesty." Honesty! This in turn means that the leaf is the cause of the leaves. We know nothing whatsoever about an essential quality called "honesty"; but we do know of countless individualized and consequently unequal actions which we equate by omitting the aspects in which they are unequal and which we now designate as "honest" actions. Finally we formulate from them a *qualitas occulta*[18] which has the name "honesty." We obtain the concept, as we do the form, by overlooking what is individual and actual; whereas nature is acquainted with no forms and no concepts, and likewise with no species, but only with an X which remains inaccessible and undefinable for us. For even our contrast between individual and species is something anthropomorphic and does not originate in the essence of things; although we should not presume to claim that this contrast does not correspond to the essence of things: that would of

---

[16]*Wesenheiten.*
[17]*Wolkenkukuksheim*: literally, "cloud-cuckoo-land."
[18]"Occult quality."

course be a dogmatic assertion and, as such, would be just as indemon-strable as its opposite.[19]

What then is truth? A movable host of metaphors, metonymies, and anthropomorphisms: in short, a sum of human relations which have been poetically and rhetorically intensified, transferred, and embel-lished, and which, after long usage, seem to a people to be fixed, canoni-cal, and binding. Truths are illusions which we have forgotten are illu-sions; they are metaphors that have become worn out and have been drained of sensuous force, coins which have lost their embossing and are now considered as metal and no longer as coins.

We still do not yet know where the drive for truth comes from. For so far we have heard only of the duty which society imposes in order to exist: to be truthful means to employ the usual metaphors. Thus, to express it morally, this is the duty to lie according to a fixed convention, to lie with the herd and in a manner binding upon everyone. Now man of course forgets that this is the way things stand for him. Thus he lies in the manner indicated, unconsciously and in accordance with habits which are centuries' old; and precisely *by means of this unconsciousness* and forgetfulness he arrives at his sense of truth. From the sense that one is obliged to designate one thing as "red," another as "cold," and a third as "mute," there arises a moral impulse in regard to truth. The venerability, reliability, and utility of truth is something which a person demonstrates for himself from the contrast with the liar, whom no one trusts and everyone excludes. As a *"rational"* being, he now places his behavior under the control of abstractions. He will no longer tolerate being car-ried away by sudden impressions, by intuitions. First he universalizes all these impressions into less colorful, cooler concepts, so that he can en-trust the guidance of his life and conduct to them. Everything which distinguishes man from the animals depends upon this ability to vol-atilize perceptual metaphors[20] in a schema, and thus to dissolve an image into a concept. For something is possible in the realm of these schemata which could never be achieved with the vivid first impressions: the con-struction of a pyramidal order according to castes and degrees, the crea-tion of a new world of laws, privileges, subordinations, and clearly marked boundaries—a new world, one which now confronts that other vivid world of first impressions as more solid, more universal, better known, and more human than the immediately perceived world, and thus as the regulative and imperative world. Whereas each perceptual metaphor is individual and without equals and is therefore able to elude

---

[19]Nietzsche criticizes Kant on just this score in *P*, 84.

[20]*die anschaulichen Metaphern*. Regarding the translation of *Anschauung,* see *P*, n. 82. The adjective *anschaulich* has the additional sense of "vivid"—as in the next sentence ("vivid first impressions").

all classification, the great edifice of concepts displays the rigid regularity of a Roman columbarium[21] and exhales in logic that strength and coolness which is characteristic of mathematics. Anyone who has felt this cool breath [of logic] will hardly believe that even the concept—which is as bony, foursquare, and transposable as a die—is nevertheless merely the *residue of a metaphor*, and that the illusion which is involved in the artistic transference of a nerve stimulus into images is, if not the mother, then the grandmother of every single concept.[22] But in this conceptual crap game "truth" means using every die in the designated manner, counting its spots accurately, fashioning the right categories, and never violating the order of caste and class rank. Just as the Romans and Etruscans cut up the heavens with rigid mathematical lines and confined a god within each of the spaces thereby delimited, as within a *templum*,[23] so every people has a similarly mathematically divided conceptual heaven above themselves and henceforth thinks that truth demands that each conceptual god be sought only within *his own* sphere. Here one may certainly admire man as a mighty genius of construction, who succeeds in piling up an infinitely complicated dome of concepts upon an unstable foundation, and, as it were, on running water. Of course, in order to be supported by such a foundation, his construction must be like one constructed of spiders' webs: delicate enough to be carried along by the waves, strong enough not to be blown apart by every wind. As a genius of construction man raises himself far above the bee in the following way: whereas the bee builds with wax that he gathers from nature, man builds with the far more delicate conceptual material which he first has to manufacture from himself. In this he is greatly to be admired, but not on account of his drive for truth or for pure knowledge of things. When someone hides something behind a bush and looks for it again in the same place and finds it there as well, there is not much to praise in such seeking and finding. Yet this is how matters stand regarding seeking and finding "truth" within the realm of reason. If I make up the definition of a mammal, and then, after inspecting a camel, declare "look, a mammal," I have indeed brought a truth to light in this way, but it is a truth of limited value. That is to say, it is a thoroughly anthropomorphic truth which contains not a single point which would be "true in itself" or really and universally valid apart from man. At bottom, what the investigator of such truths is seeking is only the metamorphosis of the world into

---

[21]A columbarium is a vault with niches for funeral urns containing the ashes of cremated bodies.

[22]I.e. concepts are derived from images, which are, in turn, derived from nerve stimuli.

[23]A delimited space restricted to a particular purpose, especially a religiously sanctified area.

man. He strives to understand the world as something analogous to man, and at best he achieves by his struggles the feeling of assimilation. Similar to the way in which astrologers considered the stars to be in man's service and connected with his happiness and sorrow, such an investigator considers the entire universe in connection with man:[24] the entire universe as the infinitely fractured echo of one original sound—man; the entire universe as the infinitely multiplied copy of one original picture—man. His method is to treat man as the measure of all things, but in doing so he again proceeds from the error of believing that he has these things [which he intends to measure] immediately before him as mere objects. He forgets that the original perceptual metaphors are metaphors and takes them to be the things themselves.

Only by forgetting this primitive world of metaphor can one live with any repose, security, and consistency: only by means of the petrification and coagulation of a mass of images which originally streamed from the primal faculty of human imagination like a fiery liquid, only in the invincible faith that *this* sun, *this* window, *this* table is a truth in itself, in short, only by forgetting that he himself is an *artistically creating* subject, does man live with any repose, security, and consistency.[25] If but for an instant he could escape from the prison walls of this faith, his "self consciousness" would be immediately destroyed. It is even a difficult thing for him to admit to himself that the insect or the bird perceives an entirely different world from the one that man does, and that the question of which of these perceptions of the world is the more correct one is quite meaningless, for this would have to have been decided previously in accordance with the criterion of the *correct perception*, which means, in accordance with a criterion which is *not available*. But in any case it seems to me that "the correct perception"—which would mean "the adequate expression of an object in the subject"—is a contradictory impossibility.[26] For between two absolutely different spheres, as between subject and object, there is no causality, no correctness, and no expression; there is, at most, an *aesthetic* relation:[27] I mean, a suggestive transference, a stammering translation into a completely foreign tongue—for which there is required, in any case, a freely inventive intermediate sphere and mediating force. "Apearance" is a word that contains many temptations, which is why I avoid it as much as possible. For it is not true that the essence of things "appears" in the empirical world. A painter without hands who wished to express in song the picture before his mind would,

---

[24]Cf. *P*, 105 and 151.

[25]See *P*, n. 68.

[26]*ein widerspruchsvolles Unding*. See *P*, n. 95.

[27]*ein ästhetisches Verhalten*. A more literal translation of *Verhalten* is "behavior," "attitude," or perhaps "disposition."

by means of this substitution of spheres, still reveal more about the essence of things than does the empirical world. Even the relationship of a nerve stimulus to the generated image is not a necessary one. But when the same image has been generated millions of times and has been handed down for many generations and finally appears on the same occasion every time for all mankind, then it acquires at last the same meaning for men it would have if it were the sole necessary image and if the relationship of the original nerve stimulus to the generated image were a strictly causal one. In the same manner, an eternally repeated dream would certainly be felt and judged to be reality. But the hardening and congealing of a metaphor guarantees absolutely nothing concerning its necessity and exclusive justification.

Every person who is familiar with such considerations has no doubt felt a deep mistrust of all idealism of this sort: just as often as he has quite clearly convinced himself of the eternal consistency, omnipresence, and infallibility of the laws of nature. He has concluded that so far as we can penetrate here—from the telescopic heights to the microscopic depths—everything is secure, complete, infinite, regular, and without any gaps. Science will be able to dig successfully in this shaft forever, and all the things that are discovered will harmonize with and not contradict each other. How little does this resemble a product of the imagination, for if it were such, there should be some place where the illusion and unreality can be divined. Against this, the following must be said: if each of us had a different kind of sense perception—if we could only perceive things now as a bird, now as a worm, now as a plant, or if one of us saw a stimulus as red, another as blue, while a third even heard the same stimulus as a sound—then no one would speak of such a regularity of nature, rather, nature would be grasped only as a creation which is subjective in the highest degree. After all, what is a law of nature as such for us? We are not acquainted with it in itself, but only with its effects, which means in its relation to other laws of nature—which, in turn, are known to us only as sums of relations. Therefore all these relations always refer again to others and are thoroughly incomprehensible to us in their essence. All that we actually know about these laws of nature is what we ourselves bring to them—time and space, and therefore relationships of succession and number. But everything marvelous about the laws of nature, everything that quite astonishes us therein and seems to demand our explanation, everything that might lead us to distrust idealism: all this is completely and solely contained within the mathematical strictness and inviolability of our representations of time and space. But we produce these representations in and from ourselves with the same necessity with which the spider spins. If we are forced to comprehend all things only under these forms, then it ceases to be amazing that in all things we actually comprehend nothing but these forms. For they must all bear within themselves the laws of number, and it is precisely number which is most astonishing in things.[28] All that conformity to law, which impresses us so much in the movement of the stars and in chemical processes, coincides at bottom with those properties which we bring to things. Thus it is we who impress ourselves in this way. In conjunction with this, it of course follows that the artistic process of metaphor formation with which every sensation begins in us already presupposes these forms and thus occurs within them. The only way in which the possibility of subsequently constructing a new conceptual edifice from metaphors themselves can be explained is by the firm persistence of these original forms. That is to say, this conceptual edifice is an imitation of temporal, spatial, and numerical relationships in the domain of metaphor.[29]

2

We have seen how it is originally *language* which works on the construction of concepts, a labor taken over in later ages by *science*.[30] Just as the bee simultaneously constructs cells and fills them with honey, so science works unceasingly on this great columbarium of concepts, the graveyard of perceptions. It is always building new, higher stories and shoring up, cleaning, and renovating the old cells; above all, it takes pains to fill up this monstrously towering framework and to arrange therein the entire empirical world, which is to say, the anthropomorphic world. Whereas the man of action binds his life to reason and its concepts so that he will not be swept away and lost, the scientific investigator builds his hut right next to the tower of science so that he will be able to work on it and to find shelter for himself beneath those bulwarks which presently exist. And he requires shelter, for there are frightful powers which continuously break in upon him, powers which oppose scientific "truth" with completely different kinds of "truths" which bear on their shields the most varied sorts of emblems.

The drive toward the formation of metaphors is the fundamental human drive, which one cannot for a single instant dispense with in

---

[28]Regarding the special epistemological significance which Nietzsche attached to number and numerical relations, see *P*, n. 46.

[29]This is where section 1 of the fair copy made by von Gersdorff ends. But according to Schlechta (in Schlechta/Anders, pp. 14-5) Nietzsche's preliminary version continued as follows:

"Empty space and empty time are ideas which are possible at any time. Every concept, thus an empty metaphor, is only an imitation of these first ideas: space, time, and causality. Afterwards, the original imaginative act of transference into images: the first provides the matter, the second the qualities which we believe in. Comparison to music. How can one speak of it?"

[30]*Wissenschaft.* See *P*, n. 14.

thought, for one would thereby dispense with man himself. This drive is not truly vanquished and scarcely subdued by the fact that a regular and rigid new world is constructed as its prison from its own ephemeral products, the concepts. It seeks a new realm and another channel for its activity, and it finds this in *myth* and in *art* generally. This drive continually confuses the conceptual categories and cells by bringing forward new transferences, metaphors, and metonymies. It continually manifests an ardent desire to refashion the world which presents itself to waking man, so that it will be as colorful, irregular, lacking in results and coherence, charming, and eternally new as the world of dreams. Indeed, it is only by means of the rigid and regular web of concepts that the waking man clearly sees that he is awake; and it is precisely because of this that he sometimes thinks that he must be dreaming when this web of concepts is torn by art. Pascal is right in maintaining that if the same dream came to us every night we would be just as occupied with it as we are with the things that we see every day. "If a workman were sure to dream for twelve straight hours every night that he was king," said Pascal, "I believe that he would be just as happy as a king who dreamt for twelve hours every night that he was a workman."[31] In fact, because of the way that myth takes it for granted that miracles are always happening, the waking life of a mythically inspired people—the ancient Greeks, for instance—more closely resembles a dream than it does the waking world of a scientifically disenchanted thinker. When every tree can suddenly speak as a nymph, when a god in the shape of a bull can drag away maidens, when even the goddess Athena herself is suddenly seen in the company of Peisastratus driving through the market place of Athens with a beautiful team of horses[32]—and this is what the honest Athenian believed—then, as in a dream, anything is possible at each moment, and all of nature swarms around man as if it were nothing but a masquerade of the gods, who were merely amusing themselves by deceiving men in all these shapes.

But man has an invincible inclination to allow himself to be deceived and is, as it were, enchanted with happiness when the rhapsodist tells him epic fables as if they were true, or when the actor in the theater acts more royally than any real king. So long as it is able to deceive without

---

[31]*Pensées*, number 386. Actually, Pascal says that the workman would be "almost as happy" as the king in this case!

[32]According to the story told by Herodotus (*Histories* I, 60) the tyrant Peisistratus adopted the following ruse to secure his popular acceptance upon his return from exile: he entered Athens in a chariot accompanied by a woman named Phye who was dressed in the costume of Athena. Thus the people were supposed to have been convinced that it was the goddess herself who was conducting the tyrant back to the Acropolis.

injuring, that master of deception, the intellect, is free; it is released from its former slavery and celebrates its Saturnalia. It is never more luxuriant, richer, prouder, more clever and more daring. With creative pleasure it throws metaphors into confusion and displaces the boundary stones of abstractions, so that, for example, it designates the stream as "the moving path which carries man where he would otherwise walk." The intellect has now thrown the token of bondage from itself. At other times it endeavors, with gloomy officiousness, to show the way and to demonstrate the tools to a poor individual who covets existence; it is like a servant who goes in search of booty and prey for his master. But now it has become the master and it dares to wipe from its face the expression of indigence. In comparison with its previous conduct, everything that it now does bears the mark of dissimulation,[33] just as that previous conduct did of distortion.[34] The free intellect copies human life, but it considers this life to be something good and seems to be quite satisfied with it. That immense framework and planking of concepts to which the needy man clings his whole life long in order to preserve himself is nothing but a scaffolding and toy for the most audacious feats of the liberated intellect. And when it smashes this framework to pieces, throws it into confusion, and puts it back together in an ironic fashion, pairing the most alien things and separating the closest, it is demonstrating that it has no need of these makeshifts of indigence and that it will now be guided by intuitions rather than by concepts. There is no regular path which leads from these intuitions into the land of ghostly schemata, the land of abstractions. There exists no word for these intuitions; when man sees them he grows dumb, or else he speaks only in forbidden metaphors and in unheard-of combinations of concepts. He does this so that by shattering and mocking the old conceptual barriers he may at least correspond creatively to the impression of the powerful present intuition.

There are ages in which the rational man and the intuitive man stand side by side, the one in fear of intuition, the other with scorn for abstraction. The latter is just as irrational as the former is inartistic. They both desire to rule over life: the former, by knowing how to meet his principle needs by means of foresight, prudence, and regularity; the latter, by disregarding these needs and, as an "overjoyed hero," counting as real only that life which has been disguised as illusion and beauty. Whenever, as was perhaps the case in ancient Greece, the intuitive man handles his weapons more authoritatively and victoriously than his opponent, then, under favorable circumstances, a culture can take shape and art's mastery over life can be established. All the manifestations of such a life will be accompanied by this dissimulation, this disavowal of indigence, this

---

[33]*Verstellung.*
[34]*Verzerrung.*

glitter of metaphorical intuitions, and, in general, this immediacy of deception: neither the house, nor the gait, nor the clothes, nor the clay jugs give evidence of having been invented because of a pressing need. It seems as if they were all intended to express an exalted happiness, an Olympian cloudlessness, and, as it were, a playing with seriousness. The man who is guided by concepts and abstractions only succeeds by such means in warding off misfortune, without ever gaining any happiness for himself from these abstractions. And while he aims for the greatest possible freedom from pain, the intuitive man, standing in the midst of a culture, already reaps from his intuition a harvest of continually inflowing illumination, cheer, and redemption—in addition to obtaining a defense against misfortune. To be sure, he suffers more intensely, *when* he suffers; he even suffers more frequently, since he does not understand how to learn from experience and keeps falling over and over again into the same ditch. He is then just as irrational in sorrow as he is in happiness: he cries aloud and will not be consoled. How differently the stoical man who learns from experience and governs himself by concepts is affected by the same misfortunes! This man, who at other times seeks nothing but sincerity, truth, freedom from deception, and protection against ensnaring surprise attacks, now executes a masterpiece of deception: he executes his masterpiece of deception in misfortune, as the other type of man executes his in times of happiness. He wears no quivering and changeable human face, but, as it were, a mask with dignified, symmetrical features. He does not cry; he does not even alter his voice. When a real storm cloud thunders above him, he wraps himself in his cloak, and with slow steps he walks from beneath it.

* *
*

Sketch of Additional Sections[35]

3

Description of the chaotic confusion characteristic of a mythical age. The oriental. Philosophy's beginnings as the director of cults and myths: it organizes the unity of religion.

4

The beginnings of an ironic attitude toward religion. The new emergence of philosophy.

---

[35] All the following notes were added by Nietzsche himself to von Gersdorff's fair copy of sections 1 and 2.

5,*etc. narration.* [36]

Conclusion: Plato's state as *superhellenic*, as not impossible. Here philosophy attains its summit as the founder of a metaphysically organized state.

* *

*

Drafts [37]

176
"Truth"

1. Considered as an unconditional duty, truth stands in a hostile and destructive relationship to the world.

2. Analysis of the ordinary sense of truth (inconsistency).

3. The pathos of truth.

4. That which is impossible, considered as a corrective for man.

5. Man's foundation is mendacious, because it is optimistic.

6. The world of the body.

7. Individuals.

8. Forms.

9. Art. The hostility toward it.

10. There can be neither society nor culture without untruth. The tragic conflict. Everything which is good and beautiful depends upon illusion: truth kills—it even kills itself (insofar as it realizes that error is its foundation). [38]

177
What is there in regard to truth which corresponds to *asceticism*? [39]

---

[36] According to Anders (in Schlechta/Anders, p. 98), this is where Nietzsche's historical presentation of Pre-Platonic philosophy was to be included.

[37] *Entwürfe.* The numbers of the following sections were added by the editors of *GOA;* again, they are *not* Nietzsche's.

[38] In the *Birth of Tragedy*, sections 14 and 15, Nietzsche had already begun to examine the way in which the search for truth turns upon itself and "bites its tail." This theme is one which he developed with greater and greater precision and mastery in his later works. It obviously bears a close relation to his final definition of nihilism: "the highest values devalue themselves." *WM*, 2.

[39] The relationship between truth, more specifically the desire for truth, and

Truthfulness, considered as the foundation of all utterances and the presupposition for the maintenance of the human species, is a eudaemonic demand,[40] a demand which is opposed by the knowledge that the supreme welfare of men depends to a far greater extent upon *illusions*. Consequently, according to the eudaemonean principle, both truth *and lies* must be utilized—which is also the way it happens.

The concept of *forbidden truth*, i.e. truth of a sort that *disguises* and *masks* the eudaemonic lie. Opposite: the *forbidden lie*, i.e. the lie which occurs in the territory where truth is permitted.

Symbol of the forbidden truth: *"fiat veritas, pereat mundus."*[41]

Symbol of the forbidden lie: *"fiat mendacium, pereat mundus."*[42]

The first thing which forbidden truths destroy is the individual who utters them. The last thing which forbidden lies destroy is the individual. In the first case, the individual sacrifices himself along with the world; in the second, the individual sacrifices the world to himself and to his existence.

Casuistry: Is it permissible to sacrifice mankind to truth?

1. It is indeed impossible! But would to God that mankind was able to perish of truth!

2. If that were possible, it would be a good death and a liberation from life.

3. Without unanimous *delusion*, no one can believe with certainty that he possesses truth: skepticism will not fail to make its appearance.

The question "Is it permissible to sacrifice mankind to a *delusion?*" must be answered in the negative. But in practice such a sacrifice does occur, since even the belief in truth is a delusion.

The belief in truth—or illusion. Elimination of all *eudaemonic* components, namely:

1. insofar as it is my *own* belief;

2. insofar as it was *discovered* by me;

3. insofar as it is a source of good opinions concerning me on the part of others—a source of fame popularity;

4. insofar as it is a domineering feeling of pleasure in resisting.[43]

---

the ascetic ideal is a question to which Nietzsche much later devoted some of the most brilliant passages of *GM*, III.

[40]I.e. a demand connected with the desire for human happiness.

[41]"Let there be truth, and let the world perish." (In *UBb*, 4 Nietzsche proposes a variant of this as the motto of historical study.)

[42]"Let there be lie, and let the world perish."

[43]*als herrisches Widerstands-Lustgefühl.*

After all of these components have been discounted, is it still possible to consider the expressing of truth purely as a *duty*? Analysis of the *belief in truth*: for all possession of truth is at bottom nothing but a belief that one possesses truth. The pathos, the feeling of duty, proceeds from *this belief*, not from the alleged truth. This belief in truth presupposes that the individual has an unconditional *power of knowledge*, as well as the conviction that no knowing being will ever have a greater power of knowledge; hence the belief in truth presupposes that the duty to speak the truth is binding upon all other knowing beings. The *relation* suspends[44] the pathos of belief, that is to say, the human limitation, with the skeptical supposition that we are perhaps all in error.

But how is *skepticism* possible? It appears to be the truly *ascetic* standpoint of thought. For it does not believe in belief and thereby destroys everything that prospers by means of belief.

But even skepticism contains a belief: the belief in logic. Therefore what is most extreme is the surrender of logic, the *credo quia absurdum est*:[45] doubt concerning reason and thereby its negation. How this occurs as a consequence of asceticism. No one can *live* within such a denial of reason, no more than within pure asceticism. This demonstrates that belief in logic and belief as such is necessary for life, and consequently, that the realm of thinking is eudaemonic. But of course when life and εὐδαιμονια[46] are counted as arguments, then the demand for lies stands out in bold relief. Skepticism turns against the forbidden truth. There then remains no foundation for pure truth in itself; the drive thereto is merely a disguised eudaemonistic drive.

Every natural process is fundamentally inexplicable to us. All we do in each case is to identify the setting in which the actual drama unfolds. Thus we speak of causality when we really see nothing but a succession of events. That this succession must always occur in a particular setting is a belief which is refuted with endless frequency.

Logic is merely slavery within the fetters of language. But language includes within itself an illogical element: metaphor, etc. The initial power[47] produces an equation between things that are unequal, and is thus an operation of the imagination. The existence of concepts, forms, etc. is based upon this.

---

[44]*aufhebt.*

[45]"I believe it because it is absurd": a famous saying attributed to Tertullian (c. 160-220).

[46]*eudaimonia:* happiness, prosperity, good fortune.

[47]I.e. the power of metaphor formation, which in section two above is considered as synonymous with that fundamental creative drive which makes us human.

"Laws of nature": nothing but relations to each other and to man.

Man as the finished and hardened *measure of things*. As soon as we think of man as something fluid and flexible, the strictness of the laws of nature ceases. The laws of sensation considered as the core of the laws of nature, the mechanics of motion. Natural science's belief in the external world and in the past.

The truest things in this world are love, religion, and art. The former sees through all dissimulations and masquerades; it penetrates to the core, to the suffering individual, suffers with him, pities him;[48] the latter, as practical love, consoles the sufferer for his sufferings by telling him about another world order and teaching him to disdain this one. These are the three *illogical* powers, which acknowledge themselves as such.

178

Does the unconditional agreement one encounters in logic and mathematics not point to a brain, to an organ which is an overseeing and abnormally derived reason? the soul? That which makes us human is something totally *subjective*. It is the accumulated ancestral estate in which everyone has a share.

179

Natural science is the process of becoming self-conscious of all one's ancestral possessions; it is the registry of the fixed and rigid laws of sensation.

180

There is no drive toward knowledge and truth, but merely a drive toward belief in truth. Pure knowledge has no drive.

181

All the drives are connected with pleasure and displeasure: there can be no drive toward truth, that is to say, a drive toward pure dispassionate truth totally apart from any results; for there pleasure and displeasure would cease, and there is no drive which does not anticipate pleasure in its satisfaction. The *pleasure of thinking* does not refer to any craving for truth. The pleasure which accompanies all sense perceptions lies in the

---

[48] . . . *sieht . . . hindurch auf den Kern, das leidende Individuum und leidet mit. Mit-leiden,* which is the ordinary German word for "pity," literally means "suffer with." Nietzsche, of course, made the most of this peculiarity of the German language in his later critique of the value of pity.

fact that they have been brought about by *inferences*. To this extent man
is always swimming in a sea of pleasure. But to what extent can the *logical
operation of inference provide pleasure*?

182

The element of impossibility in the virtues.
Man has not sprung from these higher drives; his whole nature gives
evidence of a more lax morality. With the purest morality man overleaps
his own nature.

183

Art. Necessary lies[49] and voluntary lies. However, lies of this latter
kind must in turn be traced back to a necessity.
All lies are necessary lies. The pleasure of lying is an artistic pleasure;
otherwise, only truth would possess any pleasure in itself. Artistic pleasure is the greatest kind of pleasure, because it speaks the truth quite
generally in the form of lies.
The concept of personality, and certainly the concept of moral freedom, are necessary illusions. Thus even our truth drives rest upon a
foundation of lies.
Truth within the system of *pessimism*: it would be better if thought did
not exist.

184

How is it that art is only possible as a lie?
When they are closed, my eyes perceive countless changing images
within themselves. Imagination produces these images, and I know that
they do not correspond to reality. Thus I believe in them only as images,
and not as realities.
Surfaces, forms.
Art includes the delight of awakening belief by means of surfaces. But
one is not really deceived! [If one were] then art would cease to be.
Art works through deception—yet one which does not deceive us?
What is the source of the pleasure we take in deception which we have
already tried, in an illusion which is always recognized as illusion?
Thus art treats *illusion as illusion*; therefore it does not wish to deceive;
it *is true*.[50]

---

[49]*Notlüge:* "official," or "white lies," i.e. lies thought to be required by the
exigencies of a particular situation.
[50]This and the previous section should be compared with some of Nietzsche's
later discussions of the profound truth contained in art (e.g. section 4 of the 1886
Preface to *FW*). The interpretation of passages like this one is a crucial test of any
adequate account of Nietzsche's theory of truth and knowledge.

Pure disinterested contemplation is possible only in regard to illusions which have been recognized as illusions, illusions which have no desire to entice us into belief and to this extent do not stimulate our wills at all.

Only a person who could contemplate the entire world *as an illusion* would be in a position to view it apart from desires and drives: the artist and the philosopher. Here instinctive drive comes to an end.

So long as one seeks the *truth* about the world he remains under the control of the drives. But he who desires *pleasure* rather than truth will desire the belief in truth, and consequently the pleasurable effects of this belief.

The world as an illusion: saint, artist, philosopher.[51]

185

All eudaemonic drives awaken belief in the truth of things, in the truth of the world. Thus science in its entirety is directed toward becoming and not toward being.

186

Plato as a prisoner of war, offered for sale in a slave market:[52] why indeed do men want philosophers? This may allow us to guess why they want truth.

187

I. Truth as a cloak for quite different impulses and drives.

II. The pathos of truth is based upon belief.

III. The drive to lie is fundamental.

IV. Truth cannot be recognized. Everything which is knowable is illusion. The significance of art as truthful illusion.

---

[51]This is, of course, a distinctly Schopenhauerian trinity, for according to Schopenhauer, it is the saint, the philosopher, and the artist who succeed, in varying degrees, in penetrating the veil of *maya* and in understanding how the will underlies the world of representations. This trinity occurs fairly often in Nietzsche's writings of this period, and usually in a favorable light. See e.g. *WP,* 9.

[52]This refers to an episode which is supposed to have occurred when Plato offended Dionysius, the Sicilian tyrant. He had Plato taken prisoner and turned him over to Pollis to sell him in the slave market at Aegina. He was, however, ransomed and returned to Athens. The story is told by Diogenes Laertius in his *Lives,* III, 19.

Philosophy In Hard Times

1873

V
Philosophy in Hard Times[1]

35
The Philosopher

Part 1. Medicinal morality.[2]
Part 2. Excessive thinking is ineffectual. Kleist.[3]
Part 3. The effect of philosophy, then and now.
Part 4. Popular philosophy (Plutarch, Montaigne).
Part 5. Schopenhauer.
Part 6. The priestly squabble between optimism and pessimism.
Part 7. Primitive times.
Part 8. Christianity and morality. Why [are they] not as strong as they used to be?
Part 9. Young teachers and educators as philosophers.
Part 10. Veneration of ethical naturalism.

Enormous operations: but they amount to nothing.

---

[1]The full German title is *Gedanken zu der Betrachtungen: Die Philosophie in Bedrängniss*. Of course this title was first assigned to this collection of notes by the editors of *GOA*, X. The first half of the title indicates that this material was intended for one of the projected "Untimely Meditations." The word *Bedrängniss* in the second part of the title means "distress," "affliction," or "tribulation," and I have translated it in this way when it appears in the notes themselves. However "Philosophy in Hard Times" seems to me to catch the provocative flavor of this title better than the more literal "Philosophy in Distress." As usual my translation is based upon the text printed in *MA*, VII, but I have reintroduced the convenient numbers assigned to the notes by the editors of *GOA*, X. (*PB* begins with number 35; numbers 1-34 in *GOA*, X are unused notes for *UBa* and *UBb*.)

[2]*Die medizinische Moral*. I.e. morality as a cure.

[3]Heinrich von Kleist (1777-1811), important German poet, dramatist, and novelist who committed suicide. The meaning of this reference is explained in *UBc*, 3, where Nietzsche mentions Kleist's despair concerning the consequences of Kantian philosophy.

The Tribulations of Philosophy

A. The demands made upon philosophy in the present time of need. Greater than ever.

B. The attack on philosophy greater than ever.

C. And philosophers weaker than ever.

    1. What the philosopher has been at various times.

    2. What he would have to be in our age.

    3. Portrait of the timely philosopher.

    4. The reason why he is unable to accomplish that which, according to number 2, he would have to accomplish: because there is no firm culture. The philosopher as hermit. Schopenhauer shows how nature makes an effort; nevertheless, it is insufficient.

36

To begin with: Symptoms of a decay of education[4] are everywhere, a complete extirpation: haste, the subsiding waters of religion, national conflicts, science fragmenting and disintegrating, the contemptible cash and pleasure economy of the educated classes, their lack of love and grandeur. It is clearer and clearer to me that the learned classes are in every respect a part of this movement. They become more thoughtless and loveless with every day. Everything, art as well as science, serves the approaching barbarity. Where should we turn? The great deluge of barbarity is at the door: Since we really have nothing whatsoever with which to defend ourselves and are all a part of this movement. What is to be done?[5]

The attempt to warn the actually present powers, to join with them, and to subdue those strata from which the danger of barbarism threatens while there is still time. But every alliance with the "educated" is to be rejected. That is the greatest enemy, for it hinders the physician and would disavow the disease.

37

We must seriously consider whether or not there still exist any foundations at all for the development of a culture. Is philosophy of any use as such a foundation? But it has *never* served this purpose.

My confidence in religion is boundlessly slight: after an enormous inundation one can see the waters subsiding.

---

[4]*Bildung.* See above, *P*, n. 79.

[5]Compare this striking paragraph with the similar description of the age in *UBc,* 4. Both passages are strongly reminiscent of some of Nietzsche's later descriptions of contemporary nihilism, e.g. those with which *WM* begins.

38
Toward a Description of the Present Age

I note a weariness *in regard to religion*: people have finally grown tired of and exhausted by the weighty symbols. All possible forms of Christian life have been tried: the strictest and the most lax, the most harmless and thoughtless and the most reflective. It is time to discover something new, or else one must fall back into the same old cycle over and over again. Of course it is difficult to emerge from the whirlpool after it has spun us around for a few thousand years.[6] Even mockery, cynicism, and hostility toward Christianity have run their course. What one sees is an icefield in warming weather: the ice is everywhere broken—dirty, lusterless, dotted with puddles of water, dangerous. A considerate and seemly abstention seems to me to be the only appropriate attitude: I thereby honor religion, though it is dying. Our job is to assuage and soothe, as in the case of the grievously, hopelessly ill. All we must protest against are bad, thoughtless, and bungling physicians (which is what most learned persons are). Christianity will very soon be ripe for critical history, i.e. for dissection.[7]

---

[6]Cf. *WM*, 30: "The time is coming when we will have to *pay* for having been *Christians* for two thousand years."

[7]It is instructive to compare the attitude toward Christianity evidenced in this passage and in these notebooks generally with Nietzsche's much better-known anti-Christian polemics. For the fact that Nietzsche's hostility towards Christianity *increased* over the years suggests that his eventual, very negative assessment of Christianity is based upon a more profound analysis of religion in general and Christianity in particular, rather than being in any sense a vestige of adolescent rebellion. The attitude toward religion and Christianity which Nietzsche expresses in his early published and unpublished writings is far more ambiguous than his later view. First of all, Nietzsche's early evaluations of Christianity as "one of the purest manifestations of the impulse toward culture and especially toward the ever renewed production of the saint" (*UBc*,6) were very much influenced by his rather superficial Schopenhauerianism. But apart from this, he values religion as a means of mastering the knowledge drive and facilitating cultural unity (*P*, 53) and as a source of criteria for measuring the world according to human ideals (*WWK*, 199). Christianity, in particular, is praised for the greater nobility of its moral ideas compared to those of antiquity (*UBc*, 3). However, Nietzsche was always aware that Christianity and religion were losing their power in the modern world and that an attempt to revivify religion was doomed to failure (*PB*, 37-8)—that, as he later put it, "God is dead." Finally, there are passages in the early writings which show that Nietzsche had already begun to augment his appreciation of religion and Christianity with an understanding of the profoundly world-denying character of the religious "valuation" of the world (e.g. *WP*, 158-61).

39

Wisdom independent of any knowledge of science.

The lower classes of unlearned men are now our only hope. The learned and cultivated classes must be abandoned, and along with them, the priests, who understand only these classes and who are themselves members of them. Men who still know what need is will also be aware of what wisdom can be for them. The greatest danger is the contamination of the unlearned classes by the yeast of modern education.

If a Luther were to appear now, he would rebel against the disgusting mentality of the propertied classes, against their stupidity and thoughtlessness: for they have not the least suspicion of the danger.[8]

Where should we seek the people?

Education grows worse every day because of increased haste.

40

It is all over with us if the working classes ever discover that they now can easily surpass us by means of education and virtue. But if this does not happen then all the more is it all over with us.

41

Education contradicts a man's nature.

What would happen if one allowed this nature to evolve by itself, that is to say, amid purely accidental influences? It would still be shaped,[9] but it would be shaped and formed *accidentally*, in conformity with the unlimited irrationality of nature: one fine specimen out of countlessly many. Innumerable seeds are usually destroyed, either by the discord of inner forces, or because of external influences. They are ruined either by inner discord (while the [discordant inner] forces grow stronger) or from without, because of insufficient oxygen, etc.[10]

42

Pericles speaks of the Athenian festivals, of beautiful and costly domestic furnishings, the daily sight of which chases away gloom. We Germans suffer greatly from this gloomy disposition. From the influx of

---

[8]In other words, if Luther were to appear now he would do precisely what Nietzsche is doing in the "Untimely Meditations"!

[9]*gebildet.* The word translated "education" here is, of course, *Bildung* (= "shaping" or "forming").

[10]The contrast between education and natural purposelessness occurs frequently in Nietzsche's early writings, especially in *UBc* where the image of the ruined seeds recurs (*UBc*, 7). This theme is closely related to his more general discussion of naturalness as something to be *attained*. See above, *P*, 104.

beauty and greatness, Schiller hoped for a secondary effect in the realm of moral elevation—a moral by-product of aesthetic elevation.[11] Conversely, Wagner hopes that the moral powers of the Germans will one day finally be turned to the realm of art and will demand seriousness and dignity in this realm as well. He takes art as strictly and as seriously as possible: by doing so he eventually hopes to experience its cheering effect.[12] Our situation is quite upside-down and unnatural: we place the greatest difficulties in the way of those men who want to cheer us up by means of art. Thus we demand moral brilliancy and greatness of character from them. Since the education of the most talented artists is made so difficult that they have to squander all their strength in this struggle,[13] we non-artists have on the other hand become very lax in the moral demands that we make upon ourselves. Considerations of comfort govern the principles and views of life. Thus by taking life easy, we lose the genuine need for art. When it is the case, as it was among the Athenians, that life is continually filled with duty, challenge, enterprise, and difficulty, then one knows how to esteem and to crave art, festivity, and education in general: i.e. one craves them in order to be cheered by them. And thus the moral weakness of the Germans is the chief reason why they have no culture. To be sure, they are extraordinary workers; everything is hurried. This hereditary diligence looks almost like a force of nature—in which their moral weakness proclaims itself!

43

Our age prefers vigorously one-sided people, because they at least continue to give evidence of vitality—and there must be strength before something can be cultivated.[14] If there is weakness then the effort is directed to conservation at any price; in any case nothing will be created in which one could take delight. The case is comparable to that of the consumptive who gasps for life and must always think of health, i.e. preservation. If an age has many natures of this sort, it will end up esteeming strength, even when it is coarse and hostile.

---

[11]This account of the moral effect of aesthetic elevation is provided by Schiller in his *Letters on the Aesthetic Education of Man* (1795).

[12]See *UBc*, 2 for a discussion of the way in which a work of art can "cheer us" and the difference between the falsely optimistic cheer of, for example, David Strauss and the genuine cheer associated with authors like Montaigne and Schopenhauer. The latter type of cheer always represents a victory over difficulty and has obvious parallels with Nietzsche's view of tragedy.

[13]Nietzsche makes the same indictment of the German culture of his times— viz., that it places stumbling blocks in the way of higher creative natures—in *UBa*, 4 and *ZB*, 4.

[14]*gebildet*.

44

One who becomes acquainted with the morality of antiquity will be surprised by the number of things which are now treated medically but which were in those days taken to be matters of morality. He will be amazed at how many disturbances of the soul, of the head, which were then turned over to philosophers, are now turned over to doctors—in particular, he will be amazed at the way in which alkalies or narcotics now serve to soothe the nerves. The ancients were much more moderate and more deliberately so in daily life. They knew how to abstain from and to deny themselves many things in order not to lose control over themselves. In every case their sayings concerning morality were based on the living example of those who had lived according to their sayings. I do not know what sort of distant and rare things modern moral philosophers are talking about: they take man to be a marvelous, spiritualistic being and seem to consider it indecent to deal with him in such a nakedly Greek manner and to speak of his many necessary, though base, needs. This bashfulness has gone so far that one might believe that modern man's body is merely an illusion.[15] I believe that the vegetarians, with their prescription to eat less and more simply, are of more use than all the new moral systems taken together: a little exaggeration here is of no importance. There is no doubt that the future educators of mankind will also prescribe a stricter diet. One hopes to make modern men healthy by means of air, sun, habitation, travel, etc.—including medical stimuli and toxins. But nothing which would be difficult for man seems to be ordered any longer. The maxim seems to be: be healthy and ill in an agreeable and comfortable manner. Yet it is just this incessant lack of moderation in *small* matters, this lack of self-discipline, which finally becomes evident as universal haste and *impotentia*.[16]

45

I am thinking of Diogenes' first night:[17] all the philosophy of antiquity was directed toward simplicity in living and taught a certain frugality—

---

[15]*nur noch einen Scheinleib.* The emphasis upon the philosophical importance of recognizing man as a *bodily* being is very characteristic of Nietzsche, but receives classical statement in *Z*, I, 3-4. This is one of the most *enduring* of Schopenhauer's influences upon Nietzsche's thought.

[16]"impotence."

[17]Diogenes of Sinope (423?-323 B.C.), the celebrated cynic philosopher. Presumably, Nietzsche is referring to the story of Diogenes' "conversion" to a simple, "philosophical" mode of living. According to the version related by Plutarch (*Moralia*, 77-8), there was an all-night public celebration in Athens and Diogenes was huddled in a corner feeling resentful for not being included in the feasting,

the most important remedy against all thoughts of social revolution. In this respect the few philosophical vegetarians have accomplished more for man than all the more recent philosophies. And so long as philosophers fail to muster the courage to seek a totally transformed regimen and to exhibit it by their own example, then they are of no consequence.[18]

46
The Tribulations of Philosophy

External: natural science, history (example: instinct become concept).
Internal: the courage to live a philosophy has broken down.

The other sciences (natural science, history) are only capable of explaining, not of commanding. And when they do command, they are only capable of referring to *utility*.[19] But every religion and every philosophy has in it somewhere a sublime *abnormality*, a conspicuous uselessness.[20] Is that all there is to it? Just like poetry, which is a type of nonsense.

A person's happiness is dependent upon the fact that somewhere there exists for him a truth which is *not debatable*: a crude example is the well-being of one's family considered as the highest motive for action; a more refined example is faith in the church, etc. If anything is said against it he will not listen at all.

Is the philosopher supposed to be the *brakeshoe* in the midst of this enormous agitation? Is he still able to be this?

The *mistrust* which strict scientific investigators have of every *deductive* system, *vide*. Bagehot.[21]

---

when he observed a mouse eating the crumbs of bread left from his own meal. When he realized that his crumbs were a feast for the mouse he rebuked himself for his earlier feelings and embarked upon his well-known project of simplifying his life in every possible way. (The same story is recounted by Aelian, in *Varia Historia*, XIII, 26.)

[18]Nietzsche attached considerable importance to questions of diet and health and was constantly making personal experiments with new regimens. The remarks about vegeterianism in this and the previous sections are reminiscent of some of the later views of Ludwig Feuerbach. (See also *M*, 119 and 203, and *EH*, II.) The call for a totally transformed regimen should be understood in the light of Nietzsche's interpretation of culture as an "improved *physis*." (See below, *PB*, 80.)

[19]*Nutzen*.

[20]Re. the "conspicuous uselessness" of philosophy, see *PW* and *UBc*, 7.

[21]Walter Bagehot (1826-77), English economist and writer. He was a champion of "scientific observation" of men, politics, and history: an approach pro-

47

There is a trick of holding oneself aloof from things solely by means of the words and names which one has conferred upon them: a foreign word frequently makes something which we are very well and intimately acquainted with foreign to us. When I say "wisdom" and "love of wisdom," I certainly feel something more familiar and powerful than when I say "philosophy." But as was said, the trick is sometimes precisely not to let things draw too near; for there often lies so much that is shameful in the familiar words. For who would not be ashamed to call himself a "wise man" or even merely "one who is becoming wise"! But a "philosopher"? This easily passes anyone's lips—nearly as easily as everyone uses the title "doctor," without ever thinking of the arrogant confession which this title contains: the confession that one is a "teacher."[22] Let us then assume that [the use of] the foreign word "philosopher" is prompted by shame and modesty? Or is it perhaps true that there exists no "love of truth" at all, and that the foreign designation—as in the case of the word "doctor"—is only intended to hide the lack of content, the emptiness of the concept? It is sometimes extraordinarily difficult to demonstrate something's presence, because it is so amalgamated, translated, and concealed, so diluted and weakened, whereas the names remain constant and are seducers as well. Is what we call "philosophy" today actually the love of wisdom? Does wisdom have any true friends at all today? Let us fearlessly replace the word "philosophy" with "love of wisdom": then it will become clear whether they are the same thing.

48

The philosopher is a philosopher first only for himself, and then for others. It is not possible to be a philosopher completely for oneself. For as a human being a person is related to other human beings, and if he is a philosopher, he must be a philosopher in this relationship. I mean that even if a philosopher strictly separates himself from others, even if he is a hermit, he thereby provides others with a lesson and an example and is

---

moted and exemplified in his widely translated and very influential book *Physics and Politics* (1869). Nietzsche quotes twice from this book in *UBc* (sections 3 and 8). The passage quoted in *UBc*, 8 is undoubtedly the one which prompts the present reference to Bagehot.

[22]Nietzsche is, of course, referring to the custom of calling academic Ph.D's "doctor," rather than "teacher." It may seem surprising to us that he would consider the former the more modest appelation, but this is because of the extremely high regard which Nietzsche had for the genuine teacher. In *WP*, 46 he says that "the highest and most exacting calling [is] that of the teacher and shaper of mankind." See also *ZB*, 3 and all of *UBc*.

a philosopher for them. Let him conduct himself however he pleases, as a philosopher he still has a side which faces other men.[23]

The philosopher's product is his *life* (which occupies the most important position, *before* his *works*). His life is his work of art, and every work of art is first turned toward the artist and then toward other men.

What effects does the philosopher have upon those who are not philosophers and upon other philosophers?

The state, society, religions, etc. could all ask: "What has philosophy done for us? What can it do for us today?" The same question could also be asked by culture.[24]

In general: the question concerning the cultural effects of philosophy.

Redefinition of culture: a single temperament and key composed of many originally hostile forces, which now enable a melody to be played.[25]

49

The most important feature of wisdom is that it keeps men from being ruled by the moment. Therefore, it is not "newsworthy."[26] The aim of wisdom is to enable man to face all the blows of fate with equal firmness, to arm him for all times. It is not very national.

50

Every philosophy must be able to do what I demand: it must be able to concentrate a man.[27] But no philosophy can do this now.

Two tasks: to defend the new against the old, and to connect the old with the new.

51

Philosophers have always strived for the soul's repose. Now [one

---

[23]This helps to explain Zarathustra's decision to "go down" among men at the end of section one of the preface to *Z*.

[24]*So auch die Kultur.* This might also mean "The same question could also be asked concerning culture"; however, the next sentence seems to favor the proposed reading.

[25]Re. Nietzsche's understanding of culture as stylistic unity cf. *P*, n. 35. The word "temperament" in this definition of culture is employed in the *musical* sense: the system of adjusting the intervals between the tones of an instrument of fixed intonation; tuning.

[26]*zeitungsgemäss.* This is Nietzsche's coinage: a pun on *Zeitung* ("newspaper") and *zeitgemäss* ("timely").

[27]*einen Menschen konzentrieren.* I.e. philosophy should give a man a focus which will provide him with direction and unity. Cf. *P*, 30.

strives] for unconditional unrest: so that the person is completely absorbed by his office, his trade. No philosopher will tolerate the tyranny of the press: Goethe allowed only weekly papers and pamphlets to be published.

52

Alas this brief span of time! We at least want to deal with it grandly and freely. We should not become slaves to the giver on account of such a small gift! It is most peculiar how constrained men's ideas and imaginations are: they never truly perceive life as a whole. They fear the words and opinions of their neighbors. Alas, only two more generations and then no one will any longer have those opinions which rule today and which seek to enslave you.

53

What effect has philosophy now had *upon philosophers?* They live just like all the other scholars, even like the politicians. Schopenhauer is of course an exception. They are not distinguished by a special manner of living.[28] They teach for the money. [For example:] the five thinkers of the *Augsburger Allgemeinen Zeitung.*[29] Consider the lives of their highest specimens, Kant and Schopenhauer: are these the lives of wise men? It remains [merely] science. They relate to their work as performers—thus Schopenhauer's lust for success. It is *comfortable* to be a philosopher, for no one makes any demands of philosophers. They occupy themselves with public *apices.*[30] Socrates would insist that one haul philosophy back down to man's level. Either there is no popular philosophy [today], or else it is of a wholly bad kind. Today's philosophers manifest all the vices of the age, above all its haste, and they rush into writing. They are not ashamed to teach, even when they are very young.

54

Many things only become durable when they have become weak. Until then they are threatened by the danger of a sudden and violent collapse. Health in old age becomes ever healthier. Christianity, for example, is now so diligently defended and will continue to be defended for a long time to come because it has become the most comfortable religion. Now it almost has the prospect of permanence, for it has won over to its side the most durable things in the world: human laziness and indolence.

---

[28]*Sie zeichen sich durch keine Sitten aus.*
[29]See below, *PB,* 64.
[30]The Plural of the Latin *apex.* Here it means "highest ornaments or honors," "crowns."

Similarly, philosophy is most highly esteemed and has the greatest number of champions precisely now, because now it no longer pesters people (indeed, many are supported by it), and no one hesitates to open his mouth and say whatever comes into his head. Vigorous, strong things run the danger of suddenly being ruined, cracked, and struck by lightning. The full-blooded man is seized by apoplexy. Particularly since becoming an historical discipline, philosophy has assured its own harmlessness and thereby its permanence.[31]

55

To turn *philosophy* purely into a science (after the manner of Trendelenburg)[32] means to throw in the towel.[33]

56

Philosophy's strongest tendency [has brought it to the point where it] is on the verge of being transformed into a relativistic system, approximately similar to πάντων μέτρον ἄνθρωπος.[34] With this, philosophy is finished; for nothing is more insufferable than such border patrolmen who know nothing except, "Here no further!" "One must not go there!" "This person has lost his way!" "We know nothing with absolute certainty!" etc. This is totally barren soil. Is philosophy finished then? When he was a very small boy, the Emperor Augustus was annoyed by the croaking of frogs at a villa. He commanded them to be silent, and, as Suetonius relates, they are said to have been quiet from then on.[35]

57

If contemporary philosophers were to dream up a *polis*, it would certainly be no *Platonopolis,* but rather an *Apragopolis* (city of loafers).[36]

---

[31]This brings to mind Nietzsche's deadly accurate suggested epitaph for academic philosophy: "It never hurt anybody." For Nietzsche's critique of the reduction of philosophy to the study of its own history, see *UBc,* 8 (which is also the source of this epitaph).

[32]Friedrich Adolf Trendelenburg (1802-72), Berlin philosopher and author of several important historical studies of Aristotle, Spinoza, and Kant. Today he is probably best remembered as the author of a penetrating logical critique of Hegel.

[33]*die Flinte in's Korn werfen.* Literally: "to throw the musket in the corn."

[34]"Man is the measure of all things": a famous Sophistic maxim attributed to Protagoras.

[35]Suetonius was a Roman historian of the first century A.D. The story of Ausustus and the frogs may be found in his *The Twelve Caesars,* II, 94.

[36]*Polis* is the Greek word for city (or city-state); hence, *Platonopolis* refers to the city sketched by Plato in the *Republic.*

58

The inclination toward mysticism among our philosophers is at the same time a flight from tangible ethics. In the mystical beyond there are no more demands, neither are there geniuses of goodness and transcendent sympathy. If imputability is shifted to the essence [i.e. the mystical beyond], then the ancient moral systems are meaningless.

Philosophers wish to flee from science, but it pursues them. One can see where their weakness lies: they no longer lead the way, because philosophy itself is merely science and is gradually turning into nothing but professional border patrolling.[37]

59

Sympathy for primitive conditions is certainly the favorite amusement of the age. What nonsense that a theory of evolution can be taught as if it were a religion! One is delighted that there is nothing fixed, eternal, and inviolable.

60

I hate that overleaping of this world which occurs when one condemns this world wholesale. Art and religion grow out of this. Oh, I understand this flight up and away into the repose of the One.[38]

How they lack love, these philosophers who are always thinking only of the chosen ones and have so little faith in their own wisdom! For like the sun, wisdom must shine for everyone, and a faint ray must be able to plunge down into the humblest soul.

A *possession* promised to man! Philosophy and religion as a longing for *property*.

---

[37]*Grenzwächterschaft.* What Nietzsche is alluding to here is the idea, sometimes thought to have originated with Kant's Critical Philosophy, that there is no distinctively philosophical knowledge, that the function of philosophy is merely to see that every seeker of knowledge plays by the "rules of the game"—which are usually thought to be the rules of mathematical natural science and formal logic. If anything, this conception of philosophy is more wide-spread today than it was in the 1870's.

[38]In fact, Nietzsche was only just beginning to "understand this flight into the repose of the One." He had, for example, not yet come to grasp the essential contribution of *revenge* to this flight.

61

I am unable to imagine Schopenhauer at a university. The students would run away from him and he himself would run away from his colleagues.

62

Schopenhauer is simple and honest. He seeks no catch phrases nor fig leaves; rather, he says to a world which finds itself stunted by dishonesty: "Behold, this is what man is!" What power all of his conceptions have: the will (which connects us with Augustine, Pascal, and the Indians), denial, the theory of the genius of the species! There is no agitation in his presentation, but only the clear depth of a lake which is calm, or upon which the waves surge gently while the sun shines above. He is coarse, like Luther. He is the strictest model of a German prose writer up until now. No one else has taken language—and the duty that it imposes—so seriously. One can, *e contrario*,[39] see how much dignity and greatness Schopenhauer has by observing his imitator, Hartmann (who is really his *opponent*).[40] His greatness is extraordinary: he has looked afresh into the heart of existence, without any scholarly diversions and without tiresomely dwelling upon and becoming entangled in philosophical scholasticism. The only attraction of studying the quasi-philosophers[41] who follow him is to see how they land at once in a situation in which scholarly pros and cons, brooding, and disputation are permitted, but nothing else is—where, above all, one is not permitted *to live*. Schopenhauer demolishes secularization, just as he demolishes the barbarizing power of science. He awakens the most enormous need, just as Socrates awakened a similar need. It has been forgotten what religion was, as well as the meaning that art had for life. Schopenhauer stands in contradiction to everything which now passes for culture; Plato stood in contradiction to everything that formerly *was* culture in Greece. He was ahead of his time.[42]

---

[39]"on the contrary."

[40]Eduard von Hartmann (1842-1906), extremely popular German philosopher during the late nineteenth century. Hartmann claimed to have synthesized Hegelian and Schopenhauerian metaphysics in his own system, presented in his best known book, *Die Philosophie des Unbewussten* (1869).

[41]*Viertelsphilosophen*, literally: "one-quarter-philosophers."

[42]In other words, Schopenhauer's opposition to culture was justified in a way that Plato's was not: for the culture of ancient Greece was a genuine culture, whereas the culture of nineteenth century Germany is a sham culture (see *UBa*). This remark sheds light upon the complex problem of Nietzsche's attitude toward Plato (just as the immediately preceding comparison between Socrates and Schopenhauer sheds light upon Nietzsche's attitude toward Socrates).

63

The word "philosophy," as it is applied to German scholars and authors, has recently caused me difficulty. It seems to me out of place. I wish that from now on one would avoid this word and speak straightforwardly and forcefully of nothing but *"intellectual housekeeping."*[43]
Nevertheless, I will tell how I hit upon this notion.

64

I have the presumption to speak to the "nation of thinkers"[44] on the subject of German intellectual housekeeping (in order to avoid saying "philosophy"). The foreigner will ask: "Where do these people [of this 'nation of thinkers'] dwell?" There, where dwell those five thinkers who were recently brought to our attention in an extraordinarily public place as the embodiment of present-day German philosophy: *Ulrici, Frohschammer, Huber, Carrière,* and *Fichte.*[45] True, it is easy to say something good concerning the last-named, for even Büchner,[46] that wicked he-man, has done so: "According to the younger Fichte all men have a guiding spirit from the day of their birth—only Herr Fichte has none."

---

[43]*Denkwirtschaft.* This is Nietzsche's coinage and might also be translated "intellectual economy."

[44]In former times "nation of thinkers" was a common sobriquet applied to Germany. Nietzsche often called attention to the fact that Germany had, in his view, ceased to be a "nation of thinkers" at the same time that it had become a "nation" (after the Franco-Prussian war). Cf. *MAMb,* 319.

[45]Johann Nepomuk Huber (1830-79), theologian and professor of philosophy at Munich. Huber was a leader of the "Old Catholic" party, an opponent of mechanistic world views and defender of the substantiality and freedom of spirit.

Immanuel Hermann von Fichte (1796-1879), son of the illustrious Johann Gottlieb Fichte. The "younger Fichte" expounded a highly eclectic idealist philosophy, with special emphasis upon theological issues and individual personality.

Jakob Froschammer (1821-93), priest and professor of philosophy at Munich. Froschammer claimed to have subordinated faith and revelation to idealist metaphysics.

Hermann Ulrici (1806-84), professor of philosophy at Halle. Ulrici was an idealist who criticized Hegel and proposed to erect his own metaphysics upon the foundation of natural science.

Moritz Carrière (1817-95), professor of philosophy at Munich. Carrière's philosophy, derived from Fichte and Hegel, but with a special emphasis upon aesthetic issues and individual personality, enjoyed considerable popular success during his own lifetime.

[46]Ludwig Büchner (1824-96), Darmstadt physician and author of *Kraft und Stoff* (1855). Büchner was one of the first and most influential exponents of modern philosophical materialism in Germany.

But this fanatic friend of matter would also concede to me that something phosphoresces in the remaining four men which does not do so in the younger Fichte. Thus one of the five thinkers lacks spirit, while the other four phosphoresce. Taken in a lump, they all philosophize, or rather, to speak quite plainly, they all engage in intellectual housekeeping. Yet foreigners are referred to these five so that they may recognize that we Germans are still the "nation of thinkers." With good reason Eduard von Hartmann was not included with the others; for Hartmann really possesses something that the younger Fichte would have liked. Indeed, by virtue of this something he has led the "nation of these five thinkers" around by the nose in a most unmannerly manner. As a result it appears that he no longer believes in the nation of thinkers and—what is worse—he apparently doesn't even believe any longer in the five intellectual housekeepers. But no one is pronounced blessed today unless he has faith in these five, and this is why Hartmann's name is missing from the list of the celebrated names of the German *Reich*: for he possesses spirit, and the *Reich* now belongs only to the poor in spirit.[47]

65

Is *Herr Ulrici* wise? Does he even linger in the train of wisdom as one of its admirers? No, sadly no, and I can't help it, after all, if he is not a wise man. Of course it would be so elevating to know that we Germans have a wise man in Halle, a wise man in Munich, etc. And it is with particular reluctance that we let Carrère slip away: Carrière, the discoverer of real-idealism and wooden iron.[48] If he had only been a little wiser, how happy we would have been to have accepted him completely. For it is a disgrace that the nation does not have even *one* wise man, but merely five intellectual housekeepers. And it is a disgrace that Eduard von Hartmann can reveal what he knows: that philosophers are at the moment lacking in Germany.

66

Result for our time: nothing comes of this situation. Why indeed? *They are not philosophers for themselves.*
"Physician heal thyself!" is what we must shout to them.

67

One must also note that a great deal of philosophy has already been inherited: indeed, men are almost saturated with it. Doesn't every conversation, every popular book, and every science contain within itself an

---

[47]A pun on Luke 6: 21. In German, the "kingdom of heaven" is also the *Reich*.
[48]In German this is a proverbial name for something contradictory.

applied philosophy? How countless as well are the actions which reveal that modern man has been bequeathed an infinite amount of philosophy. Even the men of Homer's time showed evidence of this inherited philosophy. I do not think that mankind would cease to philosophize, even if all the professorial chairs were permitted to go unfilled. What hasn't theology engulfed! I mean—ethics in its entirety! A world-view like the Christian one must gradually absorb all other ethics; it must combat them; it must win them over; and it must come to terms with them— indeed, if it is stronger and more persistent than they are, it must destroy them.

68

What are the effects of philosophy which one perceives among the philosophers' pupils, that is, among the *educated* people? We lack what is the best topic of conversation: refined ethics. *Rameau's Nephew.*[49]

Hypertrophy of the aesthetic viewpoint for considering greatness and life.[50]

69

The case is the same with the sciences as it is with trees: one can only cling to the stout trunk and the lower boughs and not to the most distant branches and extremities. Otherwise, one will fall, and in doing so one will, as a rule, break the lower boughs as well. The case is the same with philosophy: woe to the young who would cling to its *apices*.[51]

70

What reflections, what intimacy with the soul there was during the time of Diderot and Friedrich the Great! Even *Minna von Barnhelm*,[52] which is thoroughly grounded in the language of French society, is too refined for us today. We are raw naturalists.

I wish that someone would show the extent to which we are becoming perfect Jesuits in our glorification of ethical naturalism. Our love of what is natural is the love of aestheticians, not the love of moral philosophers.

---

[49]*Rameau's Nephew* is a famous work by Diderot, the French encyclopedist and *philosophe* (1713-84). It was translated into German by Goethe in 1805, and its wit and irony exercized a great influence upon German thought and letters in the early nineteenth century.

[50]This is one of Nietzsche's earliest indications of his growing dissatisfaction with the "artists' metaphysics" of *GT*—a dissatisfaction which only became explicit and public in Part IV of *MAMa*.

[51]"summits," "extremities."

[52]A hugely popular drama by Lessing (1767). *Minna von Barnhelm* is often cited as the first modern German stage comedy.

But there are no moral philosophers. One only has to recall Schleiermacher.[53]

71

The lack of acquaintance with Plutarch: Montaigne is better known. He is the most influential author (according to Smiles).[54] Would a new Plutarch even be possible? We all live according to a naturalistic ethic without style, and we all too easily consider the figures of antiquity declamatory.

Christianity demonstrated better form, but most [of its followers] have relapsed. It is now so difficult to return to the simplicity of the ancients.[55]

The Jesuits weakened and softened the demands of Christianity in order further to assert its power. Protestantism commenced with the enlightenment of the *adiaphora*[56] on a large scale.

Gratian[57] displays a wisdom and prudence in the experiences of life to which nothing today is comparable. We are undoubtedly the microscopists of the real. Our novelists (Balzac, Dickens) know how to observe, yet no one knows how to demand and to explain.

72

What is lacking is ethical *renown*; the ability to recognize it is definitely lacking. The "theory of force" strenuously opposes this assertion. For example, let someone say "Hegel is a poor stylist," and another will reply, "but he is so rich in original and down to earth expressions." But this only concerns the material. The stylist does not reveal himself by having

---

[53]Friedrich Daniel Ernst Schleiermacher (1768-1834), philosopher and professor of theology at Berlin. Schleiermacher is among the most influential modern protestant theologians and is always mentioned by Nietzsche with contempt. For further discussion of what Nietzsche means by "ethical naturalism" in the present context, see *UBc*, 2.

[54]Samuel Smiles (1812-1904), popular Scottish biographer and author of the widely translated *Self-Help*. Montaigne and Plutarch were, of course, always two of Nietzsche's own favorite authors.

[55]This thought is developed more fully in *UBc*, 2: "Through the elevation of its ideals Christianity surpassed the moral systems of antiquity and the naturalness which prevailed in such systems to such an extent that one became apathetic toward and disgusted by this naturalness. Afterwards however, when one still recognized the better and the higher, but was no longer capable of attaining them, one was no longer able to return to the good and the high, that is to the virtue of antiquity, no matter how much one wished to be able to do so."

[56]A word derived from the Greek for "not different," "not individual." The *adiaphora* are those who are undistinguished in any way.

[57]Flavius Gratianus Augustus (359-83), emperor of Rome, 375-383.

a beautiful piece of marble, but rather by the manner in which he carves it. The case is the same regarding matters of ethics.

73

In contrast with the ancients, *Montaigne* is also an ethical naturalist—though he is a boundlessly rich and thoughtful one. We are thoughtless naturalists, with full awareness of the fact.

74

Defectively developed *logic*! It is stunted by historical study. Even Zöllner complains: Praise of Spir and the English.[58]

---

[58]C.F. Zöllner (1836-82), one of the founders of astrophysics and an important and controversial writer on a variety of scientific subjects. Zöllner scandalized his professional colleagues with his book *Über die Natur der Kometen,* in which he argued that sensation extends throughout all of matter, and that the primary sensations are those of pleasure and displeasure. Zöllner also criticized his colleagues in the natural sciences for a failure to read and understand the works of their predecessors, for their unnecessary reduplication of experiments and compilation of useless data, for their failure to grow in logical acumen, and for their "popularizations" of scientific ideas. He also called attention to the importance of pleasure and displeasure as motives within science itself.

Afrikan Spir (1837-90), a Russian philosopher who emigrated to Germany in 1867, defended a theory of knowledge strongly influenced by the English empiricists (whom he often praises for their clear and logical way of doing philosophy). In *Denken und Wirklichkeit* (1873), Spir argued that knowledge is not obtainable, that the world is an illusion, and that "reality" is constituted from sensations and feelings. He tried to develop his entire system from nothing but immediately given sensations and the principle of identity.

Anni Anders has disucssed Nietzsche's acquaintance with the writings of Zöllner and Spir in great detail (Schlechta/Anders, pp. 118-27). Nietzsche first read Zöllner's book in November of 1872 and reread it several times thereafter. The influence of Zöllner may be detected in Nietzsche's critique of "scientific laborers" (e.g. in *UBb*) and, more specifically, in some of the remarks about the nature of matter and the sensations of pleasure and displeasure which can be found in *P.*

The influence of Spir (whose book Nietzsche first read immediately after it was first published—at a time when Spir was a quite unknown figure—and many times thereafter) was more important. Anders thinks that Spir remained the epistemologist whom Nietzsche valued most highly, even after he had moved beyond many of Spir's views, and attributes many of Nietzsche's advances in his theory of knowledge between the winter of 1872 and the summer of 1873 (i.e. between *P* and *WL*) to the influence of his reading of Spir. For example, the new stress on the relevance of the problem of language to the problem of truth shows Spir's influence on Nietzsche's thinking.

75

Professors of philosophy no longer practice skills, not even the art of debate. As it is taught, logic is quite useless. But after all, the teachers are much too young to be anything more than scientific trainees. How could they be expected to educate anyone toward wisdom?

76

Virtue is an outmoded word. One only has to think of your secondary school teachers when they try to play the role of ethical educators![59]

77

There are two maxims concerning education: First, one should quickly get to know an individual's strength and thereafter direct everything toward developing it at the expense of all the remaining secondary strengths.[60] Education thus becomes the guiding of that [primary] strength. Second, one should bring *all* existing strengths into play and should place them in harmonious relation with each other: thus the secondary strengths—those that are in need of transfusion—should be strengthened, and those that are strong should be weakened. Now where is one supposed to find a criterion [for choosing between these two maxims]?[61] The happiness of the individual? The profit which he renders the community? One-sided[62] individuals are more useful; harmonious ones are happier. At once the question arises anew: Should a great community, a state, or a people especially cultivate one-sided strength or many strengths? In the case of a state which chooses to cultivate one strength, a one-sided development of the individual will be tolerated only when the particular[62] qualities are included within the goal *of the state*, i.e. such a state will only educate a *portion* of the individuals in accordance with their particular strength. In the case of the others it will no longer look for strengths and weaknesses, but rather will look to

---

[59]These critical remarks about the "teachers" of the day and how they differ from wise men and ethical educators were developed by Nietzsche at great length in the lectures on modern education which he gave in the spring of 1872 (*ZB*) and are repeated in *UBc*.

[60]Cf. *MAMa*, 242, where Nietzsche distinguishes three matters to which educators must pay attention: first, how much energy has been inherited; second, how new energy might be aroused; third, how the individual can adapt to the manifold claims of culture without destroying his own personality.

[61]In *UBc*, 2 Nietzsche repeats these two maxims and concludes that they are not really contraries at all. They are, instead, found to be complementary: the first is the demand that man shall have a center; the second, that he shall have a periphery.

[62]*partiellen.*

see that the [state's] particular quality [i.e. the quality favored by the state]—be it originally ever so weak—is in any event *developed*. If what the state desires [for itself] is a harmony, it can still accomplish this in two ways: either by means of the harmonious development of all the individuals or by means of a harmony of one-sidedly developed individuals. In this latter case, the state wishes to produce a single temperament from powerful and openly antagonistic forces. This means that the state must restrain the one-sided exclusivity of those who are strong: it must restrain them from hostility toward one another and from actual destruction. It must unite them all through a common *goal* (church, national prosperity, etc.).

Athens is an example of the latter type of state; *Sparta* is an example of the former type. The first type is much more difficult and artificial. It is most exposed to degeneration. It requires a supervising *physician*.

In our age everything is confused and unclear. The modern state becomes more and more like Sparta. It might happen that the greatest and noblest forces will dry up and die away owing to atrophy and transfusion. For I observe that the sciences and philosophy itself are preparing the way for precisely such an occurrence. They are no longer bulwarks, because they are no longer allowed to have their own *goal*, i.e. because no commonwealth embodies their essence in its goal. Thus what is needed is the foundation of a *cultural state*, in opposition to the false ones which now go by this name and which would serve as a sort of *refugium*[63] of culture.

78

In the state the individual's happiness is subordinated to the general welfare: what does this mean? Not that the minorities are utilized for the welfare of the majorities, but rather that individuals are subordinated to the welfare of the *highest individuals*, to the welfare of the highest specimens. The highest individuals are the creative persons—be they morally the best, or else useful in some larger sense. Thus they are the purest models and are the improvers of mankind. The goal of the commonwealth is not the existence of a state at any price, but rather its goal is for the highest specimens to be able to live and create within it. This is also the goal that underlies the foundation of states, except that they often had a false opinion concerning who the highest specimens were: often conquerors, dynasties, etc. If the state's existence is no longer to be preserved in such a way that great individuals can live within it, what will then arise is the terrifying state filled with misery, the pirate state in which the *strongest* individuals take the place of the *best*. It is not the

---

[63]"refuge," or "place of refuge."

state's task that the greatest possible number of people live well and ethically within it; numbers do not matter. Instead, the task of the state is to make it generally possible for one to live well and beautifully therein. Its task is to furnish the basis of a *culture*. In short, a nobler humanity is the goal of the state. Its goal lies outside of itself. The state is a means.[64]

What is lacking today is anything which can unite all the one-sided forces: and so we observe that everything is hostile to everything else and that all the noble forces are engaged in a mutually destructive war of annihilation. Philosophy is an example of this: it *destroys*, because there is nothing to keep it within boundaries. The philosopher has become a being who is *harmful to the community*. He annihilates happiness, virtue, culture, and finally himself.

Formerly, in the role of *cultural physician*, philosophy had to be in alliance with the cohesive forces.

79

Concise writing. Winckelmann[65] said that it is difficult to write concisely and not a project for everyone. For one can less readily be taken at his word in a fuller type of writing. He who wrote to someone "I did not have enough time to make this letter briefer" understood what the concise style of writing demands.

Without any pathos. Almost no periods. No questions. Few images. Everything very terse. Peaceful. No irony. No climax. Stress upon the logical element, yet very concise.[66]

What is wisdom? In opposition to science. (Preface)

---

[64]Taken together, this and the previous section provide one of the more succinct statements of Nietzsche's view of politics and the state. Points particularly worthy of emphasis are: (1) the interpretation of the state as a means toward cultural and aesthetic ends; (2) the utopian, almost Platonic character of Nietzsche's idea of an "aristocracy of creative geniuses"; (3) the relation of the "great man" to nature and to other men—his existence justifies theirs. Most of these ideas are developed at greater length in the very important unpublished essay of 1871 on the Greek state (*GS*). They are hinted at in *UBc*, 6, but only receive explicit public presentation in *MAMa*, 439.

[65]Johann Joachim Winckelmann (1717-68), the distinguished and influential German archeologist and historian of ancient art.

[66]These notes show how deliberately Nietzsche sought to shake off the Wagnerian excesses of his first public prose style and to cultivate a style and a voice of his own—one more appropriate to the new way of thinking being worked out in the notebooks. The ideal described in this last passage is brilliantly realized in the series of five books published between *UBd* and *Z*.

Is there any striving for wisdom today? No! (Main Section)
Is a striving toward wisdom needed? Is it a necessity?
No. But it will perhaps soon be a necessity once again. When? Description. (Epilog)

80

The Tribulations of Philosophy

A. *The misery of the age. The demands upon philosophers.*

1. Haste.
2. No building for eternity (modern houses).[67]
3. Religion which has become stale.
4. Medicinal morality. Naturalism.
5. Weakening of logic (by means of history and natural science).
6. Lack of educators.
7. The uselessness and dangerous *complexity* of requirements and duties.
8. Volcanic ground.

B. *The attacks on philosophy.*

1. The mistrust of the more rigorous methods.
2. History destroys the validity of the systems.
3. The church has a monopoly upon popular influence.
4. The state demands that one live in the moment.

C. *Portrait of the philosophers.*

1. Stale. Excessive thinking is ineffectual (Kleist)
2. They discover the point where the scholar begins.
3. The priestly squabble.
4. Primitive times.
5. Lack of any models of ethical greatness.
6. The conflict between lie and thought is suffered everywhere.
7. Defective logic.
8. The absurd education of university students.
9. The life and genesis of philosophers.

---

[67]Cf. Nietzsche's remarks on modern houses in *UBc*, 1 and on the "architecture for knowing" in *FW*, 280.

D. *Can philosophy serve as the foundation of a culture?* Yes, but now no longer: it is much too refined and sharpened. One can no longer rely upon it. In fact philosophy has permitted itself to be drawn into the current of modern education. It in no way controls this education. In the best cases, philosophy has become science (Trendelenburg). Portrait of Schopenhauer: the contrast between his eudaimonean practice (the worldly wisdom of an overripe age, like that of the Spaniards) and his recently noticed, more profound philosophy. He condemns the present from two sides. Meanwhile I see no other possibility than to adopt Schopenhauer's worldly wisdom for practical matters, and for deeper needs to adopt [the more profound] wisdom. Whoever does not want to live in this contradiction must fight for an improved *physis*[68] (culture).

---

[68]*Physis* is the Greek word for "nature." It is often used in German with the sense of "natural constitution," "physiology," or "physique." Nietzsche's definition of culture as an "improved" or "transfigured" *physis* reoccurs in both *UBb*, 10 and *UBc*, 3. This definition is of fundamental importance, both for an understanding of Nietzsche's theory of culture (it must be based in nature) and of man (he is the being whose nature it is to "cultivate" or "improve" his own nature). What this cultivation amounts to is, in part anyway, the *unification* of the personality. Therefore the definition of culture as "improved *physis*" is closely related to culture as the "unifying mastery" of the drives (*P*, 46). (It is noteworthy that Nietzsche is indebted to Goethe for the idea behind *both* of these definitions. See *PtZG*, 1.)

The Struggle Between Science and Wisdom

1875

VI
The Struggle Between Science and Wisdom[1]

[[*Imitation* of antiquity.

The means for such imitation, philology, makes imitation impossible for the philologist. Knowledge without ability.[2]

Hence: philology has either become totally historical or else has been destroyed (Schiller).

Even historical knowledge of antiquity is brought about by means of reproduction and imitation.

Goethean Hellenism (the artistic σωφροσύνη[3] of the Greeks transferred to moral men).]]

[[Greek antiquity provides the classical set of examples for the interpretation of our entire culture and its development. It is a means *for understanding ourselves*, a means for regulating our age—and thereby a means for overcoming it.

The pessimistic foundation of our culture.]]

[[Simply to acknowledge the fact: *Socrates* is so close to me that I am almost continually fighting with him.]][4]

---

[1]*Wissenschaft und Weisheit im Kampfe* is the only one of the longer selections in this volume for which the original notebook has been published in *WKG*. I have tried to provide a text which will permit the reader to compare the original with the version produced by the editors of *GOA* and reprinted in later editions of Nietzsche's works. I have included within double brackets all of the passages which were not included in previous, edited versions of *WWK*. I have also arranged the notes in the order they appear in Nietzsche's notebook (an order which varies slightly from the published arrangement). All significant variations between the texts are noted. Finally, the section numbers are those which were added by the editors of *GOA*.

[2]*Kennen ohne können.* I.e. the requirements of the discipline are such that the men who are professionally employed in seeking knowledge concerning classical antiquity have become almost the polar opposites of the men of antiquity. Cf. Nietzsche's exploration of this situation in *WP*.

[3]"moderation."

[4]In *MA* this note is placed at the end of section 188. (Again, except for the section numbers the text of *MA* is identical to the text in *GOA*.)

188

The struggle between science and wisdom.[5]

Science (n.b. *before* it has become a habit and an instinct) originates:

1. when the gods are not considered to be good. The great advantage of being able to recognize something as *fixed*;
2. when egoism pushes individuals in certain enterprises, e.g. navigation, to seek their own gain by means of science;
3. as something for aristocratic people of leisure. Curiosity.
4. when the individual wants a more solid foundation amidst the turbulent flux of popular opinions.

What distinguishes this scientific drive from the general drive to learn or undertake anything whatsoever? Only its lower degree of egoism or the broader reach of the same. *In the first case,* the self is lost in the things; *in the second,* there is a selfishness which extends beyond the individual.

Wisdom shows itself:

1. in illogical generalizing and rushing toward final ends,
2. in the bearing which these results have upon life,
3. in the unconditional importance which one ascribes to his soul: "One thing is needful."

Socraticism is: *First,* wisdom in taking the soul seriously.

Second, science as fear and hatred of illogical generalization.

Third, something unique because of its demand for conscious and logically correct conduct. This generates difficulties for science and for ethical life.

[[The Struggle between Science and Wisdom, exhibited in the ancient Greek philosophers.]]

189

1. How does the world look through the eyes of these early Greeks?[6]
2. How do they behave toward those who are not philosophers?

---

[5]Though adopted as a title by earlier editors of these notes, a more accurate and informative title is the one which appears a few sections below: "The struggle between Science and Wisdom, exhibited in the ancient Greek philosophers."

[6]*Wie zeigt sich in diesen älteren Griechen die Welt gefärbt.* Literally: "In what colors does the world appear in these early Greeks."

3. Much depends upon their *persons*: the point of my consideration of their teachings is to divine their persons.[7]

4. The struggle between science and wisdom as reflected in their work.

5. Ironic supplementary clause: "all is false." How man clings to a beam.

There is also an *ironic* and *mournful* way to tell this story. In any case, I wish to avoid the even, serious tone.

At a moment when truth was *closest,* Socrates *upset everything*: that is especially *ironic*.

To depict everything against the background of myth. The boundless insecurity and fluctuating character of this. One yearns for something more secure.

The life of the Greeks is illuminated only in those places where the ray of myth falls upon it. Otherwise it is dark. The philosophers now deprive themselves of myths; how then do they endure this darkness?[8]

The individual who wishes to rely *upon himself* requires *ultimate knowledge,* philosophy. Other men require a science which is slowly augmented.

[[Or rather, what is necessary is the belief that one possesses such ultimate knowledge. Never again will there be such a degree of confidence in one's own knowledge as was possessed by those early Greeks. But they were not yet confronted with the difficulty and danger of knowing. They had a sturdy belief in themselves, with which they overcame their neighbors and predecessors. The happiness of possessing truth was never greater, but likewise neither was harshness, arrogance, and *tyranny*. Every Greek was a tyrant in his private wishes, and generally speaking anyone at all who could be a tyrant was one—with the possible exception of Solon, to judge by his own poems.[9]]]

---

[7]Compare with the following passage from the Preface to *PtZG,* in which Nietzsche explains the relation he finds between the systems and the personalities of the Greek philosophers:

"On the other hand, whoever rejoices in great men will also rejoice in such systems; even if they are also totally erroneous, they nevertheless have within themselves one irrefutable point: personal mood and color. One can use such a system to obtain a portrait of the philosopher, just as one can infer something about a soil from the plants which grow in it. *This* way of living and of viewing human matters in any case existed and is therefore possible."

[8]Except for the final clause, this paragraph is almost identical to the opening words of *MAMa,* 261.

[9]Cf. the similar passage in *MAMa,* 261.

Even the independence is only apparent: each person is finally linked with his predecessors. Phantasms linked with phantasms. It is strange to take everything so seriously.

Ancient philosophy in its entirety is a strange *labyrinthian abberation*[10] of reason. The proper note to strike is that of dreams and fairy tales.

[[*Aristotle's aesthetic judgment.*
      against Empedocles.
      regarding tragedy.
      Demosthenes.
      Thucydides.
      plastic art.
      music.]]

190

Greek *music* and *philosophy* developed side by side. They are comparable insofar as they both testify to the Hellenic nature. Of course we are acquainted with the music only from its percipitation into lyric.

Empedocles—tragedy   sacred monody
Heraclitus—Archilochus[11]   Xenophanes is *sympotisch*[12]
Democritus—Anacreon[13]
Pythagoras—Pindar[14]
Anaxagoras—Simonides[15]

All comparison of persons is distorted and stupid.

[[Compared to Greek life, *philosophies* are *shades from the underworld.* They reflect Greek life, but as if through a cloud of smoke.

---

[10]*Irrgartengang:* Nietzsche's coinage, from *Irrgang* ("mental abberation") and *Irrgarten* ("labyrinth").

[11]Greek lyric poet of the seventh or eighth century B.C., Archilocus is often called the inventor of iambic poetry. In section 5 of *GT* Nietzsche treats him as the first lyric poet.

[12]There is no such word in German. Perhaps this is Nietzsche's coinage based upon the Greek συμπότης ("drinking companion," hence "convivial," "jolly")?

[13]Greek lyricist of the sixth century B.C. Anacreon was court poet to the tyrant Polycrates of Samos and later a member of the poetic circle which gathered around Hipparchus in Athens.

[14]Most eminent of the Greek lyricists (c. 522-443). Pindar is celebrated for his odes.

[15]Greek lyricist (c. 556-469). Simonides of Ceos was a member of the literary circle surrounding Hipparchus. He was an extremely popular and influential poet, widely celebrated for his great wisdom. It is Simonides' definition of justice which is defended by Polemarchus in Plato's *Republic.*

One must stay on the heels of such men until they are re-created by a poet. The complimentary imaginations of many persons must be at work here.

Such men are too rare for us to let them get away. How little can be gained by criticizing, turning over, and shaking every fragment!

Introduction.	First Chapter.	Comparison of the earlier Greek philosophers with the sectarian philosophers who followed Socrates.
	Second Chapter.	The temporal circumstances of the early philosophers.
Narration:]]		

191

So much depends upon the development of Greek culture, since our entire occidental world received its original impulse therefrom. Destiny has ordained that the more recent and decadent Hellenism has had the greatest historical power. For this reason the older Hellenism was always falsely judged. One must be minutely acquainted with the more recent type in order to distinguish it from the older type.

There are still very many possibilities which have not yet been discovered, because the Greeks did not discover them. Other possibilities were discovered by the Greeks and then later *covered up* again.[16]

192

These philosophers demonstrate *the dangers which were comprised within Greek culture*:

Myth, taken as idleness of thought	—opposed to this, cold abstractions and strict science. Democritus.
The flabby coziness of life	—opposed to this, moderation; the strict ascetic views of Pythagoras, Empedocles, and Anaximander.
Cruelty in battle and in strife	—opposed to this, Empedocles with his reform of the sacrifices.[17]

---

[16]This note provides one of Nietzsche's clearer explanations of the *urgency* which informs all of his studies of Pre-Platonic philosophy. See above, *P*, n. 3 and cf. *MAMa*, 261.

[17]Several of Empedocles' surviving fragments are concerned with sacrificial reform, specifically they condemn meat eating and blood sacrifice (fragments 128, 135-7). See also the story of how Empedocles constructed a surrogate "sacrificial ox" of barley and honey, which may be found in Diogenes Laertius' *Lives*, VIII, 53.

Lies and deceit	—opposed to this, enthusiasm for truth, no matter what the consequence.
Pliancy and excessive sociability	—opposed to this, the pride and solitude of Heraclitus.

These philosophers indicate the vitality of a culture which produces its own correctives.[18]

How did this age perish? Unnaturally.[19] Where then are the seeds of corruption?

The flight from the world by the best people was a great misfortune. Beginning with Socrates, the individual all at once began to take himself too seriously.

In the case of Athens, the *plague* was added to this.

Then they were *destroyed* by the *Persian wars*. The danger was too great, and the victory was too extraordinary.

The death of great musical lyric poetry and of philosophy.

[[*Socrates* is the *revenge for Thersites*: the splendid Achilles slew the ugly man of the people, Thersites, out of anger over the latter's words concerning the death of Pentesilia.[20] The ugly man of the people, Socrates, slew the authority of splendid myth in Greece.]]

193

Early Greek philosophy is the philosophy of *statesmen*. How pitiful our statesmen are! Moreover, this is what best distinguishes the Pre-Socratics from the Post-Socratics.

The Pre-Socratics did not share the Post-Socratics' "detestable pretension to happiness." Everything does not yet revolve around the condition of their souls, for this is something that one does not think about without danger. Later Apollo's γνῶθι σαυτόν[21] was misunderstood.

Furthermore, these early Greeks did not *chatter* and *revile* so much; neither did they *write* so much.

---

[18]See above, *P*, n. 9.

[19]This refers to the view, widespread in the early nineteenth century, that Greek history and culture offer a paradigm of "natural development." See below, 197, and also *MAMa*, 261.

[20]Thersites was one of the Greek beseigers of Troy, who is described by Homer as deformed in mind and body. Thersites' ridicule of Achilles' grief over the death of Pethesilia angered Achilles, who then killed Thersites. See *Iliad*, II, 212ff.

[21]"Know thyself!"

Enfeebled Hellenism became Romanized, coarsened, and decorative, and then, as cultural window dressing, was accepted as an ally by enfeebled Christianity and was forcibly disseminated among uncivilized peoples: this is the history of occidental culture. The clever trick of uniting what is Greek with what is priestly has been accomplished.[22]

I wish to combine Schopenhauer, Wagner, and early Hellenism: that will provide a glimpse of a splendid culture.

Comparison of the earlier philosophy with the Post-Socratic kind.

1. The earlier kind is related to *art*. Its solution to the riddle of the universe was frequently inspired by art. The spirit of music and of the plastic arts.

2. The earlier kind is *not* the negation of the *other* life, but *grows* from it like a rare blossom. It utters its secret. (Theory and practice.)

3. The earlier kind is *not* so *individualistic* nor *eudaemonistic*: it lacks the detestable pretension to happiness.

4. Even in their lives these early philosophers possess higher wisdom and not merely cold, prudent rectitude. They picture life in a richer and more complex way. The Socratics simplify things and make them banal.

The three-part history of *dithyramb*:

1. the dithyrambs of Arion,[23] from which the older tragedy proceeds;
2. The agonistic dithyrambs of the state, parallel to domesticated tragedy;
3. the brilliantly chaotic mimetic dithyrambs.

With the Greeks it is frequently the case that an *older* form is the *higher* one, for example, in the cases of *dithyramb* and *tragedy*. The danger for the Greeks lay in *virtuosity* in all genres. With Socrates the virtuosos of living begin. Socrates, the newer dithyramb, the newer tragedy, *the invention of the rhetorician.*

The rhetorician is a Greek invention of later times! They invented "form in itself" (and also the philosopher for it).

How is Plato's struggle against rhetoric to be understood? He *envied* its influence.

Early Hellenism *revealed its strengths in its succession of philosophers.* This

---

[22]For a further development of this thought, see *WP*, 42.

[23]A semi-legendary poet of the seventh century B.C., Arion is traditionally credited with the invention of dithyrambic poetry.

revelation *comes to an end* with Socrates, who sought *to engender himself* and reject all tradition.

My general task: to show how life, philosophy, and art can have a more profound and congenial relationship to each other, in such a way that philosophy is not superficial and the life of the philosopher does not become mendacious.

It is a splendid thing that the ancient philosophers were able to live so freely *without thereby turning into fools and virtuosos.* The freedom of the individual was immeasurably great.

The false opposition between *vita practica* and *vita contemplativa*[24] is something Asiatic. The Greeks understood the matter better.

194

One can describe these early philosophers as men who experienced the Greek atmosphere and customs as a *constraint* and a *barrier*, and thus they can be described as self-liberators (Heraclitus' struggle against Homer and Hesiod, Pythagoras' struggle against secularization, the struggle of them all, but especially of Democritus, against myth). In comparison with the Greek artists, and indeed, even in comparison with the statesmen, these philosophers lack something in their nature.

I conceive of them as the *forerunners of a reformation of the Greeks,* but not as the forerunners of Socrates. On the contrary, their reformation never occurred; it remained sectarian with Pythagoras. The spirit of reformation was sustained by a single phenomenon[25]—the *development* of *tragedy. Empedocles* is the *unsuccessful reformer;* when he failed, all that remained was Socrates. Aristotle's hostility toward Empedocles is therefore quite comprehensible.

Empedocles–republic—transformation of life—popular reform— attempted with the aid of the great Hellenic festivals.

Tragedy likewise was a means. Pindar?

They did not find their philosopher and reformer. Compare Plato, who was diverted by Socrates. Attempted characterization of Plato *apart from* Socrates: tragedy—profound view of love—pure nature—no fanatical renunciation. The Greeks were evidently *on the point* of discovering a *type of man still higher* than any previous type when they were interrupted by the snip of the shears. The *tragic age* of the Greeks: that is where the matter rests.[26]

---

[24]"practical life" and "life of contemplation."

[25]*eine Gruppe von Erscheinungen.*

[26]In *FW,* 149 Nietzsche later returned to the theme of the reformation which failed to occur in Greece. But on this occasion he gives a very different and more positive interpretation to this failure: it is taken to be a sign of the maturity and health of Greek civilization that it proved itself too heterogeneous for any single

1. Portrait of the Greeks, with reference to their dangers and depravities.
2. Counter-portrait of the tragic tendency which opposed the above. The new interpretation of myth.
3. First steps toward the reformers. Attempts to acquire a world picture.[27]
4. Socrates decided the issue. *Plato was diverted.*

195

Passion in the works of Mimnermus:[28] hatred of what is *old*.

Pindar's deep melancholy: human life is illuminated only when a ray falls upon it from above.

The tragic element in tragedy is the attempt to understand the world *on the basis of suffering.*

Thales—the unmythical.

Anaximander—natural extinction and generation [interpreted] morally in terms of guilt and punishment.

Heraclitus—lawfulness and justice in the world.

Parmenides—the other world behind this one; this world as a problem.

Anaxagoras—the architect of the universe.

Empedocles—blind love and blind hatred; the profound irrationality within the most rational things in the world.

Democritus—the world is totally lacking in reason and instinctive drive; it has been all shaken together. All gods and myths are superfluous.

Socrates: there remains nothing for me but me myself; anxiety concerning oneself becomes the soul of philosophy.

Plato's attempt to think everything through to the end and to be the redeemer.

These persons are to be depicted in the way that I have depicted Heraclitus[29]—interwoven with what is historical.

---

new faith. (It is generally true that in his later works Nietzsche shows a greater appreciation of the strength and value of cultural heterogeneity than in the earlier writings.)

[27]*Weltbild,* which often has the sense of "theory of the universe," or "philosophy of life."

[28]A Greek elegiac poet of the seventh century B.C., Mimnermus of Colophon took as his themes the preciousness of life and the horror of old age.

[29]This certainly seems to refer to the account of Heraclitus which Nietzsche had provided three years earlier in *PW.*

Gradualness rules the world. The Greeks progressed quickly, but they likewise declined with frightening quickness.[30] When the Hellenic genius had exhausted its highest types, Greece declined with the utmost rapidity. An interruption had only to occur once, and the great style of life ceased to be supplied: it was finished in an instant, just like tragedy. One single powerful crank like Socrates, and the break was irreparable. The self-destruction of the Greeks is accomplished in Socrates. I consider it significant that he was the son of a sculptor.

If for once the plastic arts could speak, they would seem to us superficial. In Socrates, the son of a sculptor, their superficiality emerged.

196

Men became *more clever* during the middle ages. Calculating according to two standards, the sophistry of conscience and the interpretation of texts: these were the means for this development. Antiquity lacked such a method of *sharpening the mind* under the pressure of a hierarchy and theology. On the contrary, the Greeks became credulous and shallow under their great freedom of thought. One commenced or ceased to believe anything as one wished. For this reason they took no pleasure in forced acuteness and thus in the favorite variety of cleverness of modern times. The Greeks were not very *clever*, that is why Socrates' irony created such a sensation among them.[31] In this regard I frequently find Plato to be rather ponderous.

With Empedocles and Democritus the Greeks were well on the way toward *assessing correctly* the irrationality and suffering of human existence; but, thanks to Socrates, *they never reached the goal.* An unbiased view of man is something which eludes all Socratics, who have those horrible abstractions, "the good" and "the just," on their minds. One should read Schopenhauer and then ask himself why the ancients lacked such profound and clear insight. Did they *have to* lack it? I don't think so. On the contrary, they lost their naive impartiality thanks to Socrates. Their myths and tragedies are much wiser than the ethics of Plato and Aristotle, and their "*Stoics* and *Epicureans*" are *impoverished* in comparison with their earlier poets and statesmen.

Socrates' influence:

1. he destroyed the naive impartiality of ethical judgment,
2. annihilated science,
3. had no feeling for art,

---

[30]This sentence re-appears in *MAMa,* 261.
[31]Cf. *FW,* 82.

4. wrenched the individual from his historical bonds,

5. and promoted dialectical verbiage and loquaciousness.

197

I no longer believe in the Greeks' *"development in accordance with nature."* They were much too talented to be *gradual* in the step by step fashion of the stone and of stupidity.[32] The national misfortune was the Persian wars: the success was too great; all the bad drives broke loose. Individual men and cities were seized by the tyrannical longing to rule over all Hellas. With the domination of Athens (in the spiritual realm) a number of forces were stifled: one need only think of how long Athens remained philosophically unproductive. Pindar would not have been possible as an Athenian. Simonides proves that this is true. Neither would Empedocles or Heraclitus have been possible as Athenians. Almost all the great musicians came from outside Athens. The Athenian tragedy is not the highest form which one might be able to imagine: the heroes of these tragedies are much too deficient in the Pindaric element. In general, how terrible it is that the battle had to break out precisely between *Sparta* and *Athens*! It is impossible to meditate upon this too deeply. *It was the spiritual domination of Athens which prevented this reformation.* One really has to imagine what it was like before this domination existed. It was not something that had to happen;[33] it first became necessary as a consequence of the Persian wars: that is to say, not until after the necessity of such [spiritual] domination was demonstrated by physical and political might. Miletus, for example, was more talented, as was Agrigentum.[34]

---

[32]See above, 192 and *MAMa*, 261.

[33]This is Nietzsche's tentative answer to the question raised at the end of section 196 (above): was it necessary that the Greeks remain at a relatively immature state of development? In the present as well as the previous passage he asserts or implies a negative answer to this question. But in the previous case he appears to assign the blame for the abortive development of Greek culture to Socrates, whereas in the second case it appears that he holds the Persian wars, with their attendant economic and political consequences, responsible. The interesting tension between these two "explanations" of the failure of the Greeks to develop beyond a certain point continues to the end of *WWK*. The even more interesting question of the possible connection between these two "causes" is never explored by Nietzsche himself. The idea that Greek culture was destroyed by the political victories of individual states, which eliminated the healthy competitive struggle which was the soil upon which Greek culture blossomed, was already advanced by Nietzsche in *HW*. See also *WP*, 119-23.

[34]Miletus, birthplace of Thales, was the principal Greek city in Ionia; Agrigentum (or Acragas) was one of the largest and most prosperous of the Greek cities in Sicily.

The tyrant who can do whatever he pleases, i.e. the Greek who is held in check by no authority, is a being entirely lacking in moderation: "he overturns the customs of the fatherland; he violates women and kills men arbitrarily."[35] And the tyrannical free spirit, which the Greeks likewise feared, is just as unrestrained. Hatred of kings: a sign of the democratic way of thinking. I believe that the reformation would have been possible if a tyrant had been an Empedocles.

With his demand that philosophers occupy the throne, Plato expressed a *thought* which was formerly *feasible*: he hit upon the notion after the time when it could be realized had passed. Periander?[36]

198

Without the tyrant Pisistratus,[37] the Athenians would have had no tragedy: for Solon was opposed to tragedy, but the delight in it had previously been awakened. What did Pisistratus want with these great provocations of sorrow?

Solon's antipathy to tragedy: recall the restrictions placed upon ceremonies of mourning, the prohibition of *threnoi*.[38] The "μανιχὸν πένθος"[39] of the Miletian women is mentioned.

According to the anecdote, what offended Solon was *dissimulation*: the inartistic nature of the Athenian comes to light.

Cleisthenes,[40] Periander, and Pisistratus: promoters of tragedy as popular entertainment, of delight in the μανιχὸν πένθος. Solon desires moderation.

The tendencies to centralization produced by the Persian wars: Sparta and Athens seized upon them. In contrast, no such tendencies existed between 776 and 560, when the culture of the *polis* blossomed. I think

---

[35]Compare the discussion in *HW* of the degeneration of the Greek into a cruel and bloodthirsty seeker of revenge.

[36]Tyrant of Corinth (625-585 B.C.), generally reputed to have been a cruel despot and a successful administrator. Periander is one of the "seven sages" of Greek tradition. Presumably the point of Nietzsche's reference is that Periander was actually the type of man who might have been able to establish the city Plato could only dream of.

[37]Athenian statesman and friend of Solon, Pisistratus was tyrant from 561-560 B.C. After being overthrown he re-established his tyranny in 541. Pisistratus was a great patron of art and culture. Under his influence Thespis of Icaria is supposed to have laid the foundations of Greek drama.

[38]"funeral songs," "dirges."

[39]"frantic sorrow."

[40]Tyrant of Sicyon (c. 600-570 B.C.), Cleisthenes was renowned for his wealth and power and for re-establishing the Pythian games.

that, if it had not been for the Persian wars, they would have hit upon the idea of centralization through *spiritual reform*. Pythagoras?

The important thing in those days was the unity of festival and cult; likewise, it is here that the reform would have begun. The *thought of a Panhellenic tragedy*: an infinitely more fertile power would have then developed. Why did this not happen? —after Corinth, Sicyon, and Athens had developed this art [of tragedy]!

The greatest loss that mankind can sustain is when the highest types of life fail to occur. Such a thing happened *in those days*. There is a close parallel between this ideal and the Christian one.[41] (To use Schopenhauer's remark: "Superior and noble men quickly become aware of this education by fate and accommodate themselves to it with flexibility and profitability. They realize that instruction is indeed to be found in the world, but not happiness, and they finally say with Petrarch, *'altro diletto, che 'mparer, non provo.'*[42] This can even reach the point where they attend to their wishes and endeavors merely so to speak for the sake of appearances and in a trifling manner, while actually, in the serious-ness of their inner selves, they anticipate nothing but instruction—which gives them thereupon a contemplative, exalted air of genius." *Parerga* I, 394.[43] (Contrast this with the Socratics' and their pursuit of happiness!)

[[The terrible conversation described by Thucydides between the Athenians and the Melians![44] Hellenism had to perish because of such ways of thinking, perish from *fear* on all sides. For example, the way in which the Athenian says: "So far as the benevolence of the gods is con-cerned, we will be at no disadvantage, for we desire and do nothing which goes beyond human nature—neither regarding beliefs in the gods nor regarding that which men desire for themselves."]]

[[Luther: "I have no better labor than anger and zeal. For if I wish to compose, write, pray, and preach well, I must be angry. In this manner my blood is refreshed, my understanding sharpened, and all listless thoughts and temptations vanish."[45]]]

---

[41]Presumably the parallel is between the unfulfilled or unactualized character of the two ideals. Perhaps Paul might be thought to stand in a relationship to Christianity somewhat comparable to Socrates' relationship to Greek culture and philosophy.

[42]"I feel no happiness, except in learning."

[43]From the end of section A of Part of *Aphorismen zur Lebensweisheit* in *Parerga und Paralipomena*, I.

[44]In Book V of *The Peloponnesian War*, Chapter 7.

[45]From Luther's "Tabletalk," as recorded by C. Cordatus. *Tischreden*, II (Weimar: Böhlaus, 1913), p. 455. (The German version quoted by Nietzsche

199

It is a beautiful truth that to a person whose goal in life has become self-improvement or discernment all things serve for the best. Yet this is only true in a limited sense: [just consider] a seeker of knowledge who is forced to engage in the most exhausting kind of labor, or a seeker after self-improvement who is ennervated and unhinged by sickness! It may be admitted that on the whole what appears to be premeditated by fate is really the achievement of the individual who puts his life in order and learns from everything, absorbing knowledge in the way that the bee absorbs honey. But that fate which befalls a people is one which concerns a totality, which, unlike an individual, cannot reflect upon its existence and furnish it with goals. Thus the notion of premeditation by peoples is a fabrication of oversubtle minds. Nothing is easier to demonstrate than the lack of premeditation: e.g. when an age which is in full blossom is suddenly surprised by a snowfall which kills everything. There is just as much stupidity in this as there is in nature. Even under the most unfavorable conditions, every people probably accomplishes to a certain extent something which reminds one of their talents. But in order for a people to be able to accomplish its *best*, certain accidents must not occur. The Greeks did not accomplish their best.

Even the Athenians would have developed somewhat higher had it not been for the political furor following the Persian wars. One should recall Aeschylus, who was born in the time before the Persian wars and who was dissatisfied with the Athenians of his day.

Many conditions favorable to the formation and development of great individuals were eliminated by the unfavorable situation of the Greek cities following the Persian wars, and thus the production of genius is indeed dependent upon the fate of a people. For dispositions toward genius are very common, but the concurrence of all the necessary favorable conditions is very rare.

This reformation of the Hellenes would, as I envision it, have become a wonderful soil for the production of geniuses, a soil such as there had never been before. That would be something to describe! We lost something expressable then.

The Hellenes' higher *ethical* nature is revealed by their wholeness and simplicity. By showing us man in a *simplified* form, they delight us in the way that the sight of animals does.

---

differs slightly from the German and Latin version in the Weimar edition of Luther's Works.)

Philosophers strive to understand that which their fellow men only live through. By interpreting their own existence and coming to understand its dangers, the philosophers at the same time interpret their existence for their people.

The philosopher wishes to replace the *popular picture of the world* with a *new one*.

[[*Thales' league of cities*:[46] he saw the fatal destiny of the *polis* and saw that myth was the foundation of the *polis*. If he broke down myth then perhaps he also broke up the *polis*. Thales as statesman. The struggle against the *polis*.

Heraclitus' attitude toward the Persians: he was clear about the dangers of the Hellenic and of the barbaric.

Anaximander as a founder of colonies.

Parmenides as a lawgiver.

Empedocles, the democrat with social reform up his sleeve.]]

[[Words are the seducers of philosophers; they struggle in the nets of language.[47]]]

[[The *power of the individual* is extraordinary in Greece: the power to found cities and to establish laws.]]

Science probes the processes of nature, but it can never *command* men. Science knows nothing of taste, love, pleasure, displeasure, exaltation, or exhaustion. Man must in some way *interpret*, and thereby evaluate, what he lives through and experiences.[48] Religions gain their power by being *standards of value*, criteria. An event appears in a different light when looked at from the point of view of myth. Religious interpretations have this to be said for them: that they measure life according to human ideals.

---

[46] According to Herodotus (*Histories*, I, 170), Thales proposed a general league of Ionic cities, including a central government with its capital at Teos.

[47] Cf. *P*, 118 and n. 83.

[48] Here Nietzsche returns to a theme which had featured prominently in *P* and which was later to be central in his better-known published works, and which finds its fullest expression in the account of man as a creator of values in *Zarathustra*. See also "Appendix" to *P*, 2. (Note that Nietzsche, at the time of this note, had not yet clearly grasped the *darker* side of human evaluation, viz. that man could also come to *condemn* the world for failing to "measure up" to his human ideals. This is as true of scientific as it is of religious ideals, as Nietzsche was later to see with unsurpassed clarity. (See *PAK*, n. 5.)

Aeschylus lived and fought in vain; he came too late. This is what is tragic in Greek history: the greatest figures, like Demosthenes, came too late to be able to rescue the people.

Aeschylus vouches for a spiritual height of the Greeks, which died out with him.

Today everyone admires the gospel of the tortoise: the Greeks, alas, ran too swiftly. What I seek in history are not the happy ages, but those which offer a favorable soil for the *production* of genius. This is what I find in the times before the Persian wars. One cannot become too well acquainted with this period.[49]

1. These philosophers [considered] in isolation, each separately.
2. Then as witnesses concerning that which is Hellenic. (Their philosophies are the underworld shades of the Greek nature.)
3. Then as combatants against the dangers of that which is Hellenic.
4. Then as unsuccessful reformers in the course of Hellenic history.
5. Then as opposing Socrates and the sects and the *vita contemplativa*, by attempting to achieve a *form of life*, which has *still not* been achieved.

Many men live a *dramatic* life, many an *epic* life, and many an inartistic and confused life. Thanks to the Persian wars, Greek history has a *daemon ex machina*.[50]

[[Anaxagoras' νοῦς is an ἄθεος *ex machina*.[51]]]

Attempt at a popular culture.

The waste of the most previous Greek *spirit* and Greek *blood*! Through this it can be shown how men must learn to live much more *prudently*. In Greece tyrants of the spirit were almost always assassinated and they had

---

[49]The order of the brief notes from here to the "Notes for the Introduction" differs in the notebook and in *GOA/MA*. I have followed the order of the notebook at this point.

[50]A variant of *deus ex machina:* "god from the machine" (originally referring to a piece of stage machinery for introducing a god into the action of a theatrical drama).

[51]On *nous*, see *P*, n. 64. *Atheos* means "non-god" (as in "atheism"). But contrast this little pun with *PtZG*, 17, where Nietzsche complains that it is unjust to dismiss Anaxagoras' *nous* as a mere *deus ex machina!*

only few successors.[52] Other ages, for example the Christian era, demonstrated their strength by thinking a single great thought through to its end and following up all of its possibilities. But among the Greeks it was very difficult [for any idea] to obtain such prominence: everything there was hostile to everything else. The only kind of culture which has been *established* until now is the culture of the city. We still live within this culture today.

City culture.
World culture.
Popular culture: how weak it is among the Greeks, properly speaking, nothing but a faded form of the city culture of Athens.

200
Continuous Written Copy of the Introduction[53]

1. There undoubtedly comes for every man an hour when he stands before himself with wonder and asks: "How does one manage to live at all? Yet nevertheless one does live!"—an hour when he begins to comprehend that he possesses an inventive faculty similar to the kind that he admires in plants, an inventiveness which twists and climbs until it finally forcibly gains a bit of light for itself and a small earthly kingdom as well, thus itself creating its portion of delight from barren soil. In one's own descriptions of one's own life there is always a point like this: a point where one is amazed that the plant can continue to live and at the way it nevertheless sets to work with unflinching valour. Then there are careers, such as that of the thinker, in which the difficulties have become enormously great. And when something is related concerning careers of this sort one must listen attentively, because from such cases one learns something concerning the *possibilities of life*. And just to hear about these possibilities leads to greater happiness and strength, for they shower light on the lives of those who come after. Everything here is as resourceful, sensible, daring, desperate, and hopeful as, for instance, the voyages of the globe's greatest circumnavigators. In fact, the career of the thinker is of a somewhat similar sort: they too are circumnavigators of life's most remote and dangerous regions. What is astonishing in careers of this sort is the way in which two hostile drives, which press in opposite directions, are constrained to proceed under a *single* yoke, so to speak. The drive which desires knowledge must again and again leave the inhabited lands behind and venture forth into the unknown; and the drive which desires life must again and again grope its way back to an approx-

---

[52]A similar passage occurs in *MAMa*, 261.
[53]This heading was, of course, added by the editors of *GOA*.

imately secure place on which it can stand. We are reminded of James Cook, who for three months had to feel his way across a chain of reefs with his sounding-lead in his hand, and for whom dangers often increased to the point that he was glad to return for refuge, even to a location which he had shortly before considered to be most dangerous. (Lichtenberg IV, 152.)[54] The more powerful the two drives, the greater the struggle between life and knowledge becomes, and the rarer it is for them to remain under a single yoke. Thus the struggle increases and unity becomes rarer as life becomes more full and flourishing and as knowledge in turn becomes more insatiable and impells one more covetously toward every adventure.

2. Therefore, I never tire of setting before my mind a series of thinkers in which each individual has within himself that incomprehensibility which forces us to wonder just how he discovered his possibility of life: the thinkers who lived in the most powerful and fruitful Greek era, in the centuries before and during the Persian wars. For the possibilities of life discovered by these thinkers were, in addition, *beautiful possibilities of life*; it seems to me that the later Greeks neglected the best of these, and what people up until the present day can claim to have rediscovered them? Compare the thinkers of other ages and peoples with that series of figures which begins with Thales and ends with Democritus—yes, just compare Socrates and all the later leaders of Greek sects with these ancient Greeks. That is what we now wish to do in this book, and it is to be hoped that others will do it better still. Nevertheless, I am confident that every consideration [of these Greeks] will conclude with the exclamation "how beautiful they are!" I see among them no deformed and ruined figures, no priestly faces, no scrawny desert hermits, no fanatics looking at the world through rose-colored glasses, no theologizing counterfeiters, no depressed and pale scholars (although the seeds of all of these are present and all that is needed in addition is an evil puff of wind, and then every weed will burst into blossom).[55] I also fail to see any among them who consider the "salvation of the soul" or the question "what is happiness?" so important that they forget the world and men on that account. If only someone could rediscover *"these possibilities of life"*! Poets and historians ought to brood over this task, for such men are too rare for us to be able to afford to let them escape. On the contrary, one should not rest until he has recreated their portraits and has painted

---

[54]From G.C. Lichtenberg's essay *"Einige Lebensumstände von Capt. James Cook,"* in *Vermischte Schriften,* IV (Göttingen: Dieterichschen, 1867), p. 152.

[55]This interesting parenthetical remark in the published text of *WWK* (in both *GOA* and *MA*) inexplicably does not appear in the text of the notebook published in *WKG*.

them on the walls a hundred times—and when one has done this, then he will certainly grant himself no peace. For our age, which is so inventive, still lacks precisely that discovery which the ancient Greeks must have made: for what else could be the source of their marvelous beauty and of our ugliness? For what is beauty if not the mirror image which we behold of nature's extraordinary delight when a new, fruitful possibility of life has been discovered? And what is ugliness if not nature's self-discontent, its doubt about whether it still really understands the art of enticing us toward life?

3. Greek philosophy seems to begin with an absurd notion, with the proposition that water is the source and the maternal womb of all things. "Is it really necessary," one may ask himself, "to pause here and deliberate seriously on this absurd proposition?" Yes it is, and for three reasons: first, because it asserts something concerning the origin of things; second, because it does so without images and mythical fables; and third, because this proposition contains the thought that "all is one"—even though it contains it in an embryonic state. The first reason still leaves Thales in partnership with religion and superstition; the second removes him from this association and shows him to have been the first [scientific] investigator of nature; on the strength of the third reason Thales is considered to be the first Greek philosopher.[56] In Thales for the first time the man of science triumphs over the man of myth, and then the man of wisdom triumphs in turn over the man of science.

How was it even possible for Thales to renounce myth? Thales as statesman! Something must have occurred at this point. If the *polis* was the focal point of the Hellenic will and if the *polis* was based upon myth, then abandoning myth meant abandoning the old concept of the *polis*. Now we know that Thales proposed, though he did not accomplish, the foundation of a league of cities: he ran aground on the old mythical concept of the *polis*. At the same time he had a foreboding of the enormous danger to Greece if this isolating power of myth continued to keep the cities divided. In fact, had Thales brought his league of cities into being, the Greeks would have been spared the Persian wars and therewith the victory and predominance of Athens. All of the early philosophers took pains to alter the concept of the *polis* and to create a Panhellenic way of thinking. Heraclitus even appears to have torn down the barrier separating the barbaric and the Hellenic in order to create

---

[56]Up to this point, this paragraph is almost identical to the opening passage of *PtZG*, 3.

greater freedom and to broaden narrow points of view. [[—The significance of water and of the sea for the Greeks.]][57]

[[*Thales*: what impelled him toward science and wisdom? But above all,
[it was] the struggle against myth, against the *polis*, which is founded
upon myth: the sole means of protecting what is Hellenic, of prevent-
ing the Persian wars. All the philosophers shared a Panhellenic aim.]]

Anaximander: the struggle against myth, insofar as myth coddles people
and makes them superficial, and thus leads the Greeks into danger.

[[*Heraclitus*: the struggle against myth, insofar as myth isolates the
Greeks and opposes them to the barbarians. He ponders a superhellenic world order.]]

Parmenides: Theoretical disdain for the world as a deception. The struggle against the fanciful and unstable character of the entire [mythical?]
way of looking at the world. He wishes to grant mankind rest from
political passion. Lawgiver.

Anaxagoras: The world is irrational, yet nevertheless measured and
beautiful. This is how men should be, and this is the way he found
them to be among the early Athenians: Aeschylus, etc. His philosophy
is a mirror image of early Athens: legislation for men who have no
need of laws.

Empedocles: Panhellenic reformer; a scientifically grounded Pythago-
rean manner of living. New mythology. Insight into the irrationality of
both drives—love and hatred. Love, democracy, communal property.
Comparison with tragedy.

Democritus: The world is irrational. In addition, it is neither measured
nor beautiful, but merely necessary. The unconditional elimination of
everything mythical. The world is comprehensible. He prefers the
polis (rather than the Epicurean garden). That was a possibility of
Hellenic life.

Socrates: The tragic velocity of the Greeks. The earlier philosophers had
no effect. The virtuosos of life: the early philosophers always think
like *Icarus*.[58]

The Greeks have certainly never been *overrated*: for this would only be
possible if they had first been evaluated as they deserve to be. But just
this is impossible. How could our evaluation do them justice? We have
evaluated them only *falsely*.

---

[57]In place of this clause, which appears here in Nietzsche's notebook, *MA* and
GOA print the last clause from the paragraph on Heraclitus which follows, viz.
"he ponders the Superhellenic world order."

[58]*die alten Philosophen denken immer ikarisch.* I.e. they rose too high and soon fell,
like Icarus, who flew so close to the sun that his wax wings melted and he fell into
the sea.

Additional Plans and Outlines

1872-6

VII
Additional Plans and Outlines[1]
A
Plans from the Summer of 1872

1
The Philosopher among the Greeks

What is Hellenic about the philosophers. Their eternal types. The non-artist in an artistic world. Considered collectively, the philosophers indicate the *background* of that which is Greek, as well as the *results* of art. Contemporaries of tragedy. Those scattered requisites for the origination of tragedy [which are found] in the philosophers.

The birth of tragedy looked at from another side. Its corroboration in the philosophy of its contemporaries.
The philosophers of the tragic age. In memory of Schopenhauer.

As opposed to the freedom of myth.	*Thales and Anaximander*: Pessimism and action.
The tragic as play. Genius.	*Heraclitus*: Contest. Play.
Excess of logic and necessity.	*Parmenides*: Abstraction and language.

---

[1]The following represent no more than a representative sampling of the many draft plans and project outlines to be found in Nietzsche's notebooks of this (and every) period. The reason for including them in this volume is that, together with the plans and outlines included in some of the other sections (viz. *PAK, WL, PB,* and *WWK*), they furnish valuable information concerning Nietzsche's own intentions regarding these manuscripts on philosophy, knowledge, and the Greeks. The plans translated below are selected from the many available published texts; the section numbers (in this case alone) have been assigned by the translator. For details on the particular plans, see the "Note on the Texts."

Poet and philosopher. The concept of prose.

Anaxagoras: Free spirit. Not [the opposition of] "spirit—matter."

Love and kisses to the entire world! Will.

Empedocles: Love. The rhetorician. Panhellenic. Agonistic.

The audience. Atom—number. Natural science.

Democritus: Greeks and foreign lands. Freedom from convention.

Transmigration of souls—dramatic.

Pythagoreans: Rhythm and *metron*.² Transmigration of souls.

Metastasis of the tragic-artistic drive into science.

Socrates and Plato: Education. Now for the first time, a "school." Hostility toward the explanations of natural science.

Imagine yourself a wandering philosopher who chanced upon the Greeks: this was the case with those Pre-Platonic philosophers. They were, so to speak, strangers, astonished strangers.

Every philosopher is a stranger, and the first thing which he has to do is to experience the strangeness of what is closest to him.

Herodotus among strangers—Heraclitus among the Greeks. The historian and geographer among strangers; the philosopher at home. No prophet is honored as such in his own homeland.

2

Everything develops from one thing.

Passing away is a punishment.

Passing away and coming into being are governed by laws.

Passing away and coming into being are delusions: the one [is all that] exists.

All qualities are eternal. There is no becoming.

All qualities are quantities.

All effects are magical.

All effects are mechanical.

Nothing is fixed except concepts.

Everything about Socrates is false; concepts are not fixed, nor are they important;

knowledge is not the source of justice and is in no way fruitful; culture is disavowed.

---

²A measure or rule; also, a poetic meter.

3

Unity of the will. The intellect is nothing but a means to higher gratifications. The denial of the will is often nothing but the restoration of powerful groups among the people.

Art in the service of the will: Heraclitus.

Love and hatred in Greece: Empedocles.

Boundaries of logic: logic in the service of the will: Eleatics.

The ascetic and the deadly in the service of the will: Pythagoras.

The realm of knowledge: number: Atomists and Pythagoreans.

Enlightenment, the struggle against instinct: Anaxagoras, Socrates, Plato.

The will to characterize: its method of attaining to what is rational. Absolute logic as the essence of matter. Time, space, and causality as presuppositions of *efficacy*.[3]

Forces are left over: different forces in every briefest moment: in the infinitely shortest space of time there is always a new force, i.e. the forces are by no means *actual*.[3]

There is no real *efficacy* of [one] force upon [another] force. Rather, there actually exists nothing but an illusion, an image. Matter is, in its entirety, nothing but the outside: what truly lives and operates[3] is something entirely different. But our senses are the *product of matter and of things,* as is *our mind.* I mean to say, to arrive at a *thing-in-it-self* one must start from the *natural sciences.*

The will which remains—when one subtracts the knowing intellect.

It is possible to construct sensation materialistically—if one has only first explained organic matter materialistically. The simplest sensation is a boundlessly compounded story: there is no primal phenomenon. Brain activity and memory are required here, together with all kinds of reflex movements.

If one were in a position to construct a sensate being from matter, wouldn't half of nature then be revealed?

Sensation presupposes the infinitely complex apparatus of knowledge: knowledge is required for the acceptance of any matter. However, the belief in visible matter is pure sensory illusion.

---

[3]The verb *wirken* (noun, *Wirkung*) has several closely related, but different meanings, viz. "to effect," "to produce," "to operate," or "to work." Similarly, the noun *Wirkung* means "working," "operation," "action," "effect," "efficacy," etc. And finally, the adjective *wirklich* means "effective," but also "actual," "true," or "genuine." All three of these words occur and reoccur in this passage, though they have not always been translated by the same English word upon every occurrence.

That nature *behaves the same way* in all realms: a law that is valid for man: [is] valid for all of nature. Man is actually a microcosm.

The brain is nature's supreme achievement.

4

Introduction: Immortality of great moments.

The Greeks of the tragic age as philosophers.

How did they experience existence?

Here lies their *eternal* import. As for the rest, all systems devour themselves. Historical painting.

In a metastasis we rediscover the epic and lyric elements, all the requirements for tragedy.

How does one live without religion, with philosophy? Though, admittedly, in a tragic-artistic age.

Thales. The Pre-Socratics' in contrast to the Socratics. Their attitude towards life is *naive*. The seven wise men as representatives of the chief ethical virtues. Freedom from myth.

The Greek of the tragic age thinks about himself and bears witness. How important this is! Because in order to judge Greek tragedy we have to supply the Greeks.

The metamorphosis of the artistic drive as *philosophy*.

5

The Universal Artist and the Universal Man.
The Men of the Tragic Age.

Aeschylus as a total artist:[4] his *audience*, as it is depicted in his studio.

We wish to become acquainted with those Greeks with whom Aeschylus was acquainted as his audience. This time,[5] we will employ [for this purpose] the audience's philosopher, who *thought* during that age.

First, Aeschylus depicted as pentathlos,[6] *then the audience,* [depicted] *with reference to the types of philosophers.*

---

[4]*Gesammtkünstler. Gesammtkunst* is a Wagnerian word for that "total art form" which is supposed to integrate and supplant the various individual arts, such as music, dance, theater, painting, etc.

[5]The "other occasion" alluded to here is *The Birth of Tragedy,* in which Nietzsche had utilized Greek drama as his lens for examining Greek life.

[6]Literally, a *pentathlos* is one who enters and succeeds in the five athletic contests which make up the pentathlon; figuratively, someone who can do everything.

B
Plans from Winter 1872-Spring 1873

1

The Last Philosopher[7]

Philosophy's original purpose has been thwarted.

Against the writing of iconic history.

Philosophy apart from culture, and science.

The altered position of philosophy since Kant. Metaphysics impossible. Self-castration.

Tragic resignation, the end of philosophy.
Only art has the capacity to save us.

1. The remaining philosophers.

2. Truth and illusion.

3. Illusion and culture.

4. The last philosopher.

Classification of the philosophers' methods for arriving at what is ultimate.
The illogical drive.
Truthfulness and metaphor.

The task of Greek philosophy: mastery.
The barbarizing effect of knowledge.
Life in illusion.

Philosophy since Kant's death.
Schopenhauer the simplifier, swept away scholasticism.
Science and culture. Opposites.
The task of art.
Education is the way.
Philosophy has to produce the need for tragedy.
Modern philosophy: not naive, scholastic, loaded down with formulas.
Schopenhauer the simplifier.
We no longer permit the poetry of concepts. Only in the work of art.
Antidote against science? Where?

---

[7]This plan, from notebook P I 20, appears in the various printed edition as the last section of *P*.

Culture as the antidote. In order to be susceptible to culture one must have recognized the insufficiency of science. Tragic resignation. God only knows what kind of culture this will be! It is beginning at the end.

2

From Thales to Socrates—nothing but transferences of man onto nature—the immense shadow-play of man upon nature, as if upon the mountains!

Socrates and Plato: knowing and the good are universal.

The artists' *ideas*: beauty in the beginning.

Pythagoreans	number
Democritus	matter
Pythagoras	man is not the product of the past, but rather of recurrence. The unity of every living thing.
Empedocles	moral understanding of the world of animals and plants. The universal sexual drive and hatred. "Will" is universal.
Anaxagoras	spirit is primordial.
Eleatics	
Heraclitus	the plastic power of the artist is primordial.
Anaximander	justice and punishment are universal.
Thales	

The gods and nature [were there] beforehand. Religions are only mere undisguised expressions. Astrology. Man as goal. "*World* history." Kant's thing-in-itself as category.

The philosopher is the continuation of that drive by which we incessantly deal with nature by means of anthropomorphic illusions. The eye. Time.

3

1. Flight from the scholar and the man of cozy good nature.

2. Fame and the philosopher.

3. Truth and its value as something purely metaphysical.

Main part: system as anthropomorphism.
Life within lies.
The pathos of truth, mediated through love and self-preservation.
Copying and knowing.
Mastery of the unlimited knowledge drive by means of illusion.
Against iconic historiography.

Religions.
Art.
Impossibility and progress.
The reflections of an evil spirit concerning the value of knowledge: high astrology.
The tragic, indeed [illegible] of knowledge since Kant.
Culture and science.
Science and philosophy.
Legislation by greatness.
Procreation in the beautiful.
The logician.
Result: [knowledge] originated accidentally and without any purpose; it strives for what is impossible—morally and historically; it scorns life. The phantom which is revered as truth has the same effects [as truth itself] and is likewise considered metaphysical.

4

The question concerning the *teleology of the philosopher*—who views things neither historically nor with warm feelings.

For him this question expands to become a question of the value of knowledge.

Description of the philosopher: he needs fame; he does not think of the *advantages* which proceed from knowledge, but of the advantages which lie within knowledge itself. If he were to discover a word which would destroy the world if it were pronounced, do you think that he would not pronounce it?

What is the meaning of his belief that mankind needs truth?

What is the value of knowledge as such?

The world of lies—truth gradually comes into its own—all virtues grow out of vices.

5

Knowing the truth is impossible.
Art and the philosopher.
The pathos of truth.

All knowing is in the service of art.

What is the philosopher's relation to culture: Schopenhauer.

The unity of a culture.
Description of the present deplorable state of affairs.
Drama as nucleololus.

First rung of culture: the belief in language, as a thoroughgoing
metaphorical designation.
Second rung of culture: unity and coherence of the world of
metaphors, under the influence of Homer.

6

Concerning the Lie[8]

Heraclitus' belief in the eternity of truth.
The decline of his work—one day the decline of all knowledge.
And what is truth in Heraclitus!
Presentation of his teaching as anthropomorphism.
Similarly Anaximander. Anaxagoras.
Heraclitus' relation to the character of the Greek people. It is the
Hellenic cosmos.
The genesis of the pathos of truth. The accidental genesis of knowing.
The mendacity and illusion in which man lives.
Lying and speaking the truth—myth, poetry.
The foundation of everything great and living rests upon illusion. The
pathos of truth leads toward decline.[9] (There lies the "great.") Above all,
it leads to the decline of *culture*.

---

[8]This note is of particular interest because it shows how Nietzsche tried to
integrate his epistemological speculations with his study of the Greeks. This
outline obviously bears a close relationship to both *PW* and *WL*, but it relates the
problem of truthfulness more explicitly to the Greeks than does either of these
writings. According to the editors of *GOA*, X, Nietzsche originally intended to
use the theme of truth and lies in the introduction to his book on Greek philosophy. (*Nachbericht* I, p. 506.)

[9]Compare this statement (which states quite directly a conclusion which is
implicit in many of the passages translated in this volume) with the following
quite early note from the spring of 1870:

"The goal of science is the destruction of the world. At the same time it is
of course the case that the first effect of science is the same as the first effect of a small dose of opium: an intensification of world affirmation. We
are now at this level of development in politics.

It can be shown that this process has already been carried out in miniature in Greece, though Greek science is only of limited significance.

Art has the task of destroying the state. This also occurred in Greece.
Subsequently science also dissolves art." Notebook P I 15 (*GOA*, IX, p. 72 =
MA, III, p. 206 [= *WKG*, III, 3, p. 62]).

The contrast between the immediate and the long term effects of science and the
desire for truth had already been made in *GT*, 14 and 15, but in *GT* the illustration of
this process in the history of Greek science and philosophy had not yet been worked
out. Showing the nihilistic character of science was one of Nietzsche's purposes in
embarking upon his study of the Pre-Platonic philosophers.

Empedocles and the sacrifices (Eleatics). Plato requires the lie for his state. The Greeks were separated from culture by *sectarianism.* Conversely, we are returning to culture in a sectarian manner. We are trying once again to restrain the philosopher's measureless knowing and to convince him anew of the anthropomorphic character of all knowledge.[10]

7

The consequences of the Kantian theory: the end of metaphysics as a science.
The barbarizing influence of knowledge.
The mastery of knowledge considered as the driving force of art.
We *live* only by means of these illusions of art.
Every higher culture owes its eminence to this mastery.
The philosophical systems of the early Greeks.
The world that reveals itself [here] is the same as the one created by tragedy.
The aesthetic concept of greatness and sublimity: the task is to educate people to this concept. Culture depends upon the way in which one defines what is "great."

8

Scientific retrospect.
Theory of aggregation of the states [of matter].
Theory of matter.
Thus, a *mixture* of *physical* and *metaphysical* problems.
[The contrast between] being and becoming—this produces all [further] difference.

9

Thales[11]   Paracelsus.   Passage in Homer's allegory.
          Water in modern chemistry.
                              Lavosier.

---

[10]*Wir suchen das unermessliche Erkennen wieder in dem Philosophen züruckzudrängen und diesen wieder von dem Anthropomorphischen aller Erkenntniss zu überzeugen.* The meaning of this sentence is by no means clear in the original.
[11]This is an especially rough outline which is translated here for only one reason: because it shows the close connection between Nietzsche's study of the Pre-Platonic philosophers and his study of natural science in the winter and spring of 1872-3 (see the letter to von Gersdorff, April 5, 1873, quoted in the "Introduction" to this volume). There is no point in providing elaborate annotation for all of the esoteric references which appear in this outline. The basic plan

Clouds. Ice.
Anaximines' air (Paracelsus).

Anaximander   Becoming as the symbol of transitoriness.
Not the *infinitum,* but the *indefinitum.*
The ἄπειρον:[12] cause of the world of becoming?
(Spir's theory of emanation.)

Heraclitus   Becoming as creation. Kopp, pp. 347 and preceding.
Every becoming presupposes two elements.

Anaxagoras   Circular movement. *Dynamical* theory.
The pervasion of matter, p. 324.
Many substances.
Becoming as extraction, no longer as creation.
Penetration to points.

Empedocles   Attraction. Repulsion. Affinity. *Actio ins distans.*[13]
4 elements. 2 electricities. Kopp, p. 340.
Love and hatred—sensation as the cause of motion.
Boerhave, Kopp, p. 310.

Democritus   The atoms are all similar.
                          Buffon vs. Newton,
Various shapes. Gassendi.
                       p. 311.

Pythagoreans   Kapp, 367: the sleeping voyager in the ship.
Überweg, III, 53.
Continuation of atomism; all mechanics of motion is fi-
    nally a description of ideas.
Contiguity. *Actio ins distans.*

Parmenides   (Bernhardinus Telesius)
Contributions to a History of Physiology,
by Rixner and Silber, III.

---

is sufficiently clear; what Nietzsche is trying to do is draw parallels between the views of the ancient philosophers and various developments and theories in the history of modern science. But the outline in which he jotted down a few such parallels can only be fully understood in conjunction with the relevant passages in the two books to which Nietzsche makes constant page reference: Hermann Kopp's *Geschichte der Chemie,* Teil II (1844) and Friedrich Überweg's *Grundriss der Geschichte der Philosophie von Thales bis auf die Gegenwart* (1867). There are, in addition, cryptic references in this outline to Afrikan Spir's *Denken und Wirklichkeit* and to Nietzsche's own lengthy excursuses on Greek and modern science in his lectures on the Pre-Platonic philosophers. For detailed commentary on this outline, see Anders' discussion of it in Schlechta/Anders, pp. 88-97.

[12]"The boundless," that which is without limit or definition.
[13]"Action at a distance."

Descartes' definition of substance, see Überweg III, 52.
Reciprocal interaction of the body's total dissimilarity.
III, 53.
First principle: the principle of contradiction. Überweg
III, 81.
quidquid est, est: quidquid non est, non est.[14]

---

[14]"Whatever is, is; whatever is not, is not."

C
Two Plans from the Summer of 1873[15]

1
Assorted Servants of Truth

1. Description of science's *laisser faire*.[16] What is missing is the dictator.
2. Consequence: the right cement is lacking (—thus [we have instead] the cement of newpaper-culture!).
   In general, greater and greater crudeness.
   The stunted image of the servant of truth.
3. For this reason many have *sneaked in*. Description.
4. The attitude of German culture toward this: what is the task? (Goethe's attitude toward natural science.)

2
Assorted Servants of the Truth

First, optimistic surprise: how many investigators of truth there are! Is it permissible for the best forces to dissipate themselves in this way? Mastery of the knowledge drive: classical—antiquarian.
Pessimistic astonishment: not one of these is an investigator of truth! The reward of justice, as of the mother of the true truth drive.
Testing of "servants of truth" for their sense of justice.
It is a good thing that all of these servants of truth are *exiled,* for they would only disturb everything and cause damage. We wish to call them the hired laborers of truth; they serve it against their will and with groans.

---

[15]Just as the previous plans show the relation between Nietzsche's work on Greek philosophy and his inquiry into truth and lies, as well as the relation between his study of natural science and his study of the Pre-Platonic philosophers, so these two plans show the link between the epistemological investigations and Nietzsche's new project, the series of "Untimely Meditations"—more specifically, the link between *WL* and the *UB's*. Indeed, "Assorted Servants of Truth" is a good description of, and would have been a good title for, the *UB's*.

[16]"let act," "leave alone." Nietzsche's notebooks contain frequent remarks which draw a parallel between, what he calls the "dogma" of *laisser faire* economics and the situation of modern science. The "dictator" which is lacking is, of course, some goal or force capable of "mastering the knowledge drive."

For persons of this sort science is a house of correction, a galley. Reference to *Socrates*, who called them all crazy. At home they do not know what is good and what is evil.

Neutralization of science by means of the cloister.

Our task: to reunite and weld back together those things which have been cleft and dispersed; to establish a center for German culture, beyond all newspaper-culture and scientific popularization.[17]

---

[17]The word translated as "center" in this sentence is *Herd,* which means literally "hearth," and figuratively, "focus" or "seat." The task of finding a new "center" or "focus" for culture was perceived by Nietzsche primarily as the task of finding an overriding goal or power which could subjugate the competing lesser goals and powers within contemporary society. However, the word "center" also suggests a concrete place or institution set up for a specific purpose (e.g. a "center for biological research"); and in fact, the establishment of just such an institution was a recurrent dream of Nietzsche's. He fantasized a semi-monastic community of dedicated men of superior talents who would live in creative cooperation and devote themselves to the solution of the cultural problem of the modern age: a "center" devoted to the pursuit of a new "center" for culture. According to Nietzsche's sister, invitations were actually sent to prospective members of this association and a small castle near Graubünden was very nearly purchased for this purpose in the summer of 1873—which coincides with the date of this note. See Elizabeth Förster-Nietzsche, *The Young Nietzsche* (New York: Sturgis and Walton, 1912), p. 284ff.

D
Plans for the "Untimely Meditations" (1873-6)[18]

1
Basel, September 2, 1873

1. The cultural Philistines.

2. The Historical Sickness.

3. A Great Deal of Reading and Writing.

4. Literary Musicians (how the followers of the genius cancel his effects).

5. German and Pseudo-German.

6. Military Culture.

7. *General* Education, Socraticism, etc.

8. Educational theology.

9. Secondary Schools and Universities.

10. Philosophy and Culture.

11. Natural Science.

12. Creative Writers, etc.

13. Classical Philology.

2
(Fall 1873)

1. The Cultural Philistine.

2. History.

3. The Philosopher.

---

[18]No sooner had Nietzsche worked out for himself the general idea of a series of "Untimely Meditations," than he began making sketches and plans for the continuation of the series. Although only four were finally published, he envisaged a much longer series—often including thirteen and sometimes as many as twenty four separate titiles. I have translated a number of these plans because they show how Nietzsche was constantly working old material into his new projects. Here again the evidence points to the continuity rather than the breaks in Nietzsche's intellectual career. The selection and numbering of the individual plans are my own.

4. The Scholar.

5. Art.

6. The Teacher.

7. Religion.

8. State, War, Nation.

9. The Press.

10. Natural Science.

11. Folk Society.

12. Commerce.

13. Language.

3
(End of 1873)

1873 David Strauss.
    The Use and Disadvantage of History.
1874 Reading a lot and Writing a lot.
    The Scholar.
1875 Secondary Schools and Universities.
    Military Culture.
1876 The Absolute Teacher.
    The Social Crisis.
1877 On Religion.
    Classical Philology.
1878 The City.
    The Nature of Culture (original nature).
1879 The People and Natural Science.

4
(End of 1873)

1. Overture.

2. History.

3. The Tribulation of Philosophy.

4. The Scholar.

5. Art.

6. The Institutions of Higher Learning.

7. State, War, Nation.

8. The Social.

9. Classical Philology.
10. Religion.
11. Natural Science.
12. Reading, Writing, the Press.
13. The Path to Freedom (as an epilogue).

5

The Path to Freedom
Thirteen Untimely Meditations
(Fall 1873)

The degree of observation, of confusion, of hatred, of contempt, of unification, of clarification, of enlightenment, of struggle for, of inner peace and cheerfulness.

Attempt at a construction, at historical classification, at public classification, at [attracting] friends.

6

(Beginning of 1874)

Strauss.
History.
Reading and Writing.
The One Year Volunteer.
Wagner.
Secondary Schools and Universities.
Christian disposition.
The Absolute Teacher.
The Philosopher.
People and Culture.
Classical Philology.
The Scholar.
Newspaper Slavery.

7

(1876)[19]

1. Counterfeiting of Culture.
2. History.

---

[19]These two plans from 1886 are of special interest because of their striking resemblance to the nine parts of *MAMa*, which Nietzsche was writing in 1886-7. It may also be significant that the subtitle of *MAMa* is "a book for free spirits," for

3. The Philosopher.
4. The Artist.
5. The Teacher.
6. Woman and Child.
7. Property and Labor.
8. The Greeks.
9. Religion.
10. Liberation.
11. State.
12. Nature.
13. Social Life.

8
(1876)

1. Nature. 1883.
2. Woman and Child. 1878.
3. Property and Labor. 1881.
4. The Teacher. 1882.
5. Social Life. 1884.
6. Those Who are Frivolous. 1880.
7. The Greeks. 1879.
8. The Free Spirit. 1877.
9. The State. 1885.

---

in letters written during the year 1876 Nietzsche referred to a nearly-completed *fifth* "Untimely Meditation," to be called "The Free Spirit" and to be published in 1877. (According to the *Nachbericht* to *MA*, VI, p. 347, the draft of this unpublished "Meditation" was utilized in writing *MAMa*, which was published in 1878.)